Suffrage and the Pankhursts

WOMEN'S SOURCE LIBRARY

Series Editors:
Dale Spender and Candida Ann Lacey

This series brings together some of the most important, but still too little known, written sources which document the history of women's struggles for liberation. Taken from the principal women's archive in Britain, The Fawcett Library, and reprinted in full wherever possible, these papers illustrate major debates on a range of issues including suffrage, education, work, science and medicine as well as making the words of individual women widely available for the first time. Each volume contains a historical intro- duction to the material and biographical details of those campaigners who sought to improve the social, economic and legal status of women. The series was devised in collaboration with Catherine Ireland and David Doughan of The Fawcett Library, both of whom greatly assisted in the selection and compilation of material.

Other volumes in this series:

Barbara Leigh Smith Bodichon and the Langham Place Group
edited by Candida Ann Lacey
The Sexuality Debates edited by Sheila Jeffreys
The Education Papers edited by Dale Spender

Forthcoming volumes include:

Women's Fabian Tracts edited by Sally Alexander
The Non-Violent Militant: Selected writings of Teresa Billington-Greig
    edited by Carol McPhee and Ann FitzGerald
The Lily edited by Cheris Kramarae and Lana Rakow
Before the Vote was Won: Arguments For and Against Women's
    Suffrage, 1864–1896 edited by Jane Lewis
Sex and Social Order, 1660–1730 edited by Carol Barash and
Rachel Weil

Suffrage and the Pankhursts

Edited by
Jane Marcus

Routledge & Kegan Paul
London and New York

First published in 1987 by
Routledge & Kegan Paul Ltd
11 New Fetter Lane, London EC4P 4EE

Published in the USA by
Routledge & Kegan Paul Inc.
in association with Methuen Inc.
29 West 35th Street, New York, NY10001

Set in Linotron Bembo 10/11pt
by Input Typesetting Ltd, London SW19 8DR
and printed in Great Britain
by T. J. Press (Padstow) Ltd
Padstow, Cornwall

Library of Congress Cataloging in Publication Data

Suffrage and the Pankhursts.

(Women's source library)
Includes index.
1. Women—Suffrage—Great Britain—History—
Sources I. Marcus, Jane. II. Series.
JN979.S848 1987 324.6'23'0941 87–12868

British Library CIP Data also available
ISBN 0–7102–0903–7

Contents

Contents

Contents

Introduction

Re-reading the Pankhursts and women's suffrage

In September 1914 a young American journalist, Djuna Barnes, later to become famous as the *avant-garde* author of *Nightwood*, had herself forcibly fed in order to bring attention to the plight of the English suffragettes. The *New York World* ran her sensational story, with many graphic photographs, in their Sunday magazine. 'How It Feels To Be Forcibly Fed' was the result of an experiment undertaken by a healthy but curious young woman. She was not exhausted from a hunger strike or the rigours of imprisonment in Holloway Gaol. What began as a lark ended as a horror story. By the time her story was written, the war had turned the government's attention to less passive enemies of the state. But Djuna Barnes's newspaper pointed out that the authorities in New York were considering using forcible feeding in the case of the young I. W. W. (International Workers of the World, called the Wobblies) protester, Becky Edelson, then on a hunger strike.

Since Gandhi, the hunger strike has been a weapon of passive resistance used by the obviously weak against the powerful, Indians against colonialism, women agitating for the vote, American Blacks in the non-violent civil rights movement, the Irish in their struggle for independence, and, most recently, Russian dissidents. In each case the unorthodox form of passive resistance relies on the good conscience of the government to see the error of its ways and to recognise its own injustice. Those who protest in this way have the ethical advantage as well as the righteousness and moral superiority of those who are weak, helpless and starving in a just cause. Like children casting themselves on the mercy of an unjust father, by inflicting pain and suffering on themselves, such protesters appeal to the patriarch's humanity. Unfortunately, these tactics often enrage the authorities, who resent being cast in the role of monsters.

When woman, quintessential nurturer, refuses to eat, she cannot nurture the nation. I would argue that the tactic was a symbolic refusal of motherhood. Forcible feeding is perhaps the primary image in the public imagination regarding the 'meaning' of the suffrage movement. Consequently it is this experience as presented in suffragette poster art, as recollected in autobiography and as interpreted by historians, which one may see as symbolic of the movement as a whole. In this book I am concerned with the construction of the subject of suffrage by both historians and participants. I am also interested in several other questions – the distortions of the historians who have written about the suffrage movement, the way it shaped women's autobiographies, and the troubling issue of class and the women's movement. It is my opinion that historians have asked the wrong questions about the suffragettes. They have asked 'Why did the suffragettes abandon their roots in labour as well as democratic structures of organis-ation?' When it seems to me that the more interesting question, though infinitely more difficult to answer, is 'Why did labour reject and repudiate the suffrage movement?' I do not propose to give a full answer to this question, but I wish to raise it here to suggest areas for future research.

When Dale Spender and Candida Lacey selected the documents for this volume and asked me to introduce it, it was their intention to suggest to the reader the richness of the neglected source material on the suffragettes. This volume represents only a very small sample of the materials in the Fawcett Library. The reader who wishes to explore further may be directed as well to the splendid collections of posters, manuscript diaries and paraphernalia of the movement in the London Library, as well as local libraries in England and the Schlesinger Library at Radcliffe College in Cambridge, Massachusetts. If one uses these materials from a fresh perspective, unencumbered by preconceived notions of class divisions and predetermined dismissals by historians, the issues, the forms of struggle, the writing and speaking, the personalities of rank and file suffragettes as well as the leaders, will emerge more clearly as part of our own history.

And here it seems appropriate to state the bias of the writer. Since we all speak from inside an internalised ideology, one may at least explain one's conscious choice of position. I am arguing that we may gain new insights from studying the suffragettes from the vantage point of *Women's History*. Ever since George Dangerfield's *The Strange Death of Liberal England*, the suffrage movement has been studied as one of a number of causes of the downfall of the Liberal Party, along with the Irish question, labour and unionisation, pacifism and the First World War. As the first 'historian' to treat the movement seriously, Dangerfield invented the narrative and historical plot from which subsequent historians have seldom been able to free themselves. His narrative is so powerful an explanatory drama, his suffragette characters such moving stereotypes, simultaneously creating and satisfying a public (or patriarchal) need to label a serious women's politics as 'hysterical', that few have been able to escape from its grip. This is of course true of the power of all 'first' histories. The next generation of historians must struggle to break the grip of the *first* narrative, its choice of decisive events, its naming of heroines and villains.

Mr Dangerfield's chief metaphor is like my own. The women's suffrage movement was a 'drama', the women were 'actors' and 'actresses' in a 'scene' of the 'real' drama of the decline of the Liberal Party. My concept of the historian's 'plot' comes from Foucault and contemporary students of the rhetoric of history, like Paul Veyne, Dominick La Capra and Hayden White. Dangerfield's still-read 1935 classic uses the terms 'scene' and 'drama' to diminish and belittle the movement's accomplishments. Perhaps his most successful strategy (for its venomous view is still held in many circles) was the brilliant patriarchal ploy of labelling the suffrage movement a comedy. A light comic diversion in the Tragedy of the Liberal Demise. 'It is almost impossible to write the story of the Woman's Rebellion,' he writes disarmingly, 'without admitting certain elements of brutal comedy. An Aristophanes alone could do it justice.' Mr Dangerfield then dons the mantle of Aristophanes, and, counting on an audience of male readers of history, warms to his subject, having excused his brutality with the classical allusion which confirms his position as British patriarchal historian, *par excellence:*

> From the spectacle of women attacking men there rises, even in this day, an outrageous, an unprincipled laughter. And when a scene as ordinary as English politics is suddenly disturbed with the swish of long skirts, the violent assault of feathered hats, the impenetrable, advancing phalanx of corseted bosoms – when, around the smoking ruins of some house or church, there is discovered the dread evidence of a few hairpins or a feminine galosh – then the amazing, the ludicrous appearance of the whole thing is almost irresistible.
>
> (*Strange Death*, 154–5)

Mr Aristophanes Dangerfield consolidates his phallogocentric position. Licensing the laughter of an imagined all-male audience, he defines the suffrage movement as 'spectacle' and slips in 'unprincipled', like his earlier 'brutal', which is then a sanctioned response. The unsaid signals are received – if women make a spectacle of themselves, we, respectable men, are entitled to any 'brutal' or 'unprincipled' response. 'They brought it on themselves. We are the only actors in the great tragedy of "history". If they act, it is a comedy, a farce, a sideshow. We are the speaking subjects. If they speak, we laugh.' Of course Dangerfield, in inciting a conspiracy of unprincipled male laughter at women's actions, is not initiating a new response. The precedent is already well established in Parliament where any mention of women's causes for over fifty years (it is sadly recorded in Hansard) is greeted by hoots of laughter from the gentlemen who govern the nation. Like an experienced politician he sounds the words which trigger the laughter – corset, bosom, hat, skirt. He tickles the brutality muscle, too – those bosoms are 'impenetrable'.

From 'the dread evidence of a few hairpins or a feminine galosh' the feminist historian may reconstruct a whole different scenario. How did genteel ladies train themselves to arson and window-smashing? Imprisoned in the ideology of Victorian femininity, how did they bring themselves to march in the streets, to suffer the indignities of physical attacks by crowds of violent men, the blows of the truncheons of mounted police? But Mr Dangerfield is neither speaking to us, nor for us. He distances those paper dolls, his Punches and Judies, from conscious, lived political 'reality':

> And its chief actors – say what you please, they are not very lovable. You are forced to ascribe to Mrs. Pankhurst and her daughter Christabel certain motives of self-interest, certain moments of exhibitionism, which do not especially commend themselves. They and their associates were courageous enough; some of them stood more physical torture than a woman should be able to bear: but then, as the scene unrolls itself and their sufferings increase, how can one avoid the thought that they sought these sufferings with an enraptured, a positively unhealthy pleasure?
>
> (*Strange Death*, 155)

Here Mr Dangerfield imagines a little chivalrous discomfort on the part of his male readers – 'say what you please' – in the gentlemen's club conversation which is the structure of his discourse. He soon silences that. He puts words and opinions in their mouths, in fact the most damning words – '*You* are forced to ascribe . . . certain motives of self-interest, certain moments of exhibitionism.' Who is forced to ascribe? Forced by what? Christabel and Mrs Pankhurst are 'not lovable'. Are Asquith, Sir

4

Edward Carson, Jim Larkin, the other actors in his drama, 'lovable'? But women are supposed to be lovable; their corsets are supposed to be penetrable. Dangerfield's rhetorical strategy is brilliant in his diminishment of the militant movement as a politics on a par with any male parties or movements. He in fact uses the word 'little' several times on almost every page: 'Rather melancholy little pickets would linger in Downing Street, with little banners' (154). Notice also the passive construction of the last sentence in the long quote. A psychologist now, he attributes their martyrdom to passive masochism. The scene unrolls itself. That means they did not responsibly initiate action. But then, contradictorily, they did, as a whole mass movement of female masochists. These charges, serious charges, of 'self-interest' and 'exhibitionism' – where do they come from? They have stuck to the suffragettes for over fifty years, since the *Strange Death* was published. But no evidence is cited; no instances analysed. Where does this outrageous claim originate?

I suspect that its source is Sylvia Pankhurst's *The Suffragette Movement* (1931), the biggest and most authoritative text by one of the 'actors', the only one with a claim to be a 'history' in Dangerfield's terms, and she, too, wanted to show the 'actors in the drama' as frankly all too human 'behind the pageantry, the rhetoric and the turbulence' (*The Suffragette Movement*, vii). Sylvia Pankhurst is Mr Dangerfield's heroine. Her story, in which she plays Cinderella in a family romance, is the 'authority' for Dangerfield's text as well as the origin of his figure of the suffrage movement as a drama of clockwork dolls. Dangerfield is grateful for the facts, dates and interpretation in *The Suffragette Movement*. And there are several important consequences to his reliance on her text because, with only slight variations, the Sylvia Pankhurst/George Dangerfield version of the suffrage movement has become the standard reading of events, stubbornly held and hardly challenged. Sylvia's story conflates the personal with the political, inscribing herself as her father's daughter, the only member of the family to uphold his socialist principles of maintaining an alliance with Keir Hardie and the Labour Party and actually attributing the winning of the vote to her work with working women in the East End Federation. In Sylvia's version she is the heroine who keeps the faith, while her mother and sister become increasingly hysterical and autocratic. She paints her mother as too busy with the movement to pay attention to the ill-health of her son, Harry, and implies that she was responsible for his death. The structure of the book records the major events as splits within the movement caused by her mother and sister, while the 'winning' of the vote is claimed at the dramatic dénouement of her arrangement to get Asquith to receive her East End Delegation in June 1914. Weak from hunger-striking, she was brought to the House, surrounded by socialist men, Lansbury, Nevinson, Joseph Wedgwood – and Keir Hardie is the hero for arranging the meeting with Asquith. Sylvia Pankhurst thus claims victory in the name of socialist feminism, a victory less over the government as over her real enemies, her mother and sister, the separatist feminists who have become increasingly more aristocratic and concerned with personal power. Cinderella is liberated by her fairy godfather, Keir Hardie, from her wicked mother and sister. She and her united charwomen have won the vote.

This script is very appealing. George Dangerfield is not the only one who fell for it. Sylvia Pankhurst describes her last hunger strike as carried out against the expressed wishes of her mother after their alliance was broken, so that her script reads as a personal daughter's rebellion in which Mrs Pankhurst has become, not the powerful leader of the women's movement, but a phallic mother equated with Brittannia, the State and the Liberal Party. Christabel and Emmeline appear as isolated man-haters and hysterics and are robbed of political genius as Sylvia concludes with their 'tragic betrayal' of her father's principles in their war-time support of the government.

Mrs Pankhurst is robbed of her role as originary force of suffrage politics, and seen as merely completing her husband's work, then labelled as a traitor to his vision. The battle acted out in the pages of the *Suffragette Movement* is the battle of heterosexuality against celibacy, the sexed socialist against the unsexed viragoes; Sylvia is Athena battling Diana and Hecate. What is at stake is the reproduction of mothering, and Sylvia and the reader see suffrage as the last stand of Victorian spinsters. The 'women–identified women' are denied their own victory.

When I first came to London in 1969 to work in the old Fawcett Library near Victoria, I was a convinced socialist feminist and true believer in the Sylvia Pankhurst/George Dangerfield script. It took many hours for Jill Craigie to convince me to pay attention to Christabel Pankhurst's mind, her political genius, to escape from my own identification with Sylvia's mother–daughter drama and to begin to try to understand Emmeline Pankhurst's charismatic leadership. The plots of the first historians of suffrage, Sylvia Pankhurst's tragic family romance of the bad mother and George Dangerfield's comic farce of suffrage as a hysterical sideshow, engage the woman reader in a test of her politics and sexual orientation. Reluctant to abandon confirmation as a heterosexual socialist, I was convinced to rethink the movement by portraits of Mrs Pankhurst by two women I respected, Rebecca West and Ethel Smyth. 'Trembling like a reed,' Rebecca West wrote, 'she lifted up her hoarse, sweet voice on the platform, but the reed was of steel, and it was tremendous.' Rebecca West saw Emmeline Pankhurst as a great political champion of her sex and sought explicitly in her essay to counter the effects of Sylvia Pankhurst's matricidal prose: 'Somehow, in her terse, austere way she was as physically glorious as Ellen Terry or Sarah Bernhardt. She was glorious in her physical courage, in her obstinacy, in her integrity.' Dame Rebecca was fascinated by Mrs Pankhurst's combination of French elegance and nun-like modesty, and shrewdly shows, I believe, despite the arguments of labour historians, that she rose from 'a dusty and obscure provincial' to a leadership accepted by the people and the government, so that, in the long view, the suffragette movement could be seen as paving the way for the acceptance of the demands of labour. That no one else has analysed the movement in this way is no evidence that it might not prove to be refreshingly true:

> But the movement was neither crazy nor hysterical nor delirious. It was stone-cold in its realism. Mrs. Pankhurst was not a clever woman, but when she experienced something she incorporated it in her mind and used it as a basis for action. When she started the Women's Social and Political Union she was sure of two things: that the ideas of freedom and justice which had been slowly developing in England during the eighteenth and nineteenth centuries had grown to such maturity that there existed an army of women resentful of being handicapped by artificial disadvantages imposed simply on the grounds of their sex, and that sex-antagonism was so strong among men that it produced an attitude which, if it were provoked to candid expression, would make every self-respecting woman want to fight it.

In Dame Rebecca's view Mrs Pankhurst's popular success was due to her embodiment of democratic working-class values, as her movement was the first modern British form of popular democracy. Now, it is true that labour history is neither written nor taught in this way. The women's movement has been as segregated and isolated from 'history' as women themselves were banned from politics. Dame Rebecca's analysis gives one pause:

> But Mrs. Pankhurst's chief and most poignant value to the historian will be her demonstration of what happens to a

great human being of action in a transition period. She was the last popular leader to act on inspiration derived from the principles of the French Revolution; she put her body and soul at the service of Liberty, Equality and Fraternity, and earned a triumph for them. Then doubt seized her, as it was to seize a generation. In the midst of her battle for democracy she was obliged, lest that battle should be lost, to become a dictator. . . . She trembled under the strain of conflict, and perhaps she trembled also because she foresaw that she was to gain a victory, and then confront a mystery. She had always said and felt she wanted the vote to feed the hungry. Enfranchised, she found herself aware that economic revolution was infinitely more difficult and drastic than the fiercest political revolution. With her childlike honesty, her hate of pretentiousness, she failed to put up a good show to cover her perplexity. She spoke the truth – she owned she saw it better to camp among the ruins of capitalism than to push out into the uncharted desert. With her whole personality she enacted our perplexity, as earlier she had enacted our revolt, a priestess of the people.

(*The Young Rebecca 1911-1917*,
Macmillan/Virago, 1982, 243-62. First published 1933)

Dame Rebecca's placement of Mrs Pankhurst on the stage of the world history of democracy, the explanation of her latter-day conservatism as a failure of *vision*, offers us another way to look at this movement for social justice in the broader context of other movements for social change.

Dame Ethel Smyth, the composer, gives us another point of view, the soldier's view of her general: 'She had never set any value on her life, and at the last laid it down for her country as deliberately as any man who had volunteered for the Great War in 1914'. . . . Dame Ethel, who loved her as 'My Darling Em,' an unthinkable address for anyone else, had fled to Egypt to escape after her own two years of militant service to the cause, being in prison, and writing *The March of the Women*. She had fled her own feelings, she confesses, at their 'fiery' relationship, 'the deepest and closest of friendships'. Dame Ethel claims intimacy with her aloof heroine and in her 'portrait' shows another, more artistic side to the woman who claimed 'I am simply an agitator'; yet the essay reveals that she was attracted by the 'authority' of Mrs Pankhurst as 'master'. Dame Ethel's script includes a boast of her conquest of the leader, but her memoir, like Dame Rebecca's, concentrates on the tremendous powers of Mrs Pankhurst as a speaker:

She used little gesture beyond the rare out-stretching of both hands so wonderfully caught in her statue on the Victoria Embankment. It was all done by the expression on her face, and a voice that, like a stringed instrument in the hand of a great artist, put us in possession of every movement of her spirit – also of the great underlying passion from which sprang all the scorn, all the wrath, all the tenderness in the world. Notes bothered her and I don't think she ever used them, but no amount of preparation could have bettered the words in which her thought spontaneously clothed itself.

A genius as an orator, Mrs Pankhurst never could be convinced to write and one of Dame Ethel's anecdotes is about ghost-writing an article which Mrs Pankhurst promptly lost. Ethel Smyth prints several of Mrs Pankhurst's letters to her, marvelling at 'their stark directness, their innocence of literary intention'. In one, Emmeline Pankhurst describes her writing for the weekly *Suffragette* as

stilted and bald as usual. Oh, dear, why do I always feel as if I were in the dentist's chair when I try to write? Pity the sorrows of the poor agitator! I can't speak my mind for they won't let me speak, and I can't write it!! It is indeed a case of being driven to 'deeds not words'!

This differentiation of writing, speaking and militant action as weapons in the suffrage battle is an important one. Certainly the strategy of interrupting politician's speeches, first done by Christabel Pankhurst and Annie Kenney when they interrupted Sir Edward Grey in Manchester, in 1905, and were jailed and catapulted to national attention, is on both the real and symbolic levels the bold breaking out of the straitjacket of the female role. *'Interruption' of male political discourse*, as invented by Christabel Pankhurst, practised for a decade at by-elections and in storming the houses of Parliament and taught to thousands of women of every class and social background, is the real key to the genius of militant suffrage in giving the women of England a political voice. Trained in silence and good behaviour to modestly listen to the men, to a role, whatever her class, of 'she who may be interrupted', whose work or speech is always subservient to the male's, the women who learned from Christabel Pankhurst not only to speak in her own voice for her own cause, but to split asunder patriarchal cultural hegemony by interrupting men's discourse with each other, were taking one of the most important steps in the history of women. How difficult it was to break down women's learned silence, the culture's equation of her virtue with politeness. What emancipatory bliss to aggressively enter the space of male political debate! This was the real violence of militancy, the assumption of verbal power.

While London boasts a statue of Mrs Pankhurst, lovingly erected by her followers, Virginia Woolf in 1928, the year women finally got the vote, the year Mrs Pankhurst died, presented the world with a permanent literary tribute to the suffrage movement's giving voice to women. Constructed brilliantly around the literary tropes of interruption and absence, *A Room of One's Own* eloquently enacts the history of the struggle. The collective female narrator's voice of the victimised generic 'Marys' of the old ballad, the 'spoken' text proceeds by interrupting itself to tell the tale of the absences and gaps in literary history where women should be, eloquently articulating that absence by ellipses and in peroration calling on the voice of the absent working-class woman who is washing up the dishes to become 'Shakespeare's sister'. Woolf's figure of the pregnant suicide, Judith Shakespeare, is the literary equivalent of the abandoned pregnant servant girl who appears in all of Mrs Pankhurst's speeches.

Ethel Smyth's publication of Mrs Pankhurst's letters, one suspects, was not done out of the purest of motives, for she was angry at the request for their return when the friendship faltered during the war. But the reader is grateful, for few letters of any of the leaders remain to convey the spirit of the movement. Each letter is a story of hair-raising escape from the police, disguise and flight, defiance of the prison doctors who didn't dare to forcibly feed her. Dame Ethel also relates a story which discredits Mrs Pankhurst's devotion to downtrodden women, her stated purpose being the deflation of hero-worship, though, of course, adherents of the view that she was really a conservative autocrat will find confirmation here. They were on their way to a great Albert Hall meeting where her speeches often raised between £6,000 and £10,000:

> Suddenly the car pulled up with a jerk; a woman was down, caught by our mudguard; there was hatred and menace in the air and loud execrations. In a twinkling Mrs Pankhurst was on the pavement, her arm round the blowzy victim of Suffragette brutality, while with the innate authority that never failed her she ordered a policeman to fetch an ambulance. And so manifest was her distress, so obviously sincere her bitter regret that because of the meeting she could not herself take the injured one to the hospital, that in less time than it takes to tell the story it was the crowd that was

comforting Mrs Pankhurst assuring her (which was the case) that no harm had been done, that the lady was quite all right. And all this time Mrs Pankhurst's face, soft with pity, radiant with love, was the face of an angel, and her arm still encircled the lady, who was now quite recovered and inclined to be voluble. Finally the crowd of late enemies urged her to get back into the car, 'else you'll be late for the meeting!' Half-crowns passed, and we drove off, cheers speeding us on our way. But as she settled down somewhat violently in her seat, the nervous strain over, a furious voice muttered in my ear: 'Drunken old beast! Serve her right if we *had* run over her!'

There is a double message in this story. The whole text contains such contradictions as Dame Ethel struggles, before the reader's eye, with her conflicting feelings. She admits in the end that she has failed to present both a personal version of her heroine as all-too-human and 'the sublime and terrific violence of her soul' as a leader of the women's movement. We hear her grinding her teeth at the end (and there are at least three false endings which precede it) citing the Anacreontic Ode where the poet strikes his lyre to hymn heroism but the instrument will only sing of love. Dame Ethel feels she has failed to show her subject as human and resorts to a page of quotations on heroism from the bible. Like Dangerfield and Sylvia Pankhurst, Ethel Smyth's story has a plot. It is the story of a failed love affair. What it reveals is her own passion for the ruthless, dedicated, authoritarian leader and the death of that passion when her heroine became a simple 'civilian'. It was Mrs Pankhurst's human mistakes which were 'to silence the music between Mrs Pankhurst and myself'.

For her story begins with the claim to intimacy, suggesting that she has letters 'too sacred to print', which led to Virginia Woolf's belief that they had been lovers. But the text is not about physical but spiritual love. Try as she may, Dame Ethel cannot create 'warmth', for her script in all the brilliant autobiographical portraits is centered on the greatness of 'soul' of her friends. Mrs Pankhurst is recalled in the romantic glow of one remembered moment when they watched the dawn, two women with their noses pressed to the window on Census Night in 1910, and felt the great 'mystery' of feminism. (Quotes above are from Ethel Smyth's *Female Pipings in Eden*, Peter Davies, 1934.)

I have tried to show the operations of each author's plot in the historical representation of suffrage and the Pankhursts, what Fulford called in *Votes For Women* the range of historical tone from 'masculine condescension' to 'apostolic fervour'. Even Andrew

Rosen's *Rise Up, Women*, an attempt at a scholarly, 'objective' history, has its problems. And the books by the journalist David Mitchell, *The Fighting Pankhursts* and *Queen Christabel* were salaciously aimed at a male readership afraid of the new feminisms of the 1970s with more modern and rudely expressed sexual and psychological explanations of the political movement.

Feminist historians, notably the late Joan Kelly, whose essays have been collected as *Women, History and Theory*, have argued that women's history should not be studied only in relation to standard male periodisation by wars and reigns of kings. When Kelly asked 'Did Women have a Renaissance?' she was questioning the whole ordering of the discipline. In 'Placing Women's History in History' Betsey Fox-Genovese advocates research into women's lives and movements and the integration of that knowledge into new representations of historical material so that the voices of the powerless may be heard along with the powerful.

Fortunately we now have some good examples of ways in which such histories could be done. In Britain the powerful modern social history of the working class, led by E.P. Thompson, ignored women. Barbara Taylor's *Eve and the New Jerusalem* retraced the steps of the working–class historians and restored women socialists and religious rebels to a place in history. And yet this work continues to be ignored. That is why I suggested at the beginning of this essay that we might stimulate a new history of the suffrage struggle by asking the question, 'Why did Labour repudiate women and the struggle for the vote?' rather than writing another scenario according to Sylvia Pankhurst's script in which the movement is tarred with the 'bourgeois' brush before it is examined. Thus even Jill Liddington and Jill Norris's study of working class suffrage, *One Hand Tied Behind Us*, provides a great deal of useful information but within a monolithic and unchallenged assumption that the labour struggle was intrinsically revolutionary and that the class of the suffrage leaders must have produced a non–revolutionary movement. As Virginia Woolf wrote in *Three Guineas*, the study of men's opposition to women's freedom might be an even more interesting study than the study of women's own struggle. But this would entail a sophisticated re-thinking of modern monolithic (and sexist) labour history. The recent biographers of Keir Hardie have seen his allegiance to the woman's cause as derived from personal involvement with Emmeline and Sylvia Pankhurst rather than as an unpopular political principle, and as a 'tragic' cause of a failed career. Supposing one were to ask why his fellow labour leaders were opposed to suffrage instead? In Martha Vicinus's *Independent Women: Work and Community for*

Single Women 1850-1920 we have now an example' of a socialist-
feminist historian looking at suffrage not as an isolated phenomenon, but as the result of institution-building and the middle-class
struggle of women in the professions of religion, nursing, social
work and teaching, so that the female presence in suffrage politics
is a logical consequence of a century's processes of organisation.
Because she is concerned with women's communities of work, she
focuses on spatiality in 'homes' and institutions, as I have, as a
literary critic, looked at voice and speech. Women's public entry
into the streets and on to the platforms is what concerns her, and
the narrative of *Independent Women* is a remarkable trajectory of
middle-class women out of the confines of their parents' homes
into the public world of work and the protection of female living
communities to sustain their emotional lives. In Vicinus's account,
'the militant suffrage campaign was a radical break with the
Victorian women's movement, yet it was also its culmination'
(250), she studies the 'assault on public space' in a chapter called
'Male Space and Women's Bodies'. She deals with the charge
against the militant movement of its indifference or opposition to
a new sexual ideology for women which would include recognition
of female desire rather than stress chastity and woman's supposedly
innate spirituality:

> A closer consideration of its activities reveals a conscious
> effort on the part of the WSPU . . . to forge a new spiritu-
> ality, based upon women's traditional idealism and self-
> sacrifice but intended to reach out and transform not only
> the position of women but society itself. Women were to
> become a force in the public sphere, to take over and control
> the public arena by the strength of their superior morality.
> This naturally meant a rigorous purity in regard to sexual
> matters, combined with a strong sense of bodily control; the
> integrity of the human body – degraded by forced feeding in
> prison – in turn symbolised the inherent spiritual force of
> each woman. . . . If we make the necessary mental leap into
> a world based upon noneconomic spiritual arguments, then
> the revolutionary ideology of the suffragettes becomes clear,
> along with their adherence to sexual purity.
>
> (*Independent Women*, 252)

It might therefore be possible to connect the spirituality and
chastity of suffragette symbolism with their earlier socialist sisters
studied by Barbara Taylor in *Eve and the New Jerusalem*. On the
other hand, the text of Christabel Pankhurst's *The Great Scourge
and How to End It* is very disturbing to contemporary feminists. It

reflects the same split, particularly evident in the American feminist movement today, over pornography. As historian Judith Walkowitz points out in *Prostitution and Victorian Society*, the figures on syphilis infecting three-quarters of the male population, taken from medical treatises by American doctors, are vastly inflated. The text is couched in the language of what Nancy Cott calls Victorian 'passionlessness' as female virtue. Of course Christabel did not write in a social vacuum. There was a long history of women's struggle with prostitution in Josephine Butler's campaign over the Contagious Diseases Acts. In addition W.T. Stead and his anti White Slavery Campaign had adherents among the suffragettes. Christabel was articulating the feminist social purity position already deeply entrenched within feminism and supported by many suffragists.

Christabel Pankhurst was neither ignorant nor stupid. Her choice in linking votes for women with chastity for men was a deliberate political choice to exacerbate *difference*, to conduct the suffragette movement as a sex-war against the enemy, men. Surely she was aware of the work of the sex-radicals from the 1880s onwards, attempting, in the work of Olive Schreiner, Havelock Ellis and others, to articulate the psychic and physical realities of female desire, to campaign for birth control, which would have provided far more real relief for the destitute working women, whose victimisation Mrs Pankhurst never ceased to point out. Deliberately fanning the flames of sex hatred, the *Great Scourge* is an exercise in sexual politics like modern feminism's campaign for abortion rights. It was a political choice to champion the 'wrongs' issue rather than the 'rights' issue – venereal disease rather than birth control. Frustrated at every turn by the false promises and deceitful behaviour of the Liberals, long before abandoned by the young and struggling labour parties, Christabel Pankhurst chose to excite sex hatred in the same way that her earlier friends on the left excited class hatred, as a spur to revolutionary violence. Like the ancients carving the figure of Medusa's head on their shields, she hoped to freeze and frighten and symbolically castrate the enemy with her armed-virgin, Joan-of-Arc posture, whose sword would surgically un-womb the diseased venereal State.

The problem with her metaphor of the venereal State is the logic that it was prostitutes (the victims whom suffrage was going to save) who gave the diseases to men, who spread them to their chaste and modest wives and produced syphilitic children. There are then two meanings of the word 'women' in her text and an exciting in her middle-class women readers of fear and hatred of prostitutes. One can see that Christabel Pankhurst was attempting to reverse the stigma attached to women's bodies by the enemies of suffrage. By arguing that all of women's gynaecological diseases were caused by syphilis and gonorrhoea given to them by their husbands, she aroused more fears than she dispelled. Rather than arguing that their sexual functions did not unfit women for politics, she argued that men were the cause of all female diseases. That would leave only virgins and spinsters as fit for the vote. The text also includes a sinister subtext of eugenicist propaganda about 'race suicide'. One could argue that Christabel's tactic was effective as a political move to divide women and men as far apart as possible so that the government would at last relent, that, if men could not be moved by serious human rights arguments or the biggest demonstrations ever seen before or since, they might be moved by fear of virginal vengeance. 'Nice' women would now have access to sordid facts about syphilis and might begin to blame their husbands for their miscarriages.

There was a contemporary critique of *The Great Scourge* from the left-wing free-love feminists. Rebecca West, always a loyal and vociferously outspoken suffragette, was appalled by its arguments. In 'On Mentioning the Unmentionable' (Clarion, 26 Sept. 1913), Rebecca West attacks the hate campaign – 'One must love humanity before one can save it,' and exhorts Christabel 'as one completely ignorant young woman to another' to refrain from destroying the suffrage movement. She regrets the universal condemnation of men; 'With a sharp pang one will see Miss Pankhurst on the Day of Judgment, sweeping all our fathers and husbands and sons down amongst the goats.' Deploring Christabel Pankhurst's 'terrifying savagery' and 'old-fashioned' and 'uncharitable' position which she thinks will set back the medical treatment of syphilis by renewing moral disdain for the victims, Rebecca West urges her to reject puritanism.

Here I would like to point out that Rebecca West's socialist-feminist essays were published by Robert Blatchford in the *Clarion*, evidence that at least some sections of the left did not reject the movement as 'bourgeois'. Labour historians persist in their pursuit of women's dissociation from labour rather than asking the question the other way. The essay by Martin Pugh in the latest volume *The First Labour Party, 1906-1914* edited by K. D. Brown (Croom Helm, 1986) dismisses Middleton's *Women in the Labour Movement* and sees Labour's rejection of the women's cause as a classic dilemma of a political party with a wide range of interests confronted by 'a pressure group urging priority for its own cause'. Thus labour is forgiven in advance and labour women are quoted as finding the Pankhursts too aristocratic.

I suggest that future feminist historians may find a different story in the autobiographies of two working-class suffragettes, Hannah Mitchell in *The Hard Way Up* and Mary Gawthorpe in *Up Hill to Holloway*, where precise documentation is given of local labour groups' insistence that feminists who had spent years in labour organising must choose between suffrage or socialism. Rather than blame the Pankhursts, one might imagine their courage despite the loss of labour's support, which they had earned, in persisting outside the socialist framework in which their movement was born.

In returning now to the image with which I opened, the forcible feeding of hunger-striking suffragettes, I want to suggest ways in which we might begin to look at the iconography of suffrage in both the forcible feeding posters and the Cat and Mouse posters. The art and propaganda posters of the movement, like the rhetoric of Mrs Pankhurst's speeches, deserves the serious attention of a new generation of historians. The depictions of forcible feeding in several suffragette representations may be clearly read as rape scenes. Over a thousand women experienced this violation of their bodies and the violence of tubes thrust down their noses. The health of many women was permanently damaged. Roger Fulford reassures his readers that forcible feeding was not dangerous and had already been in use for many years on 'lunatics'. It is barbaric. Yet one is puzzled by the patriarchal power of ideology to continue to see the suffragettes as violent despite all the pictorial evidence of violence being done to them. For women readers of the suffragettes' accounts of forcible feeding and the posters, the analogy with rape is telling. One is forced to ask why the government and the medical profession colluded in classifying political rebels as madwomen and why history itself refuses to deal with why such martyrdom was called for in the winning of the basic political right in democracies, the right to vote.

Djuna Barnes faced her ordeal of imitation of the British suffragettes professionally, but she could hardly bear the anguish, the searing pain in her face and chest:

If I, play acting, felt my being burning with revolt at this brutal usurpation of my own functions, how they who actually suffered the ordeal in its acutest horror must have flamed at the violation of the sanctuaries of their spirit! I saw in my hysteria a vision of a hundred women in grim prison hospitals, bound and shrouded on tables just like this, held in the rough grip of callous warders, while white-robed doctors thrust rubber tubing into the delicate interstices of their

nostrils and forced into their helpless bodies the crude fuel to
sustain the life they longed to sacrifice.

New York World Magazine
September 6 1914

While I am not suggesting that historians of suffrage learn to re-
read the period and its actors as closely as Djuna Barnes 'read'
forcible feeding, I am interested in the results of work based on
equally close analysis of texts, posters and political strategy.
Toward this end, there are new theories which question the 'truth-
value' of historical narratives and rhetorical studies of these plots,
and there are literary critical theories of the speaking subject, which
allow us to focus on the meaning of what I call the feminist
'discourse of interruption' and other female tropes. There are also
theories, largely developed by film studies, of 'specularization' and
the problem of the male 'gaze' at the figure of the female and
women's imprisonment in it or response to it. All of these will, I
trust, produce re-readings of the suffrage movement which reflect
our present ideological concerns.

Jane Marcus
November, 1986

Christabel Pankhurst

The Commons Debate on Woman Suffrage

with a reply
(1908)

I Introductory Note

The second reading of the Women's Enfranchisement Bill has been carried by a large majority, and our object now is to force the Government to adopt the Bill. The difficulty of this task has been increased by Mr Stanger's ill-advised compromise with the opponents of the Bill. Under the new rules of procedure, the natural consequence of the second reading being carried is that a Bill is referred to a Standing Committee, where the Committee stage proceeds uninterrupted by the ordinary business of the House. Mr Stanger unfortunately went out of his way to propose, and it was carried without a division, that the Bill be referred to a Committee of the whole House. The Bill can now go no further unless the Government sets apart some of the time of the House for the purpose of its discussion. The strongest possible pressure must now be applied in order to induce the Government to take this course.

We do not expect much help in this endeavour from rank and file Members of Parliament. Most of them are so greatly lacking in influence, earnestness, and tactical skill that they are of little service to our cause. Those members who support the Government will apparently do nothing likely to embarrass their leaders. This was proved by their refusal to support Lord Robert Cecil's amendment to the Plural Voting Bill, the adoption of which would have compelled the Government to choose between making a favourable declaration on Woman Suffrage or accepting a defeat in the House of Commons. The hollowness of the average Liberal member's friendship has again been exemplified by their ready acquiescence in the proposal to shelve the present Woman Suffrage Bill.

However, although the attitude of most of our professing friends in the House of Commons is a weakness, we need not despair of success. In the past two years the National Women's Social and Political Union has done what the world deemed to be impossible, and no future difficulties can equal those already overcome. What we have to do is shortly this, to induce the Government to allot part of the time of the House for the discussion of our Bill, and to allow it to become law. The pretext for not doing this has been stated by the *Daily Chronicle* and others to be that the time of the House is already fully mortgaged, and that the withdrawal of some other piece of public business would be necessary. In reply, we have to point out that the withdrawal of other business seems no very serious calamity; and that, possibly, if less time were wasted by members of Parliament, the withdrawal of another measure might, after all, prove to be unnecessary.

In the course of his speech on behalf of the Government, Mr Herbert Gladstone made the important admission that though we have shown our claim to be just, the Government will not give the vote unless compelled to do so. He suggested that the necessary force may be applied by the holding of meetings of extraordinary size, and by the education of the constituencies. Though we suspect that his object is to induce us to abandon our direct attack upon the Government, and to undertake a campaign which he hopes will blunt our energy and exhaust our resources, we shall certainly carry out our prearranged plan of holding great meetings to demand the vote. Of these meetings, one was held on March 19th, in the Albert Hall, London, when 7,000 women paid for their seats, and another will be held in Hyde Park on Sunday, June 21st. Also our intention is to educate the constituencies not only to a belief in Woman Suffrage, but to the conviction that this Government must be compelled to grant the reform. In particular, at every bye-election we shall be found urging the electors to cast their vote against a Government which is false to its professed principles. Though we appreciate the need of continued educational work in the country, we are convinced that the education of Cabinet Ministers is even more important. The militant tactics designed to effect this object are as necessary as ever. Though the last deputations to Parliament involved heavy sacrifice on our part, the good results were so marked that we call upon our members and friends to be ready for further militant action.

Christabel Pankhurst
March, 1908.

II Answers to Opponents

In the debate in the House of Commons on the second reading of the Woman's Franchise Bill, on February 28th, 1908, a number of arguments were adduced against granting the franchise to women, by removing the disqualification of sex. I propose to answer the principal of these as shortly as possible.

1 *The security of Government rests ultimately on force.*
  With the progress of civilisation spiritual force replaces physical force as the controlling element in human affairs, and at the present day physical force is brought into play only for the purpose of restraining those anti-social and less highly evolved members of the community who are not amenable to any more subtle form of control. To this order of being, Members of Parliament who argue that Government rests on physical force unwittingly confess themselves to belong.

2 *Women are not competent to deal with Imperial and International affairs*
  In point of fact, those women who have had to deal with International and Imperial issues have done so with conspicuous success. The voters, whether men or women, do not, however, themselves transact business of this nature. Their function is to choose the persons who are to conduct the nation's business. Women are at least as competent as men to make that choice wisely.

3 *There is no precedent among Sovereign States*
  A good deal was made by Members of Parliament of the comparative unimportance of the States that do already accept the principle of Woman's Suffrage. The same men would no doubt be ready to follow the example of these States in regard to any other proposed legislation. They include, as is well known, the following: – Norway, Finland, Australia, New Zealand, and the four States of the American Union – namely, Wyoming, Colorado, Utah, and Idaho. But no Suffragist bases the argument for granting Woman's Suffrage in this country on precedent. Great Britain has not been in the habit of taking precedents in the realm of constitutional liberty from other countries, but of making them for herself, and it is to be hoped she will never abandon her leadership of the world in this respect.

4 *There is no demand for the vote by women*
  This statement is untrue. Many hundred thousand women have shown their demand for the vote in all ways permitted to them. We do not claim, however, that every woman demands the vote,

but this claim was never put forward in the case of men, nor was any attempt made to prove that the majority of men demanded the vote.

5 *No large petitions are being signed by women*
Women have learnt by experience the futility of petitions. In the seventies there were several million signatures to petitions and memorials. In 1896 a special memorial from women contained over a quarter of a million signatures. These were entirely disregarded, and, therefore, women have adopted other means of expressing their demand for the vote.

6 *The advocates of the movement are a stage army*
It is true, of course, that the leaders of the movement do not number many thousands, but this is true of all political agitations. Followers are exceedingly numerous, as proof of which may be instanced the enormous meetings of women which have been held all over the country. The recent meetings on Hunslet Moor, Leeds – one attended by 20,000 or 30,000 people, and the other by 100,000 people, of whom a great many were women – were equal in size and enthusiasm to any demonstrations held prior to the Reform Acts of the Nineteenth Century.

Other great demonstrations in favour of woman suffrage are to take place on March 19th in the Albert Hall, London, and on June 21st, in Hyde Park. Another proof of the great demand that women are making for the vote is the fact that the leading organisations of women, such as the Women's Liberal Federation and the Women's Co-operative Guild are engaged in the movement. These societies in all represent a membership of close on a million, and their interest has been aroused in spite of the refusal of the press and of politicians to educate the mass of women. If such a policy had been pursued with regard to Free Trade and Tariff Reform, or other questions of a political character, the men of the country would have shown little interest in them. Finally, men politicians seem to forget that women are much less free than men are to leave their homes and come out in the streets to demand the vote by means of big processions.

7 *The male part of the electorate is still unconverted on the question*
This was no doubt the case at one time, but the average man is now prepared to admit the justice of our claim. There is no doubt that women suffragists had enormous influence at the bye-elections in Mid-Devon, in Hereford, in Worcester, in Leeds, and in Hastings, and this in spite of the very great difficulty of persuading

men, however keenly they think on one particular question, to withdraw their support from their own party.

8 *Women have no need of the vote*

In answer to Sir W. R. Cremer's suggestion that women under the present laws are even better treated than men, it is only necessary to refer to some of the glaring inequalities which at present exist. The laws of inheritance; the laws relating to the guardianship of children, and the divorce laws, are among those which involve injustice to women. Politicians are threatening to introduce a new legal inequality by excluding women from certain industries. Other disabilities result from the fact that the adminis- tration of the law is entirely in the hands of men. The underpay- ment of women workers is another evil which only political power can remove.

9 *The homes of the country would suffer*

No such result has followed the enfranchisement of women in other countries, and it is evident that the interests of the home can best be safeguarded by women voters.

10 *All women might unite against all men*

As a matter of fact, the only question likely to unite all women against all men is the present refusal of men to grant women the vote. To place men and women on a footing of equality is the one way of rendering improbable any political war of the sexes.

11 *Women would claim admittance to all employments of men*

Women will certainly claim to be admitted to every employment suited to their powers. No legal barrier is required to exclude them from employments in which they are unfitted to engage. With regard to the entrance of women into the House of Commons, women will not sit in Parliament unless sent by the people of the country. Suffragists believe the vote to be of far greater importance than a place in the House of Commons, though they believe it to be possible that ultimately the electors may wish in some cases to be represented by competent women.

12 *The women admitted to the existing franchise would oppress the unenfranchised women*

As all classes of women, the richest and the poorest, would be represented under the present franchise, no political distinction could well be drawn between the women who had votes and those who had not. The owner of a great estate and the woman living in a one-room tenement would both be enrolled on the Parliamentary register.

We are not specially concerned with the ingenious arguments that were adduced against the particular form of Mr Stanger's Bill. The Bill proceeds along the simplest and most logical lines of removing the sex barrier, and will admit women to the same franchise as that enjoyed by men. If the Government consider this measure too limited it is open to them to carry a wider measure of enfranchisement. All we ask is that there shall be some immediate recognition of our claim to vote.

III Impressions of the Debate
By F. W. Pethick Lawrence

(1) In all Acts relating to the qualifications and registration of voters, or persons entitled or claiming to be registered and to vote in the election of members of Parliament, wherever words occur which import the masculine gender the same shall be held to include women for all purposes connected with and having reference to the right to be registered as voters and to vote in such elections.

(2) A woman shall not be disqualified by reason of marriage from being so registered and voting notwithstanding the provisions of any law or custom to the contrary.

The debate on the Women's Enfranchisement Bill on Friday, February 28th, marked a new phase of the question; not because of the result arrived at, but because of the change in the attitude of the House of Commons. I attended the debate in 1907, and I was present on this occasion, and heard the whole of the speeches. The change between the two discussions was most remarkable. This year the question was treated by every member with one exception, as a serious question of practical politics, in favour of which and against which arguments had to be brought forward.

But still more important than this change from the levity of previous years was the sense of the growing importance of the women's agitation which pervaded the atmosphere of the Chamber, and was detected even in the speeches of the most vigorous opponents of the Bill. Scarcely a single speech was made in which some reference to the militant agitation was not made, and the general feeling among the members was that however much they might disapprove of the action of the Suffragettes, nevertheless the leaders were women whose characters were above suspicion, and whose outlook was political, and not due to any desire for personal advantage.

Mr Gladstone's speech was addressed not to the members of the

House who were present at the debate, but almost entirely to the Suffragettes. He made excuses to them for the failure of the Government to tackle this question. He told them that though he sympathised with their impatience, yet a closer knowledge with politics such as he had would inform them that the Government was powerless. He recalled history for their benefit, and put his interpretation on the great meeting in Hyde Park when men had demanded the vote, and he sketched out for them the character of the agitation which he would recommend to them for their future guidance.

Another interesting feature of the debate was the sympathetic speech by Mr Pike Pease. Though Mr Pease did not, of course, speak officially on behalf of what has sometimes been called 'His Majesty's Opposition,' yet the fact that he was the sole speaker from the Opposition front bench was intended to convey the impression that the official Opposition was favourable to the measure.

Of the other speeches, that of Mr Stanger, who moved the second reading of the Bill, was undoubtedly full of strong and convincing arguments, and he dealt in a cogent manner with the principal reasons which have from time to time been made against the measure. His one mistake – unfortunately a serious one – was the ready way in which he lent himself to the shelving of the Bill by undertaking that it should go for further discussion to a Committee of the Whole House, instead of being sent, as it would otherwise naturally have been, to a Standing Committee, where it could have been discussed during the next few months, though the time of the whole House be occupied with other measures.

The principal speeches in opposition were made by Mr Cathcart Wason and Mr Mallet. The former took up the line that sex ought to be the bar to the vote. He also urged that riot should not be allowed to dominate the affairs of State. He feared the possession of the vote by women because he thought it would lead to their entrance into the House of Commons, and ultimately to women sometimes being made Speaker in that Chamber.

The only other speech which requires mention was that of Mr Rees, who talked out the Bill last year. On this occasion he was prevented from doing so by the acceptance of the closure by the Speaker. But in the quarter of an hour in which he occupied the attention of the House he demonstrated the low idea of women which finds favour among a certain section of men. His speech, which was punctuated with uproarious laughter, should be read by women in order that they may appreciate the opposition which they have to face. Such speeches demonstrate the absolute need for the possession of the vote.

The account which follows has been drawn largely from the *Times* newspaper, supplemented in one or two instances from my recollection, in particular by the reference which Mr Philip Snowden made to the great meetings in Leeds, which, as he said, demonstrated that the demand for the vote at the present time is of the same magnitude as the demand made by men thirty or forty years ago.

Details of the Discussion

Mr Stanger (Liberal Member for North Kensington), in moving the second reading, explained that its object was to remove the disability which at present attaches to women in Parliamentary elections, while the second sub-section of Clause 1 enacted that a woman should not be disqualified by reason of marriage from being registered and voting, notwithstanding any law or custom to the contrary. In answer to the criticism that the Bill did not deal at the same time with the various anomalies of the registration laws, he contended that the removal of the disability which attaches to women was a point which should be dealt with quite separately. If the Bill was read a second time he proposed to move that it be referred to Committee of the Whole House.

Mr Stanger then proceeded to sweep away a number of other objections which have from time to time been made to the possession of the franchise by women; among others, he refuted the doctrine that there was no demand. On the contrary, he held that there was a demand, both broad in volume and passionate in its intensity – a demand which no Government could afford long to refuse.

The Recent By-Elections

It was said, and with great truth, that the demand could not be conceded until the predominant partner was converted; he quite agreed, but that conversion was proceeding very satisfactorily. He was much struck by the fact that in recent bye-elections it had become almost a common form for both candidates to be in favour of woman suffrage, and he should expect to find in the lobby in support of this Bill the hon. member for South Leeds, the hon. member for Worcester City, and the hon. and gallant member for

Mid-Devon. He condemned the methods of those who had been called 'suffragettes,' he had condemned publicly and privately their acts of illegality, their concerted attempts to break up public meetings, and their invasion of the domestic privacy of Ministers. He hoped no word of his would give encouragement to such methods of campaign. But he hoped, too, that the House would not be guilty of the folly often imputed to the female sex of letting their judgment be overbalanced by a wave of emotion. (Hear, hear.) The true doctrine was that, if in the course of a political agitation excesses were committed, while preserving law and order by meeting out suitable punishments to the transgressors, they should search for the discontent which lay beneath the agitation, and apply the appropriate remedy.

Women's Service to the State

Mr Acland (Liberal Member for Yorks, Richmond), in seconding the motion, said that, though as an adult suffragist he should favour amendments at a later stage, yet he supported the principle of the Bill. The opponents of the Bill reminded them that women could not serve as soldiers and sailors, and that, if they all acted in the same way, they would be able to decide matters of military service, for instance, and all great Imperial questions against the wishes of men, upon whom the burden must fall in these important matters. With regard to that, he might perhaps venture to say that there were some things also which men could not do, and it was at any rate arguable whether the State would sooner come to grief by men ceasing to bear arms or women children. (Laughter and cheers.) He believed that the change now advocated would be good for men, good for women, and good for politics.

Mr Cathcart Wason (Liberal Member for Orkney and Shetland) said that he objected to the measure because the Liberal party had always held that property was not the foundation of the right to vote, and he would ask Liberals whether they could support a Bill which would enormously increase the number of property voters in the country, of fagot voters, and of out-voters.

He asked the House to consider whether this movement was founded on riot or revolution? If it was founded on riot, were they going to yield to clamour? If it was founded on revolution, then this was one of the most revolutionary measures ever proposed to a great assembly on a Friday afternoon by an absolutely irresponsible person.

What contribution did women make to force? It was force that ruled the world. It was force, and only force, that enabled them to put their heads on their pillows at night with any sense of security that they should wake up in the morning and find them there. (Much laughter.)

Why was it that during the long period the Conservatives had been in power they had not moved a single step forward in the direction of women franchise, although their great leaders were in favour of it? No attempts were made in those years to break up Conservative meetings. No beauteous maidens chained themselves to the door of the right hon. gentleman the Member for the City of London when he was Prime Minister, crying out 'Give, give.' (Laughter.) If the Bill were carried it would mean the giving to women the right to sit in the House, and to occupy any office in the House, even that of Mr Speaker, involving the duty of controlling an Assembly that was sometimes disorderly. (Cheers.) Surely that was a prospect at which they must all shudder. (Laughter.)

Mr Mallet (Plymouth) seconded the amendment. He thought the leaders of the suffragette party were correct when they said the action in this matter lay with the Government of the day. One grave objection to the Bill was that it would multiply the plural vote, which Liberals had been for years trying to diminish.

Creating a Precedent

Hitherto in every sovereign State in the world this right had been confined unanimously to men. This Bill asked us to reverse the rule of all the ages, which, rightly or wrongly, had based the franchise primarily upon sex. The great change needed more consideration than they could possibly give it in three short paragraphs of a private member's Bill. (Cheers.) The experience of the world must go for something. He proceeded to refer disparagingly to the colonies and other places in which woman suffrage prevailed.

One could not study these wide and generous suffrages in other parts of the world without dreaming dreams and seeing visions of a system of State-aided emigration of our suffragettes. (Cheers and laughter.)

He had the deepest respect for the motives of the advocates of woman suffrage, and he did not deny the genuineness of the movement; but he did deny it was widespread. After all, the movement now was that of a minority – a mere handful, a handful in every sense. (Laughter.) The methods resorted to proved to demonstration the weakness of the cause. He asked for proof that women desired to fill the same public duties as men, and really preferred political work and agitation to the work they had so incomparably performed for generations in forming the character of the people and in governing the family.

Government Attitude

Mr Herbert Gladstone (Leeds, W.), speaking from the Government bench, said that, as the House would have anticipated, the Government would take that day the course they pursued last year. He would remind the House that last year the Prime Minister pointed out that there was no indication of unanimity in the House of Commons, and that there were differences of opinion to be found on almost every bench. For those reasons the only course open to the Government was to leave the decision to the views of individual members.

As far as he was concerned, he was entirely in favour of the principle of the Bill, but he was not going into the question of what it contained. He had pledged himself without reservation to vote on the subject, and though this Bill might be imperfect, at any rate it removed a disqualification and an inequality which had been for so long a time a deep source of complaint with great masses of the people of this country. (Hear, hear.)

Advice to the Suffragettes

It was impossible not to sympathise with the eagerness and passion which actuated so many women. (Hear, hear.) It was impossible also not to sympathise with their disappointment, past, present, and yet to come. Women had not had the franchise up to now; therefore, through no fault of their own, they had not passed through the hard school of what were called practical, but which too often in this country were unpractical, politics. Men had had to struggle for centuries for their political rights. They had had to fight from the time of Cromwell, and for the last 130 years the contest, the warfare, had been perpetual, and full victory had not even yet been achieved on the question of male suffrage. (Hear, hear.) On this question experience showed that predominance of argument alone – and he believed that had been obtained – was not enough to win the political day. They were in the region, in the stage, of what were called academic discussions, the ventilation of pious opinions, unaccompanied, it might be, by effective action not only on the part of the Government, but of political parties and of the voters of the country. Members of the House reflected the opinions of the country not only in regard to the numbers outside, but with regard to the intensity of the feeling in support of a movement, and the Government must necessarily be a reflex of the party that brought it into being.

Then came the time when political dynamics were far more important than political argument. You had to move a great inert mass of opinion which in the earlier stages always existed in the country in regard to questions of the first magnitude, and with regard to this question opinion must be moved at the present time, not in Parliament Square, not by relieving Cabinet Ministers of the trouble of making speeches at public meetings – (laughter) – but by moving it in all the constituencies of the country. Men had learned this lesson and knew the necessity for demonstrating the greatness of their movement, and for establishing that *force majeure* which actuated and armed a Government for effective work. (Hear, hear.) That was the task before the supporters of this great movement. When he was applied to to use his influence to move the Government forward, that was very well so far as it went, but the people outside must be more actively influenced. It was not enough for the Government to bring in a Bill. Lord John Russell and Mr Disraeli four times failed to carry Bills for the extension of male suffrage. No doubt there was a great and growing movement in favour of granting the franchise to women, but the movement lacked numbers. (Hear, hear.) Looking back at the great political crisis in the thirties, the sixties, and the eighties, it would be found that people did not go about in small groups, nor were they content with enthusiastic meetings in large halls; they assembled in their tens of thousands all over the country. It had been said men had to use violence before they could get what they wanted, and the Hyde Park railings were mentioned. But the destruction of the railings was in the nature of an accident, and was due to the pressure of huge masses of people wishing to show their earnestness and to ventilate their opinions in the park, and the authorities foolishly closed the gates. Of course, it was not to be expected that women could assemble in such masses, but he was bound to say there was great force in what his hon. friend the member for Plymouth had said, that it had not yet been sufficiently demonstrated that women as a whole desired to have the vote. Power belonged to the masses, and through this power a Government would be influenced into more effective action than a Government would be likely to take under present conditions.

Mr Pike Pease (Darlington), speaking from the front Conservative bench, said that the position taken by the Home Secretary was practically this: – 'I have no objection to your lighting the fire; indeed, I should like to see it lighted; but I shall take away the matches.' It was illogical to grant electoral power to women in connection with county and borough councils, and not in regard to Parliament. Nor had it ever been explained why women were not to be regarded as worthy of the privilege they asked for. After all, the greatest ruler of the greatest country in the world – the late Queen Victoria – was a woman.

Mr Fletcher (Hampstead) said that he was informed that in New Zealand the grant of the franchise to women had been very beneficial in purifying politics, because the women declined to vote for candidates who were given to drink, or who were living apart from their wives, or who were unfavourably known on the Exchange. The result was that greater sincerity and earnestness was added to politics.

Sir M. Levy (Leicestershire, Loughborough) denounced the Bill as a retrograde measure, going back to the old reactionary days of the property qualification. (Cheers.) It would not democratise the House of Commons, but make it less representative than it was at the present time. It would exclude just that part of the womanhood of the country who were more in need of the influence and power which a vote would give than any other class.

Mr Kettle (Tyrone, E.), who admitted that the Nationalist Party, like others in the House, were divided on this question, supported the Bill, because it marked a beginning, because it would embody in the Statute-book a principle that would be found to grow and develop. He admitted that the experiment of giving women the vote would be attended with some risks; but was there ever a great social change that did not carry risks with it? They could not remove all objections by argument; and here the House was asked to make a great act of faith in the great future of humanity. He was prepared to make that great act of faith. (Cheers.)

An Undemocratic Bill

Mr A. Clement Edwards (Denbigh Borough) opposed the second reading of the Bill because he was in favour of adult suffrage. He was not prepared to support a measure of this limited and property-mongering character. Personally, he had not been frightened by the boisterous and somewhat Olympic methods of the active crusaders in favour of the women's vote, some of whose leaders might be described as belonging to the furniture vanguard of the suffrage movement. It had been suggested that the Bill ought to be supported because it was a beginning. He did not regard a Bill which clothed with the power of voting certain propertied women as a beginning. Not only would the Bill fail to enfranchise the great mass of working women, but it would have the automatic effect of actually disfranchising thousands of working men living in houses with a less rent than £20 a year or occupying lodgings of less value. If the total rent of joint occupiers was not at least £20 a year, neither was entitled to vote. In large districts of London, in colliery districts, and in the rural areas, this fact would enable landlords under the Bill to disfranchise married working men without their wives receiving votes.

The Great Demonstrations in Leeds

Mr Snowden (Blackburn) adduced facts to prove that there was a demand for the measure. He knew something of this agitation, and he had come to the conclusion that there was not in the country, at the present time, with the single exception of the Socialist movement, a movement which was so vigorous, so active – (a Ministerialist: 'So rough.') – and carrying on such persistent and consistent propaganda work as that for the enfranchisement of women. (Hear, hear.) He was convinced that the action of women in the bye-elections had done more to change the disposal of the male vote than any other factor or influence. In Leeds the women had attracted invariably larger audiences than the candidates themselves. On the Sunday before the poll they had an enormous meeting on the moor, and on the eve of the poll the great demonstration which had taken place in connection with the women's agitation was the largest in the memory of the town. If the recently returned member for the constituency were present he was sure he would corroborate this statement. Criticism had been levelled at what was called the limited character of the Bill. The Bill limited nothing. It was not an enfranchising Bill. It was simply a Bill to remove sex disability, and the position women took up was that they demanded that the vote should be given on the same terms as it was or might be given to men. They were concentrating for the present on the simple point of the removal of the sex disability, and he thought they were wise in confining their demand to that.

A Stage Army

Sir W. Cremer (Shoreditch, Haggerston) thought he would be able to prove that there was very little demand for this Bill from the women of the United Kingdom. The fact was that during the last year and a half some 4,500 more women had signed petitions to that House in favour of having the vote than had been the case during the previous 17 years. (Hear, hear.) During the last 17 years only 198,403 women had petitioned that House in favour of the suffrage, and on the basis of the last census that left 10,301,597 who would not even take the trouble to sign a petition in behalf of that cause. (Cheers.) Of course, many meetings had been held in behalf of women suffrage, but they were all organised by one little band of clever women, who were like a stage army in its progress before the curtain, the head of which was continually rushing away to appear again at the tail, and so impress the public with the idea that they were a mighty host. (Laughter.) If they had achieved any importance in the public eye it was because of the way they were boomed in the Press. So far from suffering under grievances, women, by virtue of their sex, enjoyed a great number of legal privileges which were denied to men.

Mr Guest (Cardiff district) understood that the mover of the Bill intended after the second reading to propose that the measure be committed to a Committee of the whole House. That reduced the Bill to a mere pious expression of opinion, which might have been done by a resolution. (Hear, hear.) In those circumstances, those who were opposed to the Bill would welcome a division, because the time had come when the country should realise the serious menace hanging over it.

Mr Atherly-Jones (Durham, N.W.), as a very old friend of woman suffrage, and representing a very large body of opinion outside, protested against the resolve to send the Bill to a Committee of the whole House, because it would mean relegating the question to another year.

Mr Rees (Liberal Member for Montgomery Boroughs) said that no doubt woman was a good thing – (laughter) – and suffrage was a good thing, but it did not follow that woman suffrage was a good thing. In the same way petticoat was a good thing, and government was a good thing, but it did not follow that petticoat government was a good thing. (Cheers and laughter.) An endeavour had been made to make use of the authority of Scripture. The hon. member for Orkney and Shetland began to quote St Paul, but stopped because, he supposed, he had forgotten the quotation. (Loud laughter.) He happened to remember it. 'Neither was the man created for the woman, but the woman for the man.' He put that forward as a conclusive answer against Scripture giving any support to this claim. If Scripture was to be invoked, other passages might be found of an entirely opposite description. One passage was, 'Jerusalem is ruined and Judah is fallen. As for my people, children are their oppressors and women rule over them.' (Laughter.) What kind of women were these? The prophet said, 'Because the daughters of Sion are haughty and walk with stretched forth necks' – (laughter) – 'therefore the Lord will smite with a scab the crown of the head of the daughters of Sion, and in that day the Lord will take away the bravery of their tinkling ornaments.' (Cheers and cries of 'Divide.')

Lord R. Cecil, and subsequently Mr Stanger, at two or three minutes to five o'clock, moved the closure, and on the question being put from the chair, the closure was agreed to.

The House divided, and the numbers were: –

For the amendment	92
Against	271
Majority	179

The Bill was then read a second time, and, on the motion of Mr Stanger, referred to Committee of the whole House.

Christabel Pankhurst

The Militant Methods of the N.W.S.P.U.

(Being the verbatim Report of a Speech of Christabel Pankhurst, at the St James's Hall, on October 15th, 1908)

Ladies and Gentlemen,

We have been working for the vote for forty years, but I do not think we shall have to wait very much longer. It is true that the Liberal Government is bitterly hostile to the reform that we are fighting for. The members of the present Government do not want to give votes to women. But man proposes and woman disposes; and whether they like it or not, when the womanhood of the nation demands political enfranchisement, the Government has to give in. I say the present Government is hostile to Woman Suffrage. Probably some of you will retort – those of you who are not politically experienced will retort – that we have friends in the Cabinet. What about Mr Lloyd George, what about Mr Sydney Buxton, and certain other Cabinet Ministers who tell us that they believe that women ought to have the vote? Well, we say that anybody with the smallest knowledge of constitutional matters will be well aware that membership of a Government which as a whole denies votes to women is quite incompatible with friendship to our cause. No man who believes in Woman Suffrage can possibly remain a member of the present Government. His membership of this Government means that he is hostile to our claim.

Now, where any other question than that of Woman Suffrage is concerned, everybody recognises the truth of what I have said. Would it be any good for any member of the present Government to plead that he was a Protectionist? You would say, 'My good man, then what are you doing in a Free Trade Government?' Would it be any good for a member of the present Government to try and curry favour with the opponents of the Licensing Bill by saying that he was opposed to the Licensing Bill? They would say, 'Then, my friend, your place is out of the Government, not in it!' And so with Woman Suffrage. What is the good of Mr

Lloyd George trying to persuade intelligent women like us that he is in favour of Woman Suffrage while he remains a member of this Government? Now that is why we are against the members of this Cabinet as a whole, and that is why we fight them every one. That is why we do not draw any distinctions in favour of those Cabinet Ministers who claim to be in favour of votes for women. We know perfectly well – and they will have to learn it too – that neither Mr Lloyd George nor anybody else can run with the hare and hunt with the hounds. They have got to choose between Woman Suffrage on the one hand, and a place in the present Cabinet on the other.

This is an appropriate moment, I think, to speak of the rank and file Members of Parliament who say that they support our movement, because there are a great many Liberal Members of the House of Commons, and a good many would-be Liberal Members of the House of Commons, who say, 'Why oppose us? We are in favour of Woman Suffrage.' Well, we must oppose them, because they are sailing under a hostile flag. Fancy a rank and file Member of Parliament or a Liberal candidate trying to persuade us that he is a friend to Woman Suffrage and wants to help us, when he accepts service under Mr Asquith and the present Government! The day has gone by when we could be induced to believe that Mr Jones or Mr Robinson, a follower of the Government, was a friend of our cause, although his leaders were against us. We know perfectly well where the private Member stands: we know perfectly well what the limitations of his power are. The plain fact is that rank and file Members of Parliament are counters in the game, and that they are entirely at the orders of their political leaders. That is why every follower of Mr Asquith is regarded by us as a soldier serving in a hostile army, and, just as Tommy Atkins cannot plead with the enemy not to shoot him because he does not believe in the war that he is waging, so the Liberal Member of Parliament and the Liberal candidate must realise that where we can strike at him, we shall strike at him; not for his own sake, because, poor man, he is helpless, but because he is a unit of strength on the side of the enemy that is opposing us – on the side of the Liberal Government.

You must know that what we are working for is the enactment of a Bill to remove the political disability of sex. There is a Bill now before the House of Commons that meets our views exactly – the Women's Enfranchisement Bill. That is the Bill we want carried, and we want it carried now; and we ask how it is that the Government, if only for the sake of stopping the disorderly proceedings of which they complain, do not carry that measure into law, especially as the second reading of it has already been carried. Of course, they say that they have not time, but that has been the excuse ever since this movement began. The Prime Minister, in reply to a letter we lately sent him, tells us he cannot carry this Bill because some weeks ago he said that he was not going to carry this session any private Member's Bill which was of a controversial character. But something Mr Asquith said some time ago is really no barrier against the enfranchisement of women. There is too much of this 'What I have said, I have said!' We must teach them, ladies, that when they have said and decided upon something which is not expedient from the point of view of public policy, they must learn to eat their words, and upset their own arrangements.

Now, this measure of which they all seem so much afraid – what is it? It is a Bill to give to those women who are qualified, as men voters are qualified, the right to exercise the Parliamentary franchise. They are all obliged to admit that our logical position is absolutely unassailable, and that the principle of the Bill is sound. It is sound in justice, and is in harmony with the principles of the British Constitution. What will be the immediate effect of this Bill if it is carried? It will extend the present franchise to women on the same terms as those upon which it is exercised by men. The ultimate effect of the Bill will be to enable women to share with men the benefits of any future improvement in the franchise.

The House of Lords

There are two excuses for neglecting to carry this Bill with which I propose to deal. Liberal Members of Parliament raise the first. They say, 'What is the use of carrying the Bill in the House of Commons? The House of Lords would throw it out.' Are not Liberals thankful for the House of Lords! Where could they turn for an excuse for inaction if there were no House of Lords! I know why they have dropped the House of Lords campaign; they are afraid that their mock warfare might turn into a warfare in earnest, and that somehow or other, without really intending it, they might destroy the House of Lords. This would be a terrible thing; for there would not then be a single bulwark between themselves and their Liberal principles! But what we have to say upon the question is this. Let the House of Commons deal with the matter first, let them do their duty, and if the House of Lords prove obstinate – well, we shall have to take measures to secure their adherence to the principle we have at heart. Let us take one thing at a time. The Women's Enfranchisement Bill has not got through the House of Commons yet, and I venture to prophesy that the House of Lords will not prove so obstinate or so reactionary as the House of Commons has.

One Liberal journal has said – and here comes the second excuse – that we are asking for impossibly early action when we ask for the immediate enactment of our Bill. Ladies, there is really a limit to our patience. We have worked longer for this than people have worked for some reforms that are already on the Statute Book. It seems to me that it is impossibly late, except that one knows it is better late than never. Certainly nobody, even the most inaccurate person, can claim that we are claiming the enactment of the Women's Enfranchisement Bill too early. When this Government first came into office, the Liberals' cry was, 'We cannot commit political suicide; we have only just come into power, and now you want us to go out again. We could not carry Woman Suffrage without going to the country, and that would mean an immediate dissolution.' How tender their conscience becomes when they are dealing with voters! They do not mind legislating without asking our opinion when we are outside the franchise, but they insist that when we have got the vote they must lose not a moment in giving us an opportunity of expressing our views at the ballot box. But this argument has now lost what force it ever had, because this Parliament is waxing old, not to say decrepit, and it is about time that it went in for a death-bed repentance.

We must face the position with all seriousness. If our Bill were carried this session, we should not be in a position to vote till 1910, because the Register will be made up next Autumn, and that Register will not come into operation until January 1st, 1910. If the Bill were carried next session, unless it were to receive Royal assent before the electoral lists are made up, then we should not be able to vote until 1911. The next General Election will certainly not be delayed beyond that year. Therefore, this is a matter for haste. If we do not achieve our purpose soon, this Parliament will run its course, and another Parliament will come in before we get the vote, and then will be re-told the same old story, 'You cannot expect us to enfranchise you now. Wait until this Parliament is nearing its close,' and so on, world without end. We are not prepared to face such a prospect. There is no time to be lost. Delay is dangerous. 'If it were done, it were well it were done quickly.'

The Promised Reform Bill

But, ladies and gentlemen, there is another very great reason for haste in settling this question, and that is the Reform Bill. Now, I am greatly suspicious of that measure. I view with mistrust the prospect that Mr Asquith has opened out in announcing the introduction of a Reform Bill. I am afraid he seeks to mislead us into a swamp where we must sink and sink and sink, until he hears no more of our inconvenient clamour.

What is to be the nature of this Reform Bill? It is to be introduced in a form applying, if you please, only to men! Now, why a Reform Bill for men? Are men fighting for franchise reform? Do they ever speak of it? No, my friends! The fact is that they are to be carried on our shoulders a stage further on the road to another measure of electroal reform. It is our agitation that has prompted the Government to the contemplation of this Reform Bill. Men do not think it worth while ever to ask for more votes for themselves. They think other matters more important. If they had to choose between more votes for men and, say, a measure dealing with unemployment, they would rather have the latter. They think they have a good many votes already, and they are in no haste to get more. But I do not want you to misunderstand the position. Men are prepared to stand for votes for women, because they realise that although they have three-fourths of the political loaf, the women have not even a crumb of it. Then why is Mr Asquith in hot haste to give more votes to men? The answer is, that he hopes, by improving the men's franchise, to raise up a stronger barrier against the enfranchisement of women.

Well, this Bill is to be introduced applying to men only. What chance have women of getting a claim for their enfranchisement included in that Bill? Mr Asquith makes an unprecedented suggestion. It is strange for Liberal Prime Ministers to create a precedent! It is not their custom quite; but heaven knows to what desperate straits they will be driven when they want to evade the women's claim to votes! I will tell you what is the unheard of suggestion that he makes. It is that the women's claim to vote shall depend upon the fate of a Private Member's amendment, and that the Government shall reject all responsibility in the matter. Now, I say that to deal with the question in this way is to insult the women, and to show no sense of public duty. We are not content, even if we pinned any faith whatever to the Reform Bill, even if we were sure it would be introduced, even if we were sure it would be carried, we are not content that our claim should be treated in this insolent manner.

As women have no votes, Mr Asquith mistakenly thinks – though I believe he will not think so much longer – he vainly thinks that he can afford to trifle with their claim in this manner. He tells us that it is open to a Private Member to move a Woman Suffrage amendment. Of course, it is open to a Private Member to do that. Surely, the Private Member is not quite so reduced to impotence that he has no right to move an amendment! Yes, poor man! he may still move amendments, though he cannot get them carried! But, supposing this Private Member's amendment is moved. Will Mr Asquith then give it his support? No! he is not going to do that! He is going to be neutral. No, he is not going even to be neutral. Conditional neutrality describes his attitude towards this Private Member's amendment. Now, what are the conditions with which this offer of neutrality is hedged round? Those conditions are two, and both of them may be so interpreted as to become impossible of fulfilment. The first condition is that the amendment must be drafted on democratic lines. Now, I feel full of suspicion when a Liberal begins to talk about democracy. I am sure there is something wrong somewhere. I am convinced that Mr Asquith is not speaking in good faith when he asserts that the amendment must be democratic. Why are we not told precisely upon what terms Mr Asquith will approve our enfranchisement? Because, friends, he wants, when the critical time comes, to be able to rake up this condition, and to oppose the amendment on the pretext that it is not on democratic lines. By means of this condition he thinks either to prevent the Woman Suffrage Clause getting through the House of Commons, or failing that, to leave its rejection to the House of Lords on the ground that it is too wide in its scope. But in case this first device should fail, he has another string to his bow, and I will tell you what that is. It is the threat that he will oppose the Woman Suffrage amendment unless it can be shown that the enfranchisement of women is demanded by the majority of the men and the majority of the women of the country. What do you think of that! Did they wait for the majority of men to claim the vote in the old days? Certainly not. Gladstone repudiated the idea that it was necessary to show that the majority desired enfranchisement. When the Tories argued against the Bill of '84, that the agricultural labourers did not want to vote, Mr Gladstone laughed them to scorn, and said: 'It is the business of the statesman to anticipate the people's demand for enfranchisement, not to wait until he is asked.' But, my friends, the present Liberal Government have dragged that high ideal of statesmanship into the mire; it is waiting now for others to raise it once again. The present Prime Minister is not going to give us the vote until he is badgered into giving it, shamed into giving it, until he is hounded into giving it!

Let us deal further with this point. The Prime Minister says that before women shall have the vote the majority of men must show they support the proposal. But, ladies, we are not talking about votes for men; we are talking about votes for women. Our claim to the vote would be valid, although not a man in the country were with us. Did anybody wait, before giving votes to men, to see if the women approved of it? It is equally absurd – and if some men were not so full of male arrogance that they are absolutely blind, they would see it – it is precisely as absurd to say that women must not have votes till the majority of men approve of it. But, happily, we can fulfil that condition to our satisfaction and to yours. The men and women of the country are with us to-day, as we have shown Mr Asquith at many a bye-election! – as we shall show him at many bye-elections yet. But, my friends, it would be some guarantee of his own good faith if Mr Asquith would deign, in his high-and-mightiness, to inform us what he would recognise as proof that men and women of the country believe in votes for women. As to the men, I think he will be driven to accept as proof of their support of our claim the verdict of the bye-elections. But we want to know what he will accept as proof that the women themselves want the votes. Well, somebody put that straight question to him in the House of Commons, and he refused to make any reply whatsoever. What conclusion are we to draw from that? I say the man is tricking us – or trying to trick us. He wants to retain the power to say, whatever proof of the popular demand for women's enfranchisement we adduce, that he is not satisfied yet. He is afraid of laying down terms; he is afraid of saying: 'If you do such and such a thing I shall be satisfied.' Why is he afraid of saying it? Because he knows that whatever he lays down, it is in our power to do it. Well, as he won't give us the necessary guidance, he must not complain, and nobody can complain if we try to find out for ourselves the best way of showing him that the demand is not only so wide, but so intense that he cannot stand against it any longer.

One more word on the subject of the Reform Bill. Supposing the Woman Suffrage Clause embodied in it is carried, what is going to happen to the Bill as a whole? Why, ladies, if any of you are inclined to pin your faith to the Reform Bill, take notice that Liberals are saying in the most bare-faced and open manner that they do not expect that the Bill will be carried. They think to make it a sort of battle-cry at the next General Election, and the settlement of our question is to be delayed accordingly. At all costs we must prevent that. We intend to win the vote, not only before the next General Election, but before the Reform Bill is introduced. If you doubt that to defer the enfranchisement of women until the Reform Bill is brought in would be fatal, look at what is to be the nature of that Bill. It is to be coupled with Re-distribution (so we are told by one Parliamentary correspondent, who is at the same time a Member of Parliament), and that means that the whole difficult and controversial question of Irish Representation will be raised. It is to deal, so people are saying, with Second Ballot, Payment of Election Expenses, Shorter Parliaments, and a host of other matters. Well, my friends, the Government are riding for a fall when they introduce a Bill of that kind. They want it to be thrown out; it will make something to go to the country on. We are not going to lend ourselves to that kind of thing. Let us get the sex disability removed; let us fight for that; let us wash our hands of the Reform Bill; don't let us trust in it. It is a vessel that is meant to founder. We are being sent to sea in a leaking ship, when we are invited to step on board the Reform Bill!

The attitude of the Government being so unsatisfactory, the question of methods is one of great importance. How are we to get the vote? Time presses; the cause is of great importance to us. We must get to work; we must not stand upon ceremony. Enough of this punctilio! Let us cast aside all doubts and fears, and 'let us up and at them'! Let us stop talking; let us stop arguing with our opponents. We are only degrading ourselves when we plead with people whose ear is deaf to our pleading; when we argue with people who know our arguments by heart, but do not intend to give them heed. The only womanly thing to do is to fight against the Government, who are fighting against us. I think our enemy is beginning to respect us, and to fear us. Do you remember the debates in the House of Commons in the old days? Why, they did not so much degrade us, as they degraded the men who took part in them! You remember the tone of those debates? You remember how they would have disgraced the lowest public-house in our country? There is one thing that reading those debates tells you, and that is that you want to raise the tone of the House of Commons, you want to purify the atmosphere, you want to get rid of the tittle-tattle, of the low thoughts, and of the small views and the ungenerous ways of looking at things, and the distrust of the women of the country. Ladies, you may judge of the character and the calibre of a man by the things he says about women! When you hear them mouthing platitudes on other questions, you might really not suspect what some Members of Parliament are until you have heard them discuss the Women's Question. We did not know, until Mr John Burns and Mr Lloyd George were confronted at their meetings, that they had such lack of dignity. Therefore, we say it is a very good thing that we are teaching men to respect us. We cannot blame them. How can we expect them to be better when they have not had the influence of free enfranchised women brought to bear upon their character, and upon their modes of thought? It is our conviction that all will not be well with women, and all will not be well with men until the sexes are upon an equality. Therefore, it is not with any feelings of rancour that we speak of these rulers of ours; they are the victims of the circumstances in which they have been brought up, and it would be well if they would understand that we are seeking to work the most beneficent revolution in human affairs that the world has yet seen. We are prepared to take the words of one Cabinet Minister from his own mouth, and apply them to our agitation. We are prepared to say with him that protest against injustice is the only way of keeping the soul undefiled by injustice. We are prepared to say with him that it is right to meet oppression by making constant resistance to it. That is what we are doing. We are fighting against the Government for the good of our own souls, and for the improvement of the souls of the men. We are fighting also for a practical object; we are fighting to defeat the Government, and to wrest the vote from them. Now, everybody knows that we cannot get the vote without bringing pressure to bear upon the Government. You cannot get anything done without bringing pressure to bear upon the Government, and when you are saying that you are not saying anything against the character of any particular Government; you are simply stating a fact. We are bringing pressure to bear upon the Government, and when we do that we are not doing anything more, or other than men politicians do; the sole difference is that men politicians have got a constitutional means of bringing pressure to bear – they have got the vote. Now, we have not any constitutional means of achieving our end. I know some people try to persuade us that we have. They say that we ought to abandon the militant methods, and use constitutional methods instead. Well, that is just what we are only too anxious to do, and what we shall do when the vote is ours. But they will not give us the vote, which is the sole constitutional weapon, and then they try to tantalise us by saying, 'Use the vote,' and then snatch it away. It is just like a schoolboy's trick, that. 'Would not you like it?' and then snatch it away. Well, we are grown up, and we understand business, and we understand politics, too. We say that if you won't give us a constitutional means, we will use an unconstitutional means.

The Bye-Election Policy

What means do we use? What kind of unconstitutional methods do we employ? Well, it sounds rather Irish to say that one of our unconstitutional means is a very constitutional one. It consists in asking men for the kind loan of their vote; that is to say, that at every bye-election we urge the electors to help us by voting against the Government. Is our opposition to the Government effective? Do we turn votes? Well, ask that question of any Liberal candidate. Why, in the first place, the poor man cannot even get an audience! The electors would rather listen to us, because, you see, our question is a living one. The people want to hear about votes for women. They are rather tired of the dry-as-dust political speeches that the ordinary politicians offer to them. They are much more interested in this 'side issue,' as politicians are fond of calling the votes for women question. A side issue in a politician's mouth means, you know, a question that he prefers the electors not to take any notice of, and when, as is the case nowadays, it is said on the defeat of a Liberal candidate, that side issues had much to do with that defeat, you may know that 'votes for women' has been the real issue of the election! You must have noticed, too, frequent denunciations by Liberal candidates and their supporters of the 'outside organisations' which enter the field at each bye-election in opposition to the Government, and one Member of the Government, Lord Crewe, has said that their activity must be suppressed by law. I can assure them that they will find it impossible to prevent the Women's Social and Political Union, which is the most important and active of these 'outside organisations,' from putting a finger in the pie at election times. We will allow no Act of Parliament to restrain us from making our appeal to a higher power than the Government themselves. We cannot get justice from the Government – the inferior court; we will appeal, even if it means imprisonment, against their decision, to a higher court, to the electors. Yes, if the present Government – who, after all, are the servants of the people – if they deny us justice, we shall, whatever repressive measures may be used against us, call for the support of the men who have votes. But we are interested and encouraged by the proposal in question. We know perfectly well that the outside organisation which they fear the most, that they fear more than all the others put together, is the Women's Social and Political Union. As yet they do not openly admit it. Ask a Liberal Member of Parliament whether we prevent the election of Liberal candidates. He will say, 'Oh, no; nonsense. These women have no influence at all on the elections.' Well, I ask you, why not? These Members of Parliament think they have influence themselves. They speak in support of their friend, the Liberal candidate, at a bye-election, and they think they can turn votes. Well, I am sure that the women in our Union can turn votes if they can! We are as good speakers as the men. We know as much about politics. We are not so vain as to suppose that it is by our own ability; we know it is by the greatness of our cause that we win our way in this country. It is the strength rather than the manner of our appeal that turns votes against the Government. Now, we have got a good cause, while the Liberal Party have a bad cause. So, of course, we defeat the Government at bye-elections. I have not time to lay before you all the evidence on this point, but I will give you the evidence of a Liberal Member of Parliament. Sir Charles Maclaren has publicly stated that we women are responsible for the Government defeats which have been attributed to the work of the Tariff Reformers. Well, now, let us convince our Liberal friends that it is no good trying to hide their heads in the sand. If we are influencing the electorate, we are influencing it, and no amount of denying that fact will make any difference. Liberals are apt to refuse to see a thing until it hits them in the eye. They did not believe there was a Labour Party until thirty Labour Members walked into the House of Commons. And they are now trying to believe that there is no women's movement. But this, like other illusions, will disappear as they find it more and more impossible to get elected to the House of Commons, because the women are there, barring the door against them.

Well now, that is what the men do to help us: they vote against the Government because the Government deny us political justice. How have we gained the support of men? It is by the militant methods that we have done it. It used to be said that we were alienating the country; but it is now recognised that by the new methods we have roused a feeling of chivalry in the electors and have stirred them to help us. It is quite true that when we began the militant campaign people did not understand, but now the people are with us – with us in our demand and with us in what we do to press it forward. And as we rise in the public esteem, the Government and their supporters fall. Knowing that we have the people with us, we are prepared to look our enemy straight in the face, and to fight him with more skill and more vigour and more enthusiasm than ever. The sight of women fighting for their rights, disregarding risks, hardships, penalties, has fired the imagination, touched the hearts of the people, and finally won them over to our cause. Their love of fair play, their admiration of a good fighting spirit, their desire to see the right triumph, are making them stand for us and against the Government. We have not alienated the people, we have won them by the militant methods.

Protests at Cabinet Ministers' Meetings

Apart from the opposition to the Government at bye-elections, we have two other means of attack. First, there are protests at Cabinet Ministers' meetings, and most useful and effective those protests are. This same method was adopted by men before they got the vote. In addition, they went in for storming the platform, and sending Cabinet Ministers flying in danger of their lives. We have a little more mercy for the enemy, but we adopt the same tactics in a modified form. We make no apology for doing this; we know it to be both necessary and right. Cabinet Ministers complain of being thus treated, but let them give women the vote. To deny us justice and whine at the consequent punishment is undignified and poor-spirited. Dr Cooper, a Liberal Member of the present Parliament, tells us that, 'Before the Reform Bill was carried, not a single opponent of Men's Suffrage could get in a word at a public meeting.' We ourselves are not afraid of interruptions. We go out into the market-place and we speak to our countrymen and women. We are not afraid of them; we are not afraid of their opposition. We meet it fairly. We win them over by argument. Why do not Cabinet Ministers try that method? If they were prepared with an answer to our question, 'Will you give women the vote?' all would be well. But because they will not give that answer they fear our question. They are not prepared to do us justice, and, you know, the knowledge that he is in the wrong makes anybody a coward. They can win us over by giving us the vote. And, my friends, the straits to which they are reduced are really extraordinary. They dare not face a public meeting, so their meetings are packed. In fact, in the matter of packed meetings the Liberal Party have broken the record. They can never more abuse the Tory Party; Tories have never gone to such lengths in order to escape their political opponents. Not long ago we protested at a Peace meeting addressed by a member of the Government. From this, as from other Cabinet Ministers' meetings, our members were violently ejected. The question of peace is of vital interest to women; and the question of national defence is of vital interest to us. Do we escape scot-free if the country is invaded? The questions discussed at that meeting were women's questions; and before very long we women must have the vote and take our part in deciding these great issues. When we see possible war and bloodshed ahead, do not you think that, as public-spirited human beings, we ought to fight for the vote as we have never fought for it before? Well, we went to the Peace meeting – and we did not find that the principles of peace were carried into practice. Never mind, we do not complain of that. Unlike the Prime Minister, we do not want artificial protection. We are ready to face the hardships of political life, while these frail men, the members of the Liberal Government, cannot bear to hear a word of opposition to them.

Members of the Union lately attended a Liberal meeting at Swansea. Some of us have been accused of inciting to violence. Well, we will not say more of that just now, but I want you to notice this – that Liberal Cabinet Ministers have set us a very bad example. At our meetings, when a man interrupts – as he very often does – you do not hear us say to the stewards: 'He must be ruthlessly flung out.' No; we leave that to Mr Lloyd George. But I want to point out to you that when a man in his position uses such words, it is taken by the ordinary unthinking hooligan to mean that he can do what he likes to the suffragettes. If the Government had not used force against us, if they had not had us arrested and imprisoned, if they had not insulted us by charging us with being hirelings, by telling stewards to throw us out, we should not have been in the daily physical danger that some of our women are in. We have been brought up to believe – some of us – that men's desire was to protect women from the hurly-burly and dangers of life; and yet, although Members of the present Government know that by denying us the vote and applying methods of coercion to us, they are placing us in danger of life and limb every day that we live, they continue to refuse our demand. In their own defence, however, they do not hesitate to collect 6,000 policemen, leaving the rest of London at the mercy of robbers and thieves.

My friends, before I leave this question of protesting at meetings, I will tell you why we do it. We do it, in the first place, to draw attention to our grievance and to educate the public. Cabinet Ministers will not do this for us – they shirk this question – we have got to do it for ourselves. In the second place, we know it to be an excellent way of harassing Cabinet Ministers. It is nothing to us to be interrupted, but to them it is a very serious matter. You see, they have not the sense of humour that we have got, and that means that they have no sense of proportion. Therefore Cabinet Ministers think their own speeches of vast importance. They like to deliver those speeches to a unanimous and enthusiastic audience, and as they cannot secure such an audience at an ordinary public meeting, they try to secure it by packing their meetings with partisans. They are bent on getting this unanimous support, even if it is a little artificial in its character. On the day following their meeting they like to read in the press verbatim accounts of what they said, and it makes them feel a bit sore when they find there is more in the newspapers about what the women have said than about what they have said themselves. When they get to the House of Commons – well, you know what men are about ridicule; they cannot bear it. They are very much like a pack of schoolboys in the House of Commons, you know; they tease each other so. Then they cannot go to the club or anywhere without receiving humorous condolences on account of the trouble they have had with the suffragettes. I need not say more. Everybody who knows what kind of persons these politicians are will realise what a very good idea it is to go and make protests at their meetings.

Deputations to the House of Commons

Next we must consider the deputations to the House of Commons. Recently we approached the House supported by thousands of the citizens of London. If men took this means of influencing Parliament it would be wrong, and I will tell you why – because they have representatives sitting in the House of Commons. It is right for us to do it; it is our duty to do it. It would be wrong for us not to do it, because we have nobody to represent us inside the House. If the House of Commons had any sense of logic, they would understand this point. The whole world, apart from them, understands it; and I do not – I will tell you between ourselves – I do not despair of succeeding, by constant repetition of an obvious fact, of driving that fact inside the minds of Members of Parliament. There have been leading articles in the newspapers condemning our recent action. Nobody else except the writers of those articles (perhaps not even they) has this opinion. As a matter of fact, those leading articles are most encouraging – among the best things that we have had yet. Why, they are the next best thing to getting the vote! When we are told that we are a nuisance, that we are upsetting London, that we ought to be put down with a strong hand – well, we are not far from victory.

Now, before I close, I want very briefly to speak of the example that stands before us in pursuing these militant methods. Let us begin with Magna Carta. It is a long time to go back, but still in Magna Carta we have the title-deeds of British liberty. Magna Carta was secured because of the fear that the people succeeded in implanting in the mind of King John. We must make Mr Asquith as much afraid of us as King John was of the Barons. I need not go through all the other struggles waged in this country for constitutional liberty, but I would remind you that the people who fought as we are fighting are now regarded as the saviours of this country. It may be we shall never retrieve our reputation – at least, the reputation that people pretend we have got – it may be that history will judge us as being not altogether ladylike, but, my friends, we shall have won the vote, and that is what we are fighting for.

The Reform Bills – how were they obtained? Were they obtained by milk-and-water methods? Were they obtained by coaxing the Government, by trying to win their sympathy? No. They were got by hard fighting, and they could have been got in no other way.

Now, my friends, listen to what John Bright said. If we who called on the public to help, as on October 13th, incited others to commit an unlawful act, so did John Bright. He said: 'If you fill the streets, from Charing Cross to the venerable Abbey, with men seeking a Reform Bill, you will get justice.' Why were no proceedings taken against him? Well, because there was not then such a ridiculous Government in power as now. They gave men the vote instead.

Some forty years ago there were Fenian outrages in Manchester, and the blowing up of Clerkenwell Gaol. What did those two terrible events prompt Mr Gladstone to say? He said that they had drawn the attention of England to the fact that there were grievances in Ireland. What did those two events prompt him to do? He disestablished the Irish Church! How anybody after that can say that militant methods are not effectual, I do not know. Remember, what did Mr Chamberlain say just before the passing of the County Franchise Bill in 1884? He said that if it was not carried he would march a hundred thousand men from Birmingham to London to get the vote or know the reason why. I do not know why the Liberal Government then in power did not take proceedings against Mr Chamberlain. He incited to riot – why did not he get six months? His action was discussed in the House of Commons, and even there they held him innocent. They refused to pass a vote of censure upon him, and yet we, who have spoken far less violently, we stood in the dock yesterday – I do not know where we shall be this time next week.

Let me quote what Mr Gladstone said on the subject of political revolt. I think these words should be written on the mind and heart of every member of the House of Commons, and, above all, every member of the Liberal Government. He said, in defence of Mr Chamberlain's threats and words of incitement to violence: 'I am sorry to say that if no instructions had ever been addressed in political crises to the people of this country except to remember to hate violence, love order, and exercise patience, the liberties of this country would never have been attained.' He spoke a great truth, he expounded a great law. Friends, if we are found guilty by the law of this land, we shall hold ourselves to be innocent by a higher law.

There is a thing within the memory of the youngest here, a battle for the franchise to which I must draw your attention now. The Uitlanders in South Africa found they could not wait five years to get the vote (though women wait a lifetime, and do not get it, and are by some condemned for protesting against so great a wrong). Yet in order to satisfy the impatience of these men, you plunged this country into war, you sacrificed thousands of lives, and now you say that we must not take a crowd of people to Westminster to get the enfranchisement of women. Turkey has won the constitutional rights of which we are still deprived, and the Liberal Government is loud in its congratulation. Mr Asquith is actually to be heard rejoicing at this triumph of democracy. Oh, hypocrisy beyond belief! The very Prime Minister who refuses to grant even the elementary rights of citizenship to his own country-women – who says, in answer to their call for justice, 'Go to prison,' who sees them look death in the face many a time, that Prime Minister who behaves in this wise – has the effrontery to say he approves of the revolution in Turkey. Consider, too, the action of two other Cabinet Ministers. One of them taunts women with their presumed weakness. He says: 'Do you think to succeed with a policy of pin-pricks? Why not use weapons that hurt?' Is not that inciting to violence? And yet he has never yet stood in the dock. But, my friends, he and his colleagues will be branded by public opinion in the future as wholly guilty.

Then there is Mr Herbert Gladstone, who in the House of Commons admits that argument alone is not enough to move the House of Commons. He says to the women who are hanging on his words, who are waiting for what he, on behalf of the Government, has to say upon this question – to them he says: – You have won the victory of argument, but it is not by that that you can succeed. Something more is needed. It is by *force majeure* that Governments are moved to action. And when we act upon his words, when we fight for our vote, as he has counselled us, he, as head of the police, proceeds against us, and tries to get us imprisoned, so that for a season we may be out of his way.

But we are going on with this battle. It may be six months' imprisonment for us this time; it may be more hereafter. But did you ever know a great movement for human freedom that could be crushed by repression and coercion? No. The more they repress us, the more heavily they punish us, the more they fire our indignation, the more determined they make us to get the vote for women, if it costs us life itself.

F. W. Pethick Lawrence

The Trial of the Suffragette Leaders

(1908)

Introduction

The intense interest evoked by the trial of the Suffragette leaders, Mrs. Pankhurst, Christabel Pankhurst, and Mrs. Drummond, calls for a full account of the case in an accessible form. To this only a few words by way of introduction are necessary.

The Women's Social and Political Union had for some time selected October 13, 1908, as a day on which to make a special effort to enter the House of Commons and approach the Prime Minister. This date was chosen because it was the third anniversary of the initiation of the militant methods by Christabel Pankhurst, and also the day following the opening of Parliament for the autumn after the summer recess. On several previous occasions the women had sent a deputation from Caxton Hall to the House of Commons. Sometimes these deputations had been arrested shortly after emerging from Caxton Hall; at other times they had been conducted by the police to the very doors of the House of Commons, and there turned away. Generally the women had not called upon the public to assist them in any way, but on this occasion it was decided to invite the populace to attend in large numbers to give their support to the women. Accordingly, a few days previous to October 13, it was decided to issue a special bill in the following terms:-

'Women's Social and Political Union, 4 Clements Inn. Votes for Women. Men and Women, Help the Suffragettes to Rush the House of Commons on Tuesday Evening, October 13, at 7.30.'

In support of this request Mrs. Pankhurst, Christabel Pankhurst, and Mrs. Drummond all spoke at a public meeting in Trafalgar Square on Sunday, 11th, explaining what they wished the people to do, emphasising the fact that they wished them to come unarmed, and without sticks or stones, but to give the women their support.

On Monday morning, October 12, Mrs. Pankhurst, Christabel Pankhurst, and Mrs Drummond were each served with a summons, which read as follows:-

> Information has been laid this day by the Commissioner of Police for that you in the month of October in the year 1908 were guilty of conduct likely to provoke a breach of the peace by initiating and causing to be initiated and publishing and causing to be published a certain handbill calling upon and inciting the public to do a certain wrongful and illegal act – viz., to rush the House of Commons at 7.30 p.m. on October 13 inst.
>
> You are, therefore, hereby summoned to appear before the Court of Summary Jurisdiction, sitting at the Bow-street Police Station on Monday, October 12, at the hour of 3.30, to answer to the said information, and to show cause why you and each of you should not be ordered to find sureties for good behaviour.
>
> (Signed) H. Curtis Bennett.

Instead of obeying this summons, however, they attended a great meeting at the Queen's Hall, and there addressed the audience, informing them of the steps that were being taken by the Government in the matter. At the close of the meeting they were served with a further summons, calling upon them to attend the following morning at Bow Street. This also they refused to comply with, and a warrant was at once issued for their arrest. Superintendent Wells and Inspector Jarvis came to Clements Inn forthwith to serve this upon them, but they found the women absent. A note, however, had been left for Inspector Jarvis to the effect that Mrs. Pankhurst, Christabel Pankhurst, and Mrs. Drummond would return to the office at 6 p.m., and would then be ready to go with them to Bow Street. The police then endeavoured to trace the whereabouts of Mrs. Pankhurst and the others without avail, and sat down to wait till six o'clock.

At that hour the prisoners entered the office, the warrant was read to them, and they were taken away to Bow Street. Bail was refused, and they were compelled to spend the night in the cells at the police-court. Meanwhile, the streets in the neighbourhood of the House of Commons had been carefully guarded by large masses of police, who kept the public at all points half a mile from the House. Twenty-four women were arrested on a charge of obstructing the police, and in addition twelve men were taken into custody. One woman, Mrs. Travers Symons, succeeded in entering the Chamber and addressing the House of Commons.

On Wednesday all the prisoners were brought before the magistrate at Bow Street, and the evidence of the police was given, the prisoners cross-examining in person. After taking the evidence of the police, Christabel Pankhurst asked for an adjournment in order to take legal advice and prepare a defence. This was granted for one week. During this interval Miss Pankhurst secured the assent of the Right Hon. Lloyd George, Chancellor of the Exchequer, and the Right Hon. Herbert Gladstone, the Home Secretary, as witnesses for the defence. The adjourned hearing of the case lasted the whole of October 21, the magistrate for a long time refusing a further adjournment, and keeping the prisoners in the dock from 10.30 to 7.30 at night, with only two very short intervals. At this point he asked Miss Pankhurst how many more witnesses she had to call, and on hearing that she had fifty, decided to adjourn the case until Saturday, October 24, at twelve o'clock. On the resumption of the case on Saturday the magistrate announced that he would not allow all the witnesses to be called. He consented, however, to hear three of them, and after that insisted upon the prisoners making their speeches. This they did under protest. These speeches made a profound impression upon the Court. The magistrate then gave his judgment, refusing to suspend it for a point of law to be taken to a higher court. In the account given below the speeches are printed first; following upon these is given an account of the general conduct of the case; the cross-examination of the police evidence and the examination of Mr. Lloyd George and Mr. Gladstone is given in full, but the other evidence has had to be much abridged in order that the book might not be too bulky.

In the annals of history this trial will play an important part. The brilliant conduct of the case by Christabel Pankhurst, the startling evidence given concerning a police magistrate, the presence of two Cabinet Ministers as witnesses, the profound speeches for the defence – all these will attract attention, but far beyond all in importance will be remembered the direct attack of the Government upon the leaders of the women's movement and their futile attempt to break down by coercive measures the agitation for constitutional right.

F. W. PETHICK LAWRENCE

I Speeches of the Prisoners

Christabel Pankhurst

In the first place, I want to point out that the proceedings that have been taken against us have been taken out of malice and for vexation. I think I shall have little difficulty in proving this, because of the attitude which the authorities have taken against us from the beginning of the agitation, which has been in progress for the past three years. But before I come to this point, I want to draw your attention, and the attention of the general public – (the Magistrate: Never mind the general public) – *your* attention, sir, to the very serious scandal which has been unearthed in the course of these proceedings. We have had it sworn to in the witness-box that one of the justices, Mr. Horace Smith, has allowed himself to be coerced by the Government, and has settled in conjunction with them whether a certain lady, charged in connection with this agitation, was guilty, before the evidence was heard, and Mr. Horace Smith and the Government had, moreover, decided before-hand what term of imprisonment should be inflicted upon that lady.

Now, this policy of the Government of weighting the scales against us is not of interest only to us, but is of interest to the whole community. In the course of British history we have seen many struggles for the purification of our judicial system. It is within your knowledge, sir, that in days gone by the judges have had many a fight against the King, in order to maintain their independence and to vindicate the purity of their office. It has been left to the twentieth century – it has been left to these so-called democratic days – to see our judicial system corrupted for party ends. I am glad that we have been able to perform the public duty and service of doing something to attack this evil while it is in the bud. I am quite sure that if we had not been privileged to unearth this very serious scandal, the process of corruption would have gone on until a fair trial was absolutely impossible in the case of those charged with political offences. And if injustice creeps in in political cases, it would not be long before the same corruption was prevalent in every law court in the land, and in the case of every person brought up under some charge, no matter of what kind.

I think too much attention cannot be paid to the disgraceful action of the Government; the Home Secretary and his colleagues have disgraced and degraded themselves. They have been false to their duty, they have tried to destroy the liberties which it has taken so long to build up. It is worth while standing in this dock if we have been able to do no more than do something to check a state of affairs which is going to reduce this country below the level of any other civilised country if it is not stopped and stamped out now. The Liberal Government have outdone the monarchs of old times in their attempt to corrupt the fountain of British justice; and both they and the magistrate who has allowed himself to be made a tool, who has so far forgotten his duty to us, his duty to the public, his duty to his profession, deserve to be hounded out of civilised society. I know that this action the Government have taken in corrupting the justices will not be forgotten, and will be remembered against them when next they face the verdict of popular opinion.

A Malicious Prosecution

I shall now proceed with my argument that these proceedings have been taken against us out of malice and in order to lame, in an illegitimate way, a political enemy. Take the form of the summons. We are not openly charged with the offence of illegal assembly. If we have in any way broken the law, we have broken it in that way. The only charge that could possibly be preferred against us is that of illegal assembly. Now, why have the authorities, why have the Government feared to take this course? The reason is that they want to keep us in the police-court. They believe, rightly or wrongly, that by this means they will succeed in prejudicing the public against us. We know perfectly well that up till recently the general public shunned the police-court as a disgraceful place. The fact of having been proceeded against in a police-court was in the eyes of the ordinary man or woman a stain upon the character which could hardly be wiped out in later days. Well, I think that by our presence here we have done something to relieve the police-court of that unenviable reputation. We have done something to raise its status in the public eye, and we have also done something to throw light upon the obsolete procedure and the unsuitable procedure which obtains in courts like this. But even if the procedure which we find here is suitable for committing 'drunks,' I am sure every reasonable person will agree that it is no place for the political offender. But political offenders are brought here in order that something may be done to smirch their character, and to prejudice them in the public eye.

Another reason why the authorities have feared to charge us with unlawful assembly is that they dare not see this case come

55

before a jury. They knew perfectly well that if this case were heard before a jury of our countrymen we should be acquitted, just as John Burns was acquitted years ago for taking action far more serious, far more dangerous to the public peace than anything that we have done. Yes, I say they are afraid of sending us before a jury, and I am quite sure that this will be obvious to the public, and that the Government will suffer by the underhand, the unworthy, and the disgraceful subterfuge by which they have removed this case to what we can only call a Star Chamber of the twentieth century. Yes, this is a Star Chamber, and it is in order to huddle us into prison without a fair trial that these proceedings have been taken in their present form. I daresay it was not anticipated by the prosecution that this case was ever to be defended. I am quite sure it has come to them as a surprise; they are accustomed to see us disposed of and sent to Holloway Gaol very much as the animals are dealt with in the Chicago stockyards. Prisoners are brought up here and disposed of at the rate of one a minute, or, perhaps, three in two minutes! That sort of thing has been the rule; we are accustomed to that. But those days are gone for ever. We are going to make this time a fight for our liberty. We owe it to ourselves, we owe it to our country that we should not let the disgraceful proceedings of this court go on any longer. Yes, we are deprived of trial by jury. We are also deprived of the right of appeal against the magistrate's decision. Very, very carefully has this procedure been thought out; very, very cunningly has it been thought out to hedge us in on every side, and to deprive us of our rights in the matter!

We will not be Bound Over

Then, we are also rendered liable to six months' imprisonment, and yet we are denied the privileges in making our defence that people liable to three months' imprisonment alone enjoy. We shall be told in the House of Commons no doubt – we have been told the same thing before now – that we are only bound over, we need not go to prison, if we go to prison we have only ourselves to thank. Well, if Mr. Herbert Gladstone were in the dock that would be perfectly true. He would be very willing, as a Member of Parliament★ was only yesterday, to be bound over, to express his repentance, to say he will not repeat the conduct that he has pursued up to now. But we are not prepared to betray our cause;

★ Will Thorne, M.P., in the same Court had been charged with calling upon the unemployed to 'rush the bakers' shops,' and had been bound over for twelve months to be of good behaviour.

we are not prepared to put ourselves in a false position. If the case is decided against us, if we are called upon to be bound over, it must be remembered that that amounts to imprisoning us, and that therefore the authorities cannot possibly escape their responsibility for sending us to prison by saying that we could be at liberty if we liked.

To sum up what I have just said, Magna Carta has been practically torn up by the present Government. We are liable to a term of so long as six months' imprisonment, and we have had no fair trial. We protest against that with all the force at our disposal. We think it is a disgrace; we think it is a scandal, we think the way in which we have been proceeded against disgraces the Government, and when we add to that the fact that they have attempted – and possibly still attempt – to corrupt justice, and decide the sentences upon us before we come up for trial, when we take these two facts in conjunction, I think you will agree with us that it is not we who ought to be in the dock to-day, but the people who are responsible for such a monstrous state of affairs.

I want now to deal with the reasons for issuing this bill. We do not deny at all that we issued this bill; none of us three here wishes to deny responsibility. We did issue the bill; we did cause it to be circulated; we did put upon it the words 'Come and help the Suffragettes to rush the House of Commons.' For these words we do not apologise; for our action we do not apologise. We had good reason for taking it, and what is more, at the first opportunity – on the first occasion when we think it desirable – we shall do it again!

Why We Issued the Bill

Now, it is very well known that we take this action in order to press forward a claim, which, according to the British Constitution, we are well entitled to make. After all, we are seeking only to enforce the observance of the law of the land. The law of the land is that taxation and representation must go together. The law of the land is that who obeys laws must have a share in making them. Therefore, when we claim the Parliamentary vote, we are asking the Government to abandon the illegal practice of denying representation to those who have a perfect right to enjoy it. For forty years women have claimed that the law should be obeyed; for forty years Governments have been called upon to cease from unconstitutional action, and to carry out the law of the land – to obey Magna Carta. Our agitations peacefully conducted, our petitions, our public meetings have been disregarded. Now we have in power a Liberal Government professing to believe in that principle, but refusing to carry it into practice. We have appealed to them, we have called upon them for justice, we have demanded of them that they do what we ask them – without the smallest success. We have a Prime Minister who will not even receive a deputation. Time after time have we wended our way to the House of Commons with a view to asking him to see us. Sometimes – generally – we have not called upon the general public to be with us at all, we have not asked them to come in their thousands to give us their support, we have gone alone; but that has made absolutely no difference in the case. We might go 3, we might go 6, we might go 13, we might go 60,000 strong, but the result is the same. We are sometimes escorted to the House of Commons, but we are arrested if we insist upon our right to enter. Well, what has happened? We have been arrested, and we have been imprisoned without trial – for I will not dignify these proceedings in the police-court with the name of trial – we have been imprisoned without trial. Sometimes the police have arrested us on our emerging from the Caxton Hall, sometimes they have escorted us to the door of the House of Commons, and there we have been arrested. The result has always been the same. We have been deprived of our constitutional right to see the Prime Minister, and we have been arrested for attempting to do so.

A Constitutional Right

Now, I want here to insist upon the action which we have taken in these proceedings. We have a perfectly constitutional right to go ourselves in person to lay our grievances before the House of Commons, and as one witness – an expert student of history – pointed out to you, we are but pursuing a legitimate course which in the old days women pursued without the smallest interference by the authorities. Now, the principal point we had in view in issuing the handbill for the 13th of October, was to call upon the House of Commons to carry into law a Bill, the second reading of which has already been carried. We have met with many refusals already to carry that Bill, and therefore we thought it necessary to make some demonstration of popular support. The Prime Minister has challenged us to do it. We gathered together in Hyde Park on June 21 an immense, a vast audience, but that meeting in Hyde Park was absolutely ignored. It remained for us then to summon our friends to meet us nearer the House of Commons itself. We did this on June 30. No proceedings were taken against us. No harm was done then, as no harm was done on October 13. We were allowed to do without opposition in June what we are punished for doing – or, at least, prosecuted for doing – on October 13. Well, this handbill we felt to be necessary in order to put the final pressure upon the Government, with a view to getting the measure carried this Session. The time now remaining is short; a firm stand we felt must be taken. The time of the House is being occupied by matters far less important than that which we have on hand. Juvenile smoking, the Education Bill – which nobody is eager upon – the Licensing Bill, which the Government hardly expect to carry. With these matters the time of the House is being wasted, while a far greater measure awaits their consideration. We felt we must bring pressure to bear upon the Government with a view to getting the Bill carried, but before we took the action of which the prosecution complain, we desired to make our position clear, and we therefore wrote to the Prime Minister as follows:

> I am instructed by the Committee of the National Women's Social and Political Union to write you as to the intentions of His Majesty's Government with regard to the measure introduced by Mr. Stanger, M.P., which passed second reading by a large majority.
>
> At many very large demonstrations, held all over the country, resolutions have been carried with practical unanimity, calling upon the Government to adopt this Bill, and pass it into law this year. At a succession of by-elections the voters have shown unmistakably their desire that the Government should deal with the question without further delay.
>
> We shall esteem it a favour if you will inform us whether it is the intention of the Government to carry the Women's Enfranchisement Bill during the Autumn Session of Parliament.

To that letter we had an unfavourable reply, and it was in consequence of the unfavourable nature of that reply that the arrangements for October 13 were proceeded with. In consequence of the unsatisfactory attitude of the Government, our plans went forward, and I would remind you that in making these arrangements we were but acting literally upon the advice given by John Bright in 1867. I do not know how it was that John Bright escaped being prosecuted by the Government of his day for inciting the public to the commission of an unlawful act, for he called upon the people of London, called upon the men who wanted votes, if they hoped to succeed, to gather in their thousands in the space which extends from Trafalgar-square to the Houses of Parliament.

I cannot imagine why, if this Government think it necessary to proceed against us, that earlier Government should not have done the same thing. I can only suppose that the Government of that day had more sense of proportion, more sense of their own duty, were less panic-stricken and more courteous, and more disposed to do their duty to the public, because in view of such words as John Bright used (with the possibility that the action he counselled would be taken), they resolved to give the men of this country their political rights, and the Reform Bill of 1867 was carried into law. In passing, I would suggest that to take such a course as that in regard to our movement would be more creditable to the Government than the course of instituting legal proceedings against us.

The Word 'Rush'

Now, I want to deal with the meaning of the word 'rush.' You have stated, sir, that the meaning of this word is a matter of law, but you have been good enough to allow us to ask a large number of witnesses the meaning of the word 'rush,' and all these witnesses have told us that, according to the British interpretation of the word 'rush,' no violence was counselled. Now, the word 'rush' appears to be very much the rage just now. Nobody can get away from its use. We find that at a meeting of the League for the Preservation of Swiss Scenery, Mr. Richard Whiteing, discussing the question of Swiss railways, said they ought not to be too hard on railways. Under certain atmospheric conditions a railway was the most beautiful thing in the world. He made other remarks about railways, and then he proceeded to suggest that a general rush to the Italian Alps might induce the Swiss to listen to reason. Well, I do not think that anyone here would suggest that Mr. Whiteing meant to offer any violence to the Swiss in his use of the word 'rush.' He meant to imply that a speedy advance should be made to the Italian Alps. Then we have Mr. McKinnon Wood counselling the electors to rush the County Council, and get a lady elected to that body. I want to submit that 'rush' as a transitive verb cannot mean 'attack,' 'assail,' 'make a raid upon,' or anything of that kind. The 'Century Dictionary,' which is the largest and most authoritative completed dictionary of the English language, gives numerous instances, all of which imply 'hurry' or 'hasten,' it may be to unduly hurry – although, of course, we have waited so long that undue haste is not to be wondered at. 'To unduly hurry' or 'hasten,' but never 'to assail.' Now, I have in my hand a little leaflet, which someone has been good enough to send to me. It is used in America, and it is put upon parcels which are expected to reach their destination in good time; when a parcel is wanted to be sent by an express train, they put this label, 'Rush by first train leaving.' Well, as our witnesses have one and all testified, the interpretation they placed upon the word 'rush' was that they should make haste. We have heard various meanings attributed to the word 'rush' by dictionaries. 'Rush' equals 'an eager demand'; 'urgent pressure' (as of business); a 'rusher' is 'a go-ahead person' – so says Chambers' English Dictionary. 'Rush' means 'an eager demand' – this we find in Ogilvie's Imperial Dictionary. 'Rush' means 'to go forward over-hastily'; for example, a number of Bills are rushed through Parliament – or a case is rushed through a law court. Then we have 'on the rush,' meaning 'in a hurry.' 'Into modern colloquial language,' says Farmer and Henley's Dictionary of Slang, 'rush' enters largely. As a substantive, it means 'extreme urgency of affairs,' 'an eager demand'; as a verb, it means 'to hurry,' 'to force,' or 'to advance a matter with undue haste.' 'On the rush,' or 'with a rush,' means 'with spirit,' 'energetically.' 'On the rush' means 'on the run,' 'hard at it.' One witness told us that, in her opinion, the word 'rush,' used as we have used it, might be compared with the word 'dash,' as we have it used in the expression, 'a dash for the Pole.' Everybody knows that you cannot get to the Pole in a hurry, but you can try to get there in a hurry, and that is what 'a dash to the Pole' means. Everybody knows that with a timid Government like the present one in power, having at its service the entire Metropolitan Police force, if one woman says she is going to rush the House of Commons, there will be an immense number of police to prevent her from doing it. Nobody, then, having regard to the facts I have mentioned, thought the women would rush the House of Commons, but that they would be there – it may be there with their supporters – to show their indignation against the Government, and I am glad to say that they were there. It may mean six months' imprisonment, but I think it is worth it.

Now, if we had used the expression '*storm* the House of Commons,' I could understand that a little fear would creep into the heart of Mr. Herbert Gladstone, because we know he is a rather timid person. It was all very well for him to say in the witness-box that he knows no fear, but the facts are against him. I know perfectly well that when we are in any physical danger, as we sometimes are at meetings, owing to the kind and considerate remarks of Cabinet Ministers, no such elaborate police precautions are taken for our protection as are taken for the House of

Commons in general, and Cabinet Ministers in particular, when there is thought to be any demonstration contemplated.

An Illegal Act?

Now, the next question I want to raise is this: Is it, as a matter of fact, an illegal thing to rush the House of Commons? The only woman who has done it has gone scot free. Mrs. Travers Symons rushed the House of Commons. She got in by strategy. She eluded the police, she got in, and she rushed the House of Commons. Nobody seems to mind her having done it at all; no proceedings have been taken against her. There she is! We who have not rushed the House of Commons are in the dock! Is her action illegal? She did it as the consequence of words that we had written and spoken – she is the only person who has actually succeeded in carrying out the mandate we are considered to have given to the public. She is the only person who has rushed the House of Commons, and yet she is not supposed to have broken the law of the land. Still, if she who has done it, is not to be punished, it is an extraordinary thing that we, who have not done it, are liable to imprisonment at the present moment.

We can take another instance of someone who not only 'rushed' the House of Commons, but stormed the House of Commons, and sent the members of the House of Commons flying in all directions. We have the case of Cromwell. I am not aware that he was ever made the subject of legal proceedings. It may be that by seeking to enter the House of Commons we have infringed the Speaker's regulations, but we have certainly not infringed the law of the land. We are told in our summons that it is not only illegal, but it is both wrongful and illegal. Well, you may say it is wrongful according to some moral law. We do not. It is rightful according to every law. But we want to know how it can be said that it is an illegal act. We are anxious to know by what statute it is illegal to go to the House of Commons, walk up the steps, and make our way to the strangers' entrance? We should like to know whether that is an illegal thing to do, and, if it is not illegal to go at a slow pace, we should like to know whether it is illegal to go at a quick pace, because that is what the word 'rush' means. 'To rush the House of Commons' is to go with all possible speed inside the House of Commons, and I hope that we shall be told what statute we have contravened by doing it ourselves, or sending anybody to do it, or inviting others to do it.

Now, the prosecution have drawn attention to the speeches made in Trafalgar-square on October 11. We do not in any way object to their doing this. I do not think what we have said there is strictly relevant, but I am glad they have raised this point, because it is all in our favour. We have called a number of witnesses, who have told us that they heard the speeches on that occasion, that they heard us interpreting the bill, because the speeches made there were made in interpretation of the famous bill. They have heard our speeches, and have one and all said that there was nothing inflammatory in those speeches, that there was no incitement to violence whatever. I am quite content to abide by the story of the other side in regard to this matter. The witnesses called by the prosecution all say that we used the following words, and I am sure no rational person can find in these words anything which incites to violence, and if the meaning of the word 'rush' is to be drawn from these speeches, then it will be a monstrous miscarriage of justice if we are sentenced to imprisonment. Here are the words spoken by Mrs. Pankhurst:

> On Tuesday evening, at Caxton Hall, we shall ask those who support women to come to Parliament Square. There will be a deputation of women who have no right in the House of Commons to a seat there, such as men have. The Government does not know its own mind, it changes so. But we do know that we want the vote, and mean to have it.

Then we have my own remarks:

> I wish you all to be there on the evening of the 13th, and I hope that that will be end of this movement. On June 30 we succeeded in driving Mr. Asquith underground. He is afraid of us, and so are the Government. Years ago John Bright told the people that it was only by lining the streets from Charing Cross to Westminster that they could impress the Government. Well, we are only taking a leaf out of his book. We want you to help the women to rush their way into the House of Commons. You won't get locked up, because you have the vote. If you are afraid, we will take the lead, and you will follow us. We are not afraid of imprisonment. We know we shall win because we are in the right.

These are the very dreadful words uttered on the platform that day; but what is even more important, because it comes direct from the pen of Mrs. Pankhurst, and ought to be listened to and taken into account far more than anything that we are reported to have said, are these words, written by Mrs. Pankhurst as an order to our members and to the general public:

On the 13th, in Parliament Square, there will be many thousands of people to see fair play between the women and the Government. Let us keep their support and co-operation by showing them, as we have done before, with what quiet courage, self-restraint, and determination women are fighting against tyranny and oppression on the part of a Government which has been called the strongest of modern times. It is by the exercise of courage and self-restraint and persistent effort that we shall win in this unequal contest.

Now, returning to the question of the Trafalgar-square meeting, we have been able to get evidence from a Cabinet Minister, and he tells us that he heard nothing of an inflammatory nature in Trafalgar-square. He did not hear us counsel people to do violence, he did not hear us counsel the people to do harm, he did not hear us say that we ourselves should do anything violent; in fact, if the matter were to rest upon words that he has spoken, it would certainly appear to everybody that we have said nothing to the public which could be taken as inciting them to do anything violent or illegal. We are quite prepared to take our stand upon what Mr. Lloyd George said of the words we spoke in Trafalgar-square.

The Events of the 13th

Now, let us come to the events of the 13th of October. The prosecution suggested – it was in some way raised by them – that Mrs. Pethick Lawrence, the chairman of the Caxton Hall meeting, had counselled violence to the women who were going forth into the streets to seek an interview with the Prime Minister. Well, we were able to call a great deal of evidence to show that that was an absolute fabrication. Mrs. Pethick Lawrence did not counsel the use of force; she urged the women to meet physical force with spiritual force; to show determination, and to make their way forward so far as they could, and not to be deterred lightly from entering the House; but as for the use of force directed against the police, directed against property, directed against Members of Parliament or Cabinet Ministers, she deprecated the use of such force, and discountenanced it. So that we have been able to clear ourselves of any suggestion that wild or inflammatory language was spoken in the Caxton Hall on the 13th.

Now, as to what happened outside on the 13th. We have heard over and over again that this was the most orderly crowd that has ever been known within the memory of living people to assemble in the streets of London. Mr. Lloyd George thought so little of its dangers that he actually brought with him his young daughter of six years. It is all very well for him to say that he relied upon the police arrangements. It is obvious to any intelligent person that 6,000 police are no match for £5660,000 if they really desired to force a way through the police lines. If there had been a violent spirit in the crowd, the police would have been as nothing, they would not have been able to restrain the crowd, and Mr. Lloyd George and his daughter, and even the police line would have been brushed aside, had the people been incited by us to do any violence. As a matter of fact, they knew what we wanted them to do, and they did it, and the fact that this child was brought into the crowd by her father shows that there was no apprehension in anybody's mind of any harm being done. But it is not because of anything serious that occurred on that night, or was expected to occur, that we are here; we are here in order that we may be kept out of the way for some months, and may cease from troubling the Government for as long a period as they can find it in them, or for which the public will allow them, to deprive us of our liberty.

We have had Mr. Herbert Gladstone telling us that he was not afraid on that night. Well, if there had been any danger, he would have been afraid. It was because he knew perfectly well that the public had no hostile intention, and that we had no hostile intention, that he ventured to come into the streets. If there had been a riot, if there had been a violent mob, he would have kept very carefully in the House of Commons, and it is perfectly absurd to argue that he thought the crowd was a disorderly one.

While we can show from our evidence that this was an orderly crowd, what have we got on the other side? We have two police officers. That has been the only evidence that has been brought against us. I think it is a monstrous thing if the evidence of two police officers, however reliable, however worthy they may be, is to be believed against the host of witnesses that we have already called, and the large number of witnesses that we could have called to say the same thing. It seems to me that there is no justice in this court if the word of the police is to be believed against the public. I want to call your attention to the fact that the prosecution have been unable to bring forward any impartial person to say that the events of the 13th were a danger to the public streets. This state of affairs must end. It is in the public interest that it should. It is not right that police evidence should be the only evidence upon which we are to be judged. It seems to me that the prosecution, the witnesses, the authorities, the magistrates, are all on one side, they are all in the same box, and the prisoner charged with an offence is absolutely helpless whatever facts he may bring forward. Those facts are set aside. It is indeed a waste of time to bring forward evidence in a police-court. Over the doors of this court ought to be the motto: 'Abandon hope all ye who enter here.' We do not care for ourselves, because imprisonment is nothing to us; but when we think of the thousands of helpless creatures who come into this monstrous place, and know perfectly well that they are found guilty before they have a chance of defending themselves, it is almost too terrible to think of the horrible injustice that is done day after day in these courts. Nobody to help them, nobody to plead for them. But I am thankful to think that we have been able, by submitting ourselves to the absurd proceedings that are conducted here, to ventilate this fearful wrong.

Well, I say that the crowd was orderly, and nobody could compare it with other crowds. The Eucharistic Procession drew together a far more disorderly crowd than that which we assembled, and yet, who has been proceeded against for that? Nobody has. Somebody ought to be in the dock, because they brought together a crowd which might possibly have led to riot and bloodshed. As for the Protestants who threatened that if they did not get their own way there would be bloodshed, no proceedings have been taken against them. Why are they not bound over? How anybody can say that we are treated with fair play I do not know. These things will be written up against the Government in the time to come.

Take the crowd which assembled for the C.I.V.'s, and the crowd which assembled on Mafeking night – we all know, and our witnesses have said, that there was a disorderly crowd, yet nobody was proceeded against. Why, even at the Churchill wedding the crowd was far more violent than that of the 13th. The crowds that try to get in and hear a popular preacher are more disorderly than the crowd which came to support us on the 13th. Of the Jubilee procession the same thing has been said. The crowds at Lord Mayor's Shows, too, are more disorderly, while at a meeting in Trafalgar-square some years ago bloodshed was narrowly averted, and yet the man who was responsible for it was acquitted by his countrymen.

Now, the prosecution have said that owing to the crowd brought together by us on the 13th forty watches and purses were stolen. Are we to take the responsibility for that? Are we to be responsible for the stealing of forty watches and purses? Why, I daresay sixty watches are stolen when the King goes to open Parliament!

There is not a single arrest which is traceable to the issue of our bill. Are we to understand that, once arrested, you are deemed guilty before you are tried? We know that in the higher courts the assumption is that a prisoner is innocent before he is proved to be guilty, but in this Court the assumption is that the prisoner is guilty before he is tried, and in ninety-nine cases out of a hundred he has no chance of getting off. People would have been there whether there had been a bill or not. Members of our Union would have been there whether there had been a crowd or not. The arrests have nothing to do with our action on the 13th, and therefore we deny absolutely the statement that because we issued that bill arrests were made. We are not responsible for pickpockets, they may be arrested whether we have a bill or not; we are not responsible for 'drunks,' and we are not responsible for the unemployed; we are responsible for ourselves, and as for the deputation, they were arrested not because we had issued a bill, but because they wanted to see the Prime Minister.

It is very interesting to notice what very elaborate police arrangements were made on the 12th. It just shows that members of the Government are afraid of their own shadow. I am glad they are reduced to this state of panic, because we shall get justice out of them. At present they are in fear lest they be a little inconvenienced, lest they be unable to get home and back again because of the crowds round the House of Commons.

Following the Advice of Statesmen

Now I come to another point – that in taking the course we are taking we have been encouraged by statesmen, and especially by Liberal statesmen. The whole of our liberties have been won by action such as ours, only of a far more violent kind. We have not broken the law, though we have offended certain persons who seem to think they can do injustice and escape with impunity. They seem to think they can have their cake and eat it. Well, we are prepared to show them that they cannot.

Therefore, we repudiate the charge that we are law-breakers. Still, we are prepared to say that even if we were law-breakers, we should be justified in doing so. Magna Carta itself was won by a threat of a breach of the peace. Hampden, whom we all honour now, was a law-breaker. Charles I, because he did not rule in a manner acceptable to his subjects – just as Mr. Asquith is not ruling to-day in a manner acceptable to us – was beheaded. Revolution after revolution has marked the progress of our country. The Reform Bills were got by disorder. We are told that, prior to 1832, the Mansion House, the Custom House, the Bishop's Palace, the Excise Office, three prisons, four toll-houses, and 42 private dwellings and warehouses were burnt. There was a general rebellion, but as a consequence the Reform Bill of 1832 was won. Then we have the Reform Bill of 1867. That was won in consequence of the breaking down of the Hyde Park railings. In 1884 we had the Aston Park riots. They made it impossible for the legislators or any section of them to withstand the enfranchisement of the agricultural labourers.

I think I have already quoted the example set us by John Bright. Although he got off scot-free, we are now liable to a long term of imprisonment. Then there were the Fenian outrages, the killing of a policeman in Manchester, and the blowing up of Clerkenwell Gaol.

Mr. Gladstone himself said:

The whole question of the Irish Church was dead; nobody cared for it, nobody paid attention to it in England. Circumstances occurred which drew the attention of people to the Irish Church. When it came to this, that a great gaol in the heart of the metropolis was broken open under circumstances which drew the attention of English people to the state of Ireland, and when a Manchester policeman was murdered in the exercise of his duty, at once the whole country became alive to Irish questions, and the question of the Irish Church revived.

And in a subsequent explanation he said:

When at an election you say that a question is out of the range of practical politics, you mean it is not a question likely to be dealt with in the Parliament you are now choosing. That is the meaning of it. It was said, and truly said, that in the year 1867 there happened certain crimes in England – that is to say, a policeman was murdered in circumstances of riot and great excitement at Manchester; the wall of Clerkenwell Prison was blown down in a very alarming manner – in consequence of which, it was said, I changed my mind about the Irish Church.

To explain how the matters referred to had had the effect of drawing the attention of the people of this country to the Irish question, he says that agitation of this kind is like the ringing of the church bell; it reminds those who are forgetting to go to church, that it is time they were up and doing, to perform their religious duty.

Mr. Chamberlain

Then there was Chamberlain threatening to march one hundred thousand men on London. Now, what difference is there between his action and ours, except that his action was far more likely to lead to law-breaking than any action we have taken? He proposed to bring a mob to storm the House of Commons. Was he prosecuted? No! The Gladstone of those days was a less absurd and hesitating and cowardly and peaceful person than the Gladstone of this time and the colleagues of the present Gladstone, and therefore Mr. Gladstone took the statesmanlike action of pressing forward the Reform Bill instead of taking proceedings against Mr. Chamberlain. And so Mr. Chamberlain was not legally proceeded against, and when a vote of censure was moved in the House of Commons, even that was defeated. On that occasion Mr. Gladstone said that if no instructions had been issued to the people of this country in political crises save only to remember to hate violence and love order and exercise patience, the liberties of this country would never have been attained.

Then there was Lord Randolph Churchill, who spoke words which were literally disgraceful for a public man addressing those who were voters. He counselled the voters – and, mind you, those who have votes have not the excuse for violence that those who have not got votes have – he counselled the voters to resort to the supreme arbitrament of force. He said, 'Ulster will fight, and Ulster will be right,' and as a consequence of what he said, dangerous riots, increasing in fury until they almost amounted to warfare, occurred in the streets, firearms were freely used by the police and by the combatants. Houses were sacked, and men and women were killed. So savage, repeated, and prolonged were the disturbances, breaking out again and again in spite of all efforts to suppress them, that they became in the end the subject of a Parliamentary Commission. But the author of these riots was not made the victim or prosecution. What a monstrous thing it is that we who have led to no trouble, who have not caused the loss of a single life, who have not caused damage to property, who have not done any harm at all, we should be imprisoned, or threatened with imprisonment, while a man who spoke those words, who counselled action which resulted in the death of his fellow countrymen, should be allowed to escape without even a vote of censure. If the Government had been as vindictive as the present one, penal servitude for life would have been the fate of Lord Randolph Churchill because of his encouragement to murderous attacks. He certainly was deserving of some punishment. But we, who have broken no law, or urged others to do so, we are threatened with this long term of imprisonment.

Then there was John Burns, who was far, far more violent; who was absolutely unrestrained in his language, which was utterly irresponsible – this man was brought up at the Old Bailey, and acquitted. If we were at the Old Bailey, I feel sure we should be acquitted; that is why we are not allowed to go there. He said in his speech that he was a rebel, because he was an outlaw. Well, that fact will support us in all that we have done. If we go to far greater lengths than we have done yet, we shall only be following in the footsteps of a man who is now a member of the Government.

We have been told by Mr. Haldane that we are entitled to fight the Government, but were fighting them with pin-pricks. Why not use weapons? We do not want to use weapons, even though we are taunted in this way with our restraint. They know that if we have a fault, it is that we are too gentle – not formidable enough. How, then, can anybody contest my statement that we have been incited to real violence, which we have not yet committed.

Mr. Herbert Gladstone himself, though in the witness-box he denied that he counselled our action, yet in a speech which I read to him, told us that the victory of argument alone is not enough. As we cannot hope to win by force of argument alone, it is necessary to overcome the savage resistance of the Government to our claim for citizenship by other means. He says: 'Go on. Fight like the men did.' And then, when we show our power and get the people to help us, he comes forward in a manner which would be disgraceful even in the old days of coercion, and in a manner which would be thought disgraceful if it was practised in Russia.

Then there is Mr. Lloyd George, who, if any man has done so, has set us an example. His whole career has been a series of revolts. Even as a child he counselled the breaking of school regulations. Then he incited the Welsh Councils to disobey the law. He has authorised the illegal and lawless action of the Passive Resisters, and even to us he has given counsel that we should break the law. He has said that if we do not get the vote – mark these words – we should be justified in adopting the methods which men had to adopt, namely, in pulling down the Hyde Park railings.

Then, as a sign of the way in which men politicians deal with men's interests, we have Lord Morley saying: 'We are in India in the presence of a living movement, and a movement for what? For objects which we ourselves have taught them to think are desirable objects, and unless we can somehow reconcile order with satisfaction of those ideas and aspirations, the fault will not be theirs; it will be ours; it will mark the breakdown of British statesmanship.'

Apply those words to our case. Remember that we are demanding of Liberal statesmen that which for us is the greatest boon and the most essential right. Remember that we are asking for votes, that we are demanding the franchise, and if the present Government cannot reconcile order with our demand for the vote without delay, it will mark the breakdown of their statesmanship. Yes, their statesmanship has broken down already. They are disgraced. It is only in this Court that they have the smallest hope of getting bolstered up. It is only by keeping us from the judgment of our countrymen that they can expect to be supported in the action that they are taking.

We make no Apology

Whatever be the result of the proceedings to-day, we know that by public opinion we shall be acquitted, and I do not want you, sir, to suppose that in all I have said I have wished to make any apology. Far from it. We are here to-day to say that if you call upon us to be bound over we shall go to prison, because our honour forbids us to do anything else, and if we go to prison, when we come out, we shall be ready to issue another bill calling upon the public to compel the House of Commons and compel the Government to do us justice.

Mrs. Pankhurst

Sir, I want to endorse what my daughter has said, that in my opinion we are proceeded against in this Court by malice on the part of the Government. I want to protest as strongly as she has done. I want to put before you that the very nature of your duties in this Court – although I wish to say nothing disrespectful to you – make you perhaps unfitted to deal with a question which is a political question, as a body of jurymen could do. We are not women who would come into this Court as ordinary law-breakers, and we feel that it is a great indignity – as have felt all the other women who have come into this Court – that for political offences we should come into the ordinary police-court. We do not object to that if from that degradation we shall ultimately succeed in winning political reform for the women of this country.

Mrs. Drummond here is a woman of very great public spirit; she is an admirable wife and mother; she has very great business ability, and she has maintained herself, although a married woman, for many years, and has acquired for herself the admiration and respect of all the people with whom she has had business relations. I do not think I need speak about my daughter. Her abilities and earnestness of purpose are very well known to you. They are young women. I am not, sir. You and I are older, and have had very great and very wide experience of life under different conditions. Before you decide what is to be done with us, I should like you to hear from me a statement of what has brought me into this dock this morning.

Why I am in this Dock

I was brought up by a father who taught me that it was the duty of his children, boys and girls alike, to realise that they had a duty towards their country; they had to be good citizens. I married a man, whose wife I was, but also his comrade in all his public life. He was, as you know, a distinguished member of your own profession, but he felt it his duty, in addition, to do political work, to interest himself in the welfare of his fellow countrymen and countrywomen. Throughout the whole of my marriage I was associated with him in his public work. In addition to that, as soon as my children were of an age to permit me to leave them, I took to public duties. I was for many years a Guardian of the Poor. For many years I was a member of the School Board, and when that was abolished I was elected on to the Education Committee. My experience in doing that work brought me in contact with many of my own sex, who in my opinion found themselves in deplorable positions because of the state of the English law as it affects women. You in this Court must have had experience of women who would never have come here if married women were afforded by law that claim for maintenance by their husbands which I think in justice should be given them when they give up their economic independence and are unable to earn a subsistence for themselves. You know how inadequate are the marriage laws to women. You must know, sir, as I have found out in my experience of public life, how abominable, atrocious, and unjust are the divorce laws as they affect women. You know very well that the married woman has no legal right of guardianship of her children. Then, too, the illegitimacy laws; you know that a woman sometimes commits the dreadful crime of infanticide, while her partner, the man who should share her punishment, gets off scot-free. I am afraid that great suffering is inflicted upon women because of these laws, and because of the impossibility that women have of getting legal redress. Because of these things I have tried, with other women, to get some reform of these laws. Women have petitioned members of Parliament, have tried for many, many years to persuade them to do something to alter these laws, to make them more equal, for they believe, as I do, that in the interests of men quite as much as of women it would be a good thing if laws were more equal between both sexes. I believe it would be better for men. I have a son myself, and I sometimes dread to think that my young son may be influenced in his behaviour to the other sex by the encouragement which the law of the land gives to men when they are tempted to take to an immoral life. I have seen, too, that men are encouraged by law to take advantage of the helplessness of women. Many women have thought as I have, and for many, many years women have tried by that influence we have so often been reminded of, to alter these laws, but we have found for many years that that influence counts for nothing. When we went to the House of Commons we used to be told, when we were persistent, that Members of Parliament were not responsible to women, they were responsible only to voters, and that their time was too fully occupied to reform those laws, although they agreed that they needed reforming.

I have tried constitutional Methods

Ever since my girlhood, a period of about thirty years, I have belonged to organisations to secure for women that political power which I have felt was essential to bringing about those reforms which women need. I have tried constitutional methods. I have been womanly. When you spoke to some of my colleagues the day before yesterday about their being unwomanly, I felt that bitterness which I know every one of them felt in their hearts. We have tried to be womanly, we have tried to use feminine influence, and we have seen that it is of no use. Men who have been impatient have invariably got reforms for their impatience. And they have not our excuse for being impatient.

You had before you in this Court yesterday a man who has a vote, a man who had been addressing other men with votes, and he advised action which we would never dream of advising. But I want to say here and now, as a woman who has worked in the way you advised, that I wonder whether this womanly way is not a weakness that has been taken advantage of. I believe that Mr. Will Thorne was right when he said that no action would have been taken against him if his name had not been mentioned in this Court, because it is a very remarkable thing that the authorities are only proceeding against him when goaded to it by the observations which women made here.

Now, while I share in the feeling of indignation which has been expressed to you by my daughter, I have lived longer in the world than she has. Perhaps I can look round the whole question better than she can, but I want to say here, deliberately, to you, that we are here to-day because we are driven here. We have taken this action, because as women – and I want you to understand it is as women we have taken this action – it is because we realise that the condition of our sex is so deplorable that it is our duty even to break the law in order to call attention to the reasons why we do so.

I do not want to say anything which may seem disrespectful to you, or in any way give you offence, but I do want to say that I wish, sir, that you could put yourself into the place of women for a moment before you decide upon this case. My daughter referred to the way in which women are huddled into and out of these police-courts without a fair trial. I want you to realise what a poor hunted creature, without the advantages we have had, must feel.

I have been in prison. I was in Holloway Gaol for five weeks. I was in various parts of the prison. I was in the hospital, and in the ordinary part of the prison, and I tell you, sir, with as much sense of responsibility as if I had taken the oath, that there were women there who have broken no law, who are there because they have been able to make no adequate statement.

You know that women have tried to do something to come to the aid of their own sex. Women are brought up for certain crimes, crimes which men do not understand – I am thinking especially of infanticide – they are brought before a man judge, before a jury of men, who are called upon to decide whether some poor, hunted woman is guilty of murder or not. I put it to you, sir, when we see in the papers, as we often do, a case similar to that of Daisy Lord, for whom a great petition was got up in this country, I want you to realise how we women feel; because we are women, because we are not men, we need some legitimate influence to bear upon our law-makers.

Now, we have tried every way. We have presented larger petitions than were ever presented for any other reform, we have succeeded in holding greater public meetings than men have ever had for any reform, in spite of the difficulty which women have in throwing off their natural diffidence, that desire to escape publicity which we have inherited from generations of our foremothers; we have broken through that. We have faced hostile mobs at street corners, because we were told that we could not have that representation for our taxes which men have won unless we converted the whole of the country to our side. Because we have done this, we have been misrepresented, we have been ridiculed, we have had contempt poured upon us. The ignorant mob at the street corner has been incited to offer us violence, which we have faced unarmed and unprotected by the safeguards which Cabinet Ministers have. We know that we need the protection of the vote even more than men have needed it.

I am here to take upon myself now, sir, as I wish the prosecution had put upon me, the full responsibility for this agitation in its present phase. I want to address you as a woman who has performed the duties of a woman, and, in addition, has performed the duties which ordinary men have had to perform, by earning a living for her children, and educating them. In addition to that I have been a public officer. I enjoyed for ten years an official post under the Registrar, and I performed those duties to the satisfaction of the head of the department. After my duty of taking the census was over, I was one of the few Registrars who qualified for a special bonus, and was specially praised for the way in which the work was conducted. Well, sir, I stand before you, having resigned that office when I was told that I must either do that or give up working for this movement.

I want to make you realise that it is a point of honour that if you decide – as I hope you will not decide – to bind us over, that we shall not sign any undertaking, as the Member of Parliament did who was before you yesterday. Perhaps his reason for signing that undertaking may have been that the Prime Minister had given some assurance to the people he claimed to represent that something should be done for them. We have no such assurance. Mr. Birrell told the woman who questioned him the other day that he could not say that anything would be done to give an assurance to the women that their claims should be conceded. So, sir, if you decide against us to-day, to prison we must go, because we feel that we should be going back to the hopeless condition this movement was in three years ago if we consented to be bound over to keep the peace which we have never broken, and so, sir, if you decide to bind us over, whether it is for three or six months, we shall submit to the treatment, the degrading treatment, that we have submitted to before.

Although the Government admitted that we are political offenders, and, therefore, ought to be treated as political offenders are invariably treated, we shall be treated as pickpockets and drunkards: we shall be searched. I want you, if you can, as a man, to realise what it means to women like us. We are driven to do this, we are determined to go on with this agitation, because we feel in honour bound. Just as it was the duty of your forefathers, it is our duty to make this world a better place for women than it is to-day.

I was in the hospital at Holloway, and when I was there I heard from one of the beds near me the moans of a woman who was in the pangs of child-birth. I should like you to realise how women feel at helpless little infants breathing their first breath in the atmosphere of a prison. We believe that if we get the vote we will find some more humane way of dealing with women than that. It turned out that that woman was a remand prisoner. She was not guilty, because she was finally acquitted.

We believe that if we get the vote it will mean better conditions for our unfortunate sisters. We know what the condition of the woman worker is. Her condition is very bad. Many women pass through this Court who I believe would not come before you if they were able to live morally and honestly. The average earnings of the women who earn their living in this country are only 7s. 6d. a week. There are women who have been driven to live an immoral life because they cannot earn enough to live decently.

We believe your work would be lightened if we got the vote. Some of us have worked, as I have told you, for many years to help our own sex, and we have been driven to the conclusion that only through legislation can any improvement be effected, and that that legislation can never be effected until we have the same power as men have to bring pressure to bear upon our representatives and upon Governments to give us the necessary legislation.

Now, sir, I do want to say this, that we have not wished to waste your time in any way; we have wished to make you realise that there is another side of the case than that put before you by the prosecution. We want you to use your power – I do not know what value there is in the legal claims that have been put before you as to your power to decide this case – but we want you, sir, if you will, to send us to trial in some place more suitable for the trial of political offenders than an ordinary police-court. I do not know what you will do; I do not know what your powers are; but I do think, speaking as a woman to a man, I do say deliberately to you – I think your experience has been a large one – I come here not as an ordinary law-breaker. I should never be here if I had the same kind of power that the very meanest and commonest of men have – the same power that the wife-beater has, the same power that the drunkard has. I should never be here if I had that power, and I speak for all the women who have come before you and the other magistrates.

This is the only way we can get that power which every citizen should have of deciding how the taxes she contributes to should be spent, and how the laws she has to obey should be made, and until we get that power we shall be here – we are here to-day, and we shall come here over and over again. You must realise how futile it is to settle this question by binding us over to keep the peace. You have tried it: it has failed. Others have tried to do it and have failed. If you had power to send us to prison, not for six months, but for six years, for sixteen years, or for the whole of our lives, the Government must not think that they can stop this agitation. It will go on.

I want to draw your attention to the self-restraint which was shown by our followers on the night of the 13th, after we had been arrested. It only shows that our influence over them is very great, because I think that if they had yielded to their natural impulses, there might have been a breach of the peace on the evening of the 13th. They were very indignant, but our words have always been, 'be patient, exercise self-restrain, show our so-called superiors that the criticism of women being hysterical is not true; use no violence, offer yourselves to the violence of others.' We are going to win. Our women have taken that advice; if we are in prison they will continue to take that advice.

Well, sir, that is all I have to say to you. We are here not because we are law-breakers; we are here in our efforts to become law-makers.

Mrs. Drummond

I want to point out to you why I came into this Court. I think, if you wished to find out, you will not find that I have ever been in this Court as an ordinary law-breaker; in fact, I am proud to say that I never entered a police-court until I came here to fight for my liberty.

I am charged with issuing a bill. I wish to say here, and now, that I do not want to apologise for circulating that bill. I want to say that we did circulate it because we had lost all faith in the Government, and because we trusted the people. We knew that if we could get the people to the House of Commons there would be a better chance of getting what we have been asking for so many years. Mrs. Pankhurst has pointed out to you how women have tried to get the vote in a quiet way, and have been no nearer gaining it.

Superintendent Wells has told you that I am an active organiser of this Union, and I rather think that is the reason why I have been included in these proceedings. The Government find that this organisation is becoming so powerful, and so determined, and that women are coming in in every way, coming forward to us, giving all their lives to gain this point. The Government can see for themselves that this agitation is extending all over the country.

Now, I want to say why I am an organiser in this Union, and why I am in this position to-day. It is because I want my sex to be recognised as a person in the eyes of the law. To-day, if I had appeared to you as a mother asking for exemption from vaccination of my child, I should have been told by you and your colleagues that I was not a person in the eyes of the law, and that you could not deal with me. Now, I stand before you on another charge, and in that position you will deal with me. I want my political rights, and I am not sorry at all that I caused that bill to be published, because I made up my mind that nothing else would gain that for which we have been fighting.

It has also been brought to your notice that I spoke in Trafalgar-square. I want to tell you that our two leaders, Mrs. Pankhurst and Miss Christabel Pankhurst, restrained us. They said: 'No, you must not be impatient; you must be prepared to try some peaceful means.' Now, I say to you that in our speeches we have done what we could to instil into the minds of the people the fact that we did not want them to practise violence. If the people who were round the House of Commons had believed that we had invited them to violence, not even 6,000 policeman would have prevented those people from getting into the House of Commons.

You say we have broken the peace. I should really like you to tell us what is meant by breaking the peace. Mrs. Pankhurst left the Caxton Hall with twelve other women; she was arrested and imprisoned for six weeks. Later on, under the same circumstances, that same number of women left the Caxton Hall, and they were not arrested. Now, in the first place, they broke the peace; in the second place, they did not. We women are fairly at sea as to what is a breach of the peace.

Do you realise what I, as a wife and mother, am wanting? I want women to be looked upon as human beings in the eyes of the law. I do not want the little boy in the street – and I put it down to the status of women legally – to say: 'Votes for women, votes for dogs!' I want you to realise, you men, that we want to look after our own interests, and we want justice to be done to our sex.

It is not that we go out into the streets to break the law. I should say that you know that you would never see us before you in any other circumstances.

I do not know what you intend to do to us, but whatever you intend to do, whatever sentence you intend to give us, we look only upon the sentence, we shall take no notice whatever of the binding over to keep the peace. I want to say to you that the agitation will go on – and I can speak on good authority – that it will go on stronger than it has ever done before, because the action which the Government have taken has fired the bosoms of women, who are determined to take up the flag that we women have had to lay down to-day.

I have been twice to prison, and I am prepared to go as many times as necessary; and I say again, we women are prepared to do it for this agitation. I am glad to say, also, that we have left everything in working order, and that the agitation will go on, and we shall find it stronger than it was when we left it. I should like to assure you that whatever you do, it will not stop the agitation that is going on at the present time.

II The Hearing of the Case

The first hearing of the case was on Wednesday, October 14, before the magistrate, Mr. H. Curtis Bennett. Mr. Muskett appeared for the Commissioner of Police (the prosecutor).

Mrs. Pankhurst, Miss Christabel Pankhurst, and Mrs. Drummond were placed in the dock at the outset.

Miss Christabel Pankhurst, addressing the magistrate, said she wished to apply that this case should be sent for trial, and not be dealt with summarily. They were informed that under Section 17 of the Summary Jurisdiction Act, 1879, they were entitled to the option of being tried where they desired, and they desired that the case should go before a jury.

The Magistrate: Yes; but we will go on.

Miss Pankhurst: Can I have your answer at once, sir?

The Magistrate: I cannot say what is in my power until I have heard the case.

Miss Pankhurst: Then I apply for an adjournment, in order that we may be properly legally advised and represented.

The Magistrate: That will come later on. We must go on with the case at present.

Mr. Muskett said the defendants were all prominent leaders in the agitation which had been disturbing the metropolis for so long, and they were brought up upon warrants for having disobeyed a summons to appear on Monday, October 12, charging them with having been guilty of conduct likely to provoke a breach of the peace. It was alleged that they had circulated, and caused to be circulated and published, a certain handbill calling upon members of the public to 'rush' the House of Commons on Tuesday evening, October 13. When process was issued, it was only known to the police authorities that the conduct of which the defendants were alleged to have been guilty was likely to lead to a breach of the peace, but now it was known as a fact that an actual breach of the peace had occurred owing to the incitement to riot, for which the prosecution said these ladies were responsible. The fact that between thirty and forty persons were to come before the Court that morning in connection with the demonstration was sufficient evidence of the fact that a serious breach of the peace had occurred.

On October 8, Inspector Jarvis had occasion to attend at the offices of the Union, and he saw Mrs. Drummond, who was a very active agitator, and Miss Christabel Pankhurst. That young lady said to the inspector, 'What about the 13th? Have you seen our new bills?' and she produced a handbill which, in substance, formed the foundation of the present charge. It was worded:

'Votes for Women. – Men and women, help the Suffragettes to rush the House of Commons on Tuesday, October 13, at 7.30 p.m.'

With regard to it, Miss Pankhurst said that the words 'to rush' were not in sufficiently large type, and they were going to have them made much more distinct. On Sunday last, October 11, a meeting of these ladies took place in Trafalgar-square, causing an enormous amount of additional labour to be thrown upon the shoulders of the police.

At this meeting speeches were delivered by Mrs. Pankhurst and her daughter and others, inciting the people who were present in the square to carry out the programme of rushing the House of Commons. The magistrate would agree that such conduct as that could not be tolerated in this country, and the authorities accordingly set the law in motion. It was not necessary to adduce any legal authority for the general proposition which was submitted on behalf of the Commissioner of Police, namely, that all persons who were guilty of of such conduct as was attributed to these three ladies might, and ought to be, ordered to find sureties for their future good behaviour. It could not be allowed with impunity that persons should incite other people to riot.

Evidence of Superintendent Wells

Superintendent Wells then went into the witness-box, and spoke as to what took place upon the occasion of his visit to the offices of the Women's Social and Political Union. He was given a copy of a letter which had been addressed to Mr. Asquith, and Mrs. Pankhurst said their action would depend upon the reply, there would be nothing but a great cheer for the Government, but if it was unsatisfactory there would be a demonstration, and they would try to get into the House of Commons. Witness said, 'You cannot get there, because the Police will not allow you unless you come with cannon.' Mrs. Pankhurst said no lethal weapons would be used, and no breaking of windows would form part of the programme, but witness pointed out the great danger of bringing so large a concourse of people into the vicinity of Parliament. Mrs. Pankhurst replied, 'Mr. Asquith will be responsible if there is any disorder and accident.' Witness, however, expressed the opinion that the Suffragists would be responsible. They then discussed the window-breaking matter, and Miss Pankhurst said that although it was not in their programme, they could not always control the women of their union. This was the substance of the interview reported to the Commissioner.

In the course of the meeting in Trafalgar-square on Sunday last Mrs. Drummond was distributing the handbills complained of. She was an active leader of the Suffragists, and she wore a uniform with the word 'general' or 'generalissimo' on the cap. (Laughter.) Witness told her that she and Mrs. Pankhurst would be prosecuted.

Mr. Muskett: Did a very large demonstration take place last evening in the vicinity of the House of Commons?

Witness: Yes; the traffic was wholly disorganised for four hours, and for three hours the streets were in great disorder. At ten o'clock I had to clear them.

Did this entail the employment of a very large body of police to maintain order? – A very large body indeed. Ten persons were treated at Westminster Hospital, and seven or eight constables and sergeants were more or less injured.

Miss Pankhurst's Cross-examination

Mr. Wells, I should like in the first place to ask you whether you are aware of our having given any undertaking to appear at the Court either on Monday or Tuesday? You are not aware of any promise to come in answer to the summons, are you? – Your mother and Mrs. Drummond left me under that impression.

They gave you a definite undertaking to appear? – Not in actual words.

And then, in the second place, I should like to ask you whether you are in the habit of reading our official organ, VOTES FOR WOMEN, and whether you read that issue which appeared on October 8 – I do not read it.

Then you are not aware that Mrs. Pankhurst wrote the following words:

> On the 13th, in Parliament-square, there will be many thousands of people to see fair play between the women and the Government. Let us keep their support and co-operation by showing them, as we have done before, with what quiet courage, self-restraint, and determination women are fighting against the tyranny and oppression on the part of a Government which has been called the strongest of modern times. It is by the exercise of courage and self-restraint and persistent effort that we shall win in this unequal contest.

There is nothing very inflammatory in those words, which were the official statement. Does it occur to you that those words were calculated to incite to riot? – I am not complaining of that article, I am complaining of those bills.

Well, I submit to you that the whole of our utterances ought to be taken together.

Now, I want to ask you further a question about the crowd in Trafalgar-square. – Was it a disorderly crowd? – It was quite an orderly crowd.

Are you aware that any member of the Government was there? – I don't know that I should answer that.

The Magistrate: You can say: 'Yes' or 'No.'

The question was repeated, and witness said: 'I saw one there.'

Was it Mr. Lloyd George? (Laughter.)

Witness did not answer, and the magistrate said the defendant must be satisfied with the answer.

Was there anything inflammatory in anything? – No reply.

At a later stage I shall have to require the presence of Mr. Lloyd George as one of the witnesses. But that is another matter. Now, I should like to ask one or two questions about the nature of our speeches in Trafalgar-square. That has not been brought out in evidence yet. On Sunday last was there anything inflammatory in anything that these speakers said? – I am not dealing with any speeches, but with the pamphlets.

Oh, but you see, I must press this question. . . . We must take the whole thing together. Was there anything in our speeches which was inflammatory? Did we incite the people to do personal violence, or to do damage to property? – You asked them to come within the vicinity of the House of Commons, and to rush the House of Commons.

Now, what do you understand by the word 'rush'? – To attempt an unlawful entry.

But do we say that violence may be used? Could it not be said to imply a request to enter, and if that request was denied, that pressure should be used? – I fully explained to you that your action in bringing people to the House of Commons –

Oh, yes, but then you see, that is rather different from inciting to riot? – What I am complaining of is your bringing them there.

But does not all hang upon the word 'rush'? I think I am right in saying that it was not until the handbill was issued that it was decided to take proceedings? You did not propose to take proceedings until you thought it possible to say we intended to do violence, and to incite to riot. Before the word 'rush' was used no proceedings were intended? – You don't know what was in my mind.

But I know the people above you – the Government. Do you think it was their dilatoriness, such as was displayed at the time of the Eurcharistic Procession, which induced them to delay these proceedings so long, or was it the word 'rush' that decided the matter? – I do not know.

I should like to ask you whether your mind takes you back to the meeting in Trafalgar-square at which John Burns was present many years ago. Did you ever hear the speeches made by Mr. John Burns? – I did not.

I see. You did not hear the speeches. But are you aware that the words he used at that time were very much more inflammatory – were very much more calculated to lead to destruction and damage to property than anything we have said? – I am not aware of it.

You are aware, however, that John Burns is a member of the present Government, and is responsible jointly with his colleagues for the action that has been taken against us? – Yes.

You are aware of that. That the law-breaker is now sitting in judgment upon those who have done far less than he did himself? You are aware of that?

Were you in Trafalgar-square when Mr. Thorne, M.P., made a speech? Did you hear him call upon the people to rush the bakers' shops? – I did not hear it, but it was reported to me.

Well, does it occur to you that his language was far more dangerous to the public peace than the language we have used? –

I am not complaining of your language, I am complaining of the bills.

Well, the language that was used on the bills, he used. He spoke the word 'rush,' and he incited people to riot and violence. Does it occur to you that his action is more reprehensible than ours? – It occurs to me that he might be prosecuted the same as you are.★

You are not aware whether proceedings will be taken? Can you tell me anything now as to whether – (Question interrupted).

You have seen Mr. Gladstone's reply in the House of Commons to the effect that these proceedings are not instituted by the Government, but by the police, and that the police are responsible? – You have kept me so busily engaged that I have not had time to look at the papers this morning.

I am sorry, but we are really not responsible for that. Can you tell me whether Mr. Gladstone and other members of the Government were consulted before these proceedings were taken? – I cannot.

Can you tell me whether the Government considers we should be tried by jury or not? – I cannot say.

You cannot say. Can you tell me whether anything has been decided already as to the length of the sentences to be imposed upon us? – I cannot.

Are you aware that in a London drawing-room Mr. Horace Smith asserted that in sentencing one of our members to six weeks' imprisonment he was only doing what he had been told to do? – I cannot say.

You are not aware of it. Can you tell me now what our letter to Mr. Asquith contains? Do you desire me to read it? – Yes. (The letter given on page 9 was read in Court by Mr. Wells.)

Now, Mr. Wells, is it not a fact that we assured you, on our word of honour, that if a satisfactory reply were forthcoming to that letter the attempt to rush the House of Commons would not be made? – The Magistrate: Well, he has already said that you said that.

Have you had time to peruse the columns of the morning papers for to-day? – I have not.

You have not. Then you have not seen a leading article which appears in the *Daily Chronicle*, which, I believe, is contempt of Court, prejudging this issue, and calling upon the magistrate to give us drastic punishment? – I have not seen that article. Do you wish me to express an opinion upon what is in a newspaper?

★ A summons was issued for Mr. Will Thorne on the following day.

What can you tell me as to the demeanour of the crowd last night? Did they show any inclination to attack people, and injure them, or to destroy property? – They were rowdy.

Rowdy, but not violent or menacing? – They were violent in a measure.

In a measure, but there was nothing seriously wrong? – There were two or three policemen badly hurt.

Were there any persons at all detained in hospital? – No.

The injuries were, then, so slight as to make it possible to discharge them? – One man had his head bandaged this morning.

There was practically no danger to life or loss of property? – There was a window broken.

A window broken. But no serious consequences have followed upon yesterday's demonstrations, having regard to the enormous number of people?

Cross-examination by Mrs. Pankhurst

You have recognised from the beginning that this is a political movement? – I have.

Well, it is quite a matter of opinion how far a politcal movement can go. But perhaps, although you have not had time to read the daily papers, you may know that in previous franchise demonstrations Mr. John Bright and Mr. Gladstone have advised us to do exactly what we have done? – To a certain extent.

But farther than that. To assemble in Parliament-square, from Parliament-street down to Charing Cross, if the Government continued to resist their just demands. Well, now, throughout the whole of this movement, I I think you will admit that, though a large number of people feel a very great interest in this movement, yet self-restraint has been exercised by the women engaged in the agitation, and exceedingly little damage has been done? – There has been great inconvenience.

No doubt. We regret that exceedingly, but it is necessary. Now, on the occasion when Mr. John Burns came to Trafalgar-square, was there not a great deal more violence shown by the crowd – fighting and stone-throwing – and was it not really a very much worse demonstration in every way, although not so large in number, as anything in which we took part? – Yes, more violent.

I just want to ask this last question: You have recognised, Mr. Wells, that this is a political movement? – Yes.

Cross-examination by Mrs. Drummond

Mr. Wells, you said that you heard Mrs. Pankhurst and myself speaking in Trafalgar-square. Do you remember what I said in my speech regarding the gathering on the 13th? Can you take your mind back to what I said? It was this: I asked the people to bring no weapons, to go there without weapons of any kind, but to carry their argument, which argument is that taxation without representation is tyranny, and that if the women were refused, then the men should be admitted, as voters. Was not that what I said? – No, I did not hear it.

Was there anything else in my speech which you thought inciting to riot? – There was nothing in your speech to take particular exception to.

Further Cross-examination by Miss Pankhurst

The fact that these proceedings are taken by the Commissioner of Police is no proof that the Government is not pulling the strings in the background? – The proceedings are instituted by the Commissioner of Police, and they may be made without referring, as far as I am aware, to any Government official. The Commissioner of Police has certain duties to perform, and in a breach of regulations, he has orders to proceed.

But the fact that the proceedings are nominally instituted by the Commissioner of Police is no proof that the Government are not the moving spirit in the matter? – The Commissioner of Police can institute proceedings.

He can do so, but does not. Yes, quite so, but in some cases they do go to the Government. Is not that so? – I do not know it.

You do not know it. But you are aware that this is sometimes the case? – I should suspect that it was.

Yes, and so would everybody else.

Evidence of Inspector Jarvis

Inspector Jarvis said that he called at the offices of the Union and saw Miss Pankhurst.

'Miss Pankhurst said, "What about the 13th?" I said, "Yes, what are you going to do?" and she said, "What are *you* going to do?" Then she said, "have you seen our new bill?" I said, "No, what about that?" She said, "I will fetch you one," and went into another room and came back again with a bill.'

Mr. Muskett: Were you present at the meeting in Trafalgar-square on Sunday afternoon last?

Yes.

Did any of these three defendants address the public?

Yes, sir, all three of them.

86

Did you particularly notice what Miss Christabel Pankhurst said? – Yes, sir, amongst other things, she said:

I wish you all to be there on the evening of the 13th, and I hope that that will be the end of this movement. On June 30 we succeeded in driving Mr. Asquith underground. He is afraid of us, and so are the Government. Years ago John Bright told the people that it was only by lining the streets from Charing Cross to Westminster that they could impress the Government. Well, we are only taking a leaf out of his book. We want you to help the women to rush their way into the House of Commons. You won't get locked up, because you have the vote. If you are afraid, we will take the lead, and you will follow us. We are not afraid of imprisonment. We know we shall win, because we are in the right.

And Mrs. Pankhurst? Did she address the crowd? Did you take any note of what she said? – She said:

On Tuesday evening, at Caxton Hall, we shall ask those who support women to come to Parliament Square. There will be a deputation of women who have no right in the House of Commons to a seat there, such as men have. The Government does not know its own mind, it changes so. But we do know that we want the vote, and mean to have it. When the people in Parliament Square –

Mr. Muskett interrupted: Did Mrs. Drummond address the meeting? – Yes, sir.

She is one of the active leaders? – Oh yes, very active.

I only want this fact. We summoned the defendants to appear in the morning, and you served that summons that morning for them to attend here on Monday afternoon at half-past three? – Yes.

I want to know about this question as to whether they promised to attend here or not? – Well, Miss Christabel. I saw her alone, and she said, 'We are not afraid. We shall be there.'

Then they were served with a summons to appear on the following morning at eleven o'clock? – Yes.

And as they did not put in an appearance then, a warrant was issued? – Yes.

And you had to wait there for them until they surrendered to you? – Yes.

Cross-examination by Miss Pankhurst

Miss Pankhurst began by questioning Mr. Jarvis as to whether they had promised to attend the police-court on the summons being served, and eventually drew from him the admission that they had made no definite statement to that effect, though the impression that they were coming had existed in his mind. He added that he regarded the word of the Suffragettes as reliable.

Miss Pankhurst: Well, now, with regard to this bill. Are you aware that the bill which we gave you was a proof, and that when we spoke of enlarging the word *rush* we were referring to an instruction to the printer? – Very likely that was so.

Now, you were in Trafalgar-square on Sunday. You saw the crowd? It was an orderly crowd? – It was an orderly crowd.

Don't you think it was a more orderly, more respectable crowd than most crowds which assemble there? – I don't know about that. As a rule they are orderly.

But still, it was a very orderly crowd? Did you see Mr. Lloyd George amongst the crowd? – I did not see him.

But you heard he was there? – Yes.

You heard the speeches. Did you think them very inflammatory in their character? – You meant to get everybody down to Parliament-square to rush the House.

Did we advise them to use weapons, to throw stones? Did we advise them to attack any persons? Did we advise them to destroy property? – No.

We did not advise them to rush private premises or damage any property. We simply urged them to come and rush the House of Commons. Now, did the word 'rush' convey to your mind the idea that we wanted to get inside the House? – Yes.

And it was obvious to you that if no resistance were offered we should make a peaceable entry? We expressed no desire to do damage to property? – No.

Very good. I wonder if your memory goes back, Mr. Jarvis, to the days of the riots in which Mr. John Burns was concerned? – No, it does not.

But, of course, you are familiar with the facts, and you know that the crowd on that occasion was far more disorderly than that which assembled in Parliament-square. compare the actual damage done – I mean on the 13th – with John Burns' Trafalgar-square meeting, and you agree that there was far more violence, more damage done? – I did not hear his speech.

You did not hear his speech, but, of course, it is a matter of common knowledge that he incited people to violence, and you know, of course, that he is in the Government to-day, and from being a law-breaker he is now a law-maker? Does it occur to you that we may follow the same course? – I beg your pardon?

Does it occur to you that we may become law-makers – at the ballot-box? (No answer.)

Did you hear Mr. Thorne, M.P., advise people to make a rush? Now, does it occur to you that it is because this gentleman is a member of Parliament that (on the principle of there being honour among thieves) the Government would not proceed against him? Or do you think the reason rather is that because he is a man and a voter the Government have less courage in dealing with him than with us?

Can you say that the crowd last night showed any feelings of great anger? – They threw themselves upon the police in the usual way. Some of them were very fiery indeed.

But less violent than they were in Trafalgar-square in the days of '86? – Yes.

Now, as to the injuries. Is it within your knowledge that 10 people were injured and taken to hospital? – Yes, there were 10 went to the hospital.

On the whole, however, very little permanent trouble has ensued as the result of that demonstration? – Well, the police were very lenient.

As a matter of fact, no damage was done worth mentioning, either to person or property? – That is so.

Cross-examination by Mrs. Pankhurst

I should like to ask one question about the report of my speech. You said that I said 'women had not seats in the House of Commons' – was it not that I said 'women had no representatives in the House of Commons?' – I am not sure.

Now, with regard to the serving of the summons. You are no doubt aware that I was in the office, and that I had been there to take full responsibility, so that proves that I was not likely to evade in any way. Now, when you finally served the summons upon me at Clements Inn, I did not say that I should or should not *go*, did I? – No, but the impression I formed was that you were all coming in the afternoon.

But nothing that I said to you led you to form that impression? – Except what I have just said.

Well now, do you remember on the occasion of the Trafalgar-square meeting addressed by John Burns there was stone throwing in Northumberland-avenue? – I have heard of it.

You did not see it yourself? – No.

Like Mr. Wells, you have known this agitation, and have seen a great deal of it. We have never either threatened or shown any desire to do damage to property or person? – No.

Cross-examination by Mrs. Drummond

With reference to my speech on Sunday, I should like to ask you, did you find that my speech was more violent or inciting to violence than the unemployed speeches on the Saturday before? – Well, at any rate, it was quite illegal to ask them to come and rush the House of Commons.

You do not think that my efforts were to incite the people to violence and destroy property? – You wanted to get as many people as you possibly could in Parliament-square and rush the House.

Of course, you remember that we acted on the advice of John Bright? – (No reply.)

Do you remember the remarks made by Mr. Lloyd George in Swansea the other day? He incited his stewards to 'ruthlessly fling the women out.' Do you not agree with me that this is inciting to violence? – I cannot say.

Don't you really think that it was more inflammatory than my speech on Sunday? – As a matter of fact, I never heard Mr. Lloyd George.

Well, I am just telling you. Do you not think that he was inciting to violence more than I did in my speech on Sunday? – (No reply.)

Well, I think the Court will agree with me that he was.

After a further inspector had been called whose evidence was not material, the case for the prosecution closed.

Miss Pankhurst again applied for an adjournment, which was granted for a week. Bail was allowed; £100 from each person with two sureties of £50 each.

The Hearing on Wednesday, October 21

On Mr. Curtis Bennett, the magistrate, taking his seat,

Mr. Muskett said the case for the prosecution was concluded last week.

The magistrate, addressing the defendants, said: I would just make one suggestion. It may be for the benefit of two gentlemen who are here, that before you make any remarks their evidence should be taken, because they have, I know, important engagements elsewhere.

Miss Pankhurst: I desire first to submit that, as a matter of law, you ought not to bind us over at all, having regard to the form of the summonses and the nature of the evidence that has been adduced by the prosecution in support of them.

The Magistrate: Won't you submit that afterwards?

Miss Pankhurst: I think, with your permission, it might be well to submit it now.

The Magistrate: I am only suggesting that you should call these two gentlemen first.

Miss Pankhurst: Do I understand that if I take their evidence now it will be open for me to raise this later?

The Magistrate: Certainly.

Mr. Lloyd George's Evidence

Mr. Lloyd George then went into the witness-box.

Miss Pankhurst: You are Mr. Lloyd George? – Yes.

Privy Councillor and Chancellor of the Exchequer? – Yes.

Were you present at the meeting addressed by Mrs. Pankhurst, Mrs Drummond, and myself in Trafalgar-Square on October 11? – I think I was there for about ten minutes. I believe I heard Mrs. Pankhurst – partly.

Did you see a copy of the bills which were being distributed to members of the audience? – Yes. A young lady gave it to me the moment I arrived – it invited me to rush the House of Commons.

How did you interpret the invitation conveyed to you as a member of the audience? What did you think we wanted you to do? – I really should not like to place an interpretation upon the document. I don't think it is quite my function, Miss Pankhurst.

Well, I am speaking to you as a member of the general public. – I heard what Mrs. Pankhurst said, and I thought she placed the interpretation you desired to be put upon the document.

I want to deal with the matter in this way. First of all to get the meaning conveyed by the bill, quite apart from anything you may have heard said; and then we must throw some light upon the meaning of the bill by examining the words which were spoken on the platform. Let us take the bill itself. Imagine you were not at the meeting at all, but were walking up the Strand, and someone gave you a copy of this bill, and you read it – 'Help the Suffragettes to rush the House of Commons.' And suppose you forgot you were a member of the Government and regarded yourself just as an ordinary person like myself – quite unofficial. You get this bill. What would you think you were called upon to do? – Really, I should not like to be called upon to undertake so difficult a task as to interpret that document.

Now, this word 'rush,' which seems to be at the bottom of it all. What does it mean? – I understand the invitation from Mrs. Pankhurst was to force an entrance to the House of Commons.

No, no. I want you to keep your mind centred on the bill. Let us forget what Mrs. Pankhurst said. What did the bill say? – I really forget what the bill said.

I can refresh your memory. The bill said, 'Help the Suffragettes to rush the House of Commons.' – Yes; that's it.

I want you to define the word 'rush'? – I cannot undertake to do that.

You can't offer any definition of the word 'rush'? – No, Miss Pankhurst, I cannot.

Well, I will suggest some to you. I find that in Chambers' English Dictionary one of the meanings of the word is an 'eager demand.' Now, what do you think of that? – I can't enter into competition with Chambers' Dictionary. I am prepared to accept it.

'Urgent pressure of business.' That is another meaning. Ogilvie gives the same meaning – 'eager demand.' Now, if you were asked to help the Suffragettes to make an eager demand to the House of Commons that they should give votes to women, would you feel we were calling upon you to do an illegal act? – That is not for me to say.

The Magistrate: The witness is perfectly right. That is for me to say on the evidence. I have not interfered so far.

Miss Pankhurst: Here is another sense in which the word 'rush' is used, and I think it will be of some interest to you. We use it in this connection – to rush bills through Parliament.

Witness: Yes, I think I have some experience of that!

Miss Pankhurst: 'On the rush,' we are told in another dictionary, means in a hurry. There is nothing unlawful in being in a hurry?

The Magistrate: I have already said you must address those remarks to me afterwards.

Miss Pankhurst: Did you understand we asked you to go in a hurry to the House of Commons to make this eager demand for enfranchisement? Was that the meaning which the bill conveyed to you? – I cannot express any opinion as to that. I can only give evidence as to what I really saw.

You can't tell me what you, as a member of the public, understood?

The Magistrate: Miss Pankhurst, you must take my ruling, please.

Miss Pankhurst (to witness): Can you tell me at all what were the words you heard Mrs. Pankhurst use in Trafalgar-square? – I really could not, Miss Pankhurst. If you insist upon my giving my vague recollection I shall do so.

I should like to have it. – My vague recollection is that Mrs. Pankhurst insisted upon the right of women to have access to the House of Commons, and she said if that was refused they meant to force an entrance, and she invited the crowd to assist her. I am only giving a vague impression of the words that were used.

Did you hear this: 'On Tuesday evening, at Caxton Hall, we shall ask those who support the women to come to Parliament-square. There will be a deputation of women, who have no rights in the House of Commons such as men have. The Government does not know its own mind, it changes so; but we know we want the vote and mean to have it'? – Yes; I was there when Mrs. Pankhurst said that.

She was the only speaker you heard? – Yes.

Now, what impression did you form from the demeanour of the crowd in Trafalgar-square as to whether they were likely to respond to this invitation to rush the House of Commons? – I thought they were a very unlikely crowd to respond.

You didn't think they would come? – Not from the demeanour of the crowd – certainly not.

You thought that although we issued the invitation it would not be accepted? – Not by that particular crowd.

Did you think on other grounds that there would be a large public response to this invitation? – That I should not like to say.

Did you hear the speaker threaten any violence to you or to any member of the Government? – Oh, no, Miss Pankhurst.

She didn't invite others to attack you in any way? – Oh, no.

She didn't urge the people to come armed? – Oh, no; I never heard anything of that sort.

There was no suggestion that public or private property should be in any way damaged? – Oh, I do not suggest anything of that sort.

You heard nothing of that kind? – No, Miss Pankhurst.

What did you anticipate that the consequence would be to you yourself personally if the public responded to the invitation to rush the House of Commons? – Well, I didn't think it was very formidable.

You didn't think you would be hurt? – (The witness smiled and shook his head.)

Or that any of your colleagues would be hurt? – Oh, there was no suggestion of any personal violence to anybody.

No suggestion of violence at all. Then you are able to tell me that the speeches were not inflammatory. They were not likely to incite to violence? – I should not like to express an opinion as to what the result would be of inviting a crowd of people to force an entrance to the House of Commons. I should not have thought it possible to do that without some violence.

You didn't hear the word 'force'? – I have only a very vague impression as to the words used. If Mrs. Pankhurst says she didn't use the word force I would not contradict her.

There were no words so likely to incite to violence as the advice you gave at Swansea, that women should be ruthlessly flung out of your meeting?

Mr. Muskett: That is quite irrelevant.

The Magistrate: That was a private meeting, and not of the same character.

Miss Pankhurst: A public meeting.

The Magistrate: Well, it is private in a sense.

Miss Pankhurst: They are private nowadays. That is quite true. (To witness): You didn't hear any speeches made by myself or by Mrs. Drummond?

The Magistrate: The witness has already said he only heard Mrs. Pankhurst.

The Witness: I only heard Mrs. Pankhurst for about ten minutes or a quarter of an hour.

Am I right in assuming that you read the official organ of our society? – Well, I only read, I think, one copy that was kindly sent me by Mrs. Pethick Lawrence.

You didn't read the copy in which Mrs. Pankhurst issued a manifesto dealing with the plans for the 13th? – No; I don't think it was included in that.

Listening to the speeches in Trafalgar-square, what did you gather as to the object we had in view in planning a rush to the House of Commons? – I was not quite clear.

You were not quite clear as to the object? – No, except to force an entrance to the House of Commons; that is all I heard.

Did you gather for what reason this rush had been planned?

The Magistrate: You are not entitled to cross-examine your own witness. I am loth to stop you. I should have stopped counsel before this.

Miss Pankhurst: I rather anticipated this difficulty, and I looked up 'Taylor on Evidence,' and I saw words which I thought gave me a good deal of latitude. (To witness): Were you in the neighbourhood of the House of Commons on the evening of the 13th? – I was in the House of Commons, Miss Pankhurst.

Before you reached the House of Commons you were necessarily in the street, and you saw something of what took place? – Yes, I saw a little bit.

You were not alone, I think? – No, I had my little girl with me. How old is she? – She is six.

Did you think it safe to bring her out? – Certainly. She was very amused.

You thought it was quite safe for a child of those tender years to be amongst the crowd? – I was not amongst the crowd.

You thought that, in spite of the contemplated rush, you were safe to have her inside and outside the House of Commons? – Yes, considering the police arrangements.

Were the streets crowded? – Not by the House. You see I only brought her from Downing-street to the House, and I think that was clear.

Were you in the crowd yourself? – No; it was quite clear.

Did you see any women you supposed to be members of our Union? – I don't think I did.

Did you see any women arrested? – I was not anywhere near that.

Had you any opportunity of noticing the attitude of the crowd? – I don't think there was much of a crowd by the House of Commons. I think it was on Embankment; so I heard.

Had you any opportunity of seeing any arrests or what was going on in the crowded part? – No, Miss Pankhurst, I did not see the crowd at all.

Were you yourself attacked or assaulted in any way? – Oh! dear me, no.

Did you apprehend any attack or assault? – No.

Can you tell me, according to your own knowledge, what harm has resulted from the events of the 13th? – I don't think I can tell you that.

You can't tell me? – No, Miss Pankhurst.

Do you know of any serious injury having taken place? – I should not like to express any opinion. It is hardly my function in the witness-box.

The prosecution asserts that a serious breach of the peace took place. Do you concur with that statement?

The Magistrate: The Chancellor of the Exchequer would have nothing to do with that.

Miss Pankhurst: I believe you are a lawyer? – Well, I hope I am.

Don't you think the offence alleged against us would be more properly described as unlawful assembly? – There again, I was not put in the witness-box to express an opinion of that sort.

The Magistrate: That has nothing to do with Mr. Lloyd George.

Miss Pankhurst: Of course, I am subject to your guidance, your worship. (To witness): You have seen the form of summons issued against us? – No.

You don't know with what we are charged? – No, I don't really.

The Magistrate: Have you any other question?

Miss Pankhurst: Well, I think it is desirable he should know. But I am subject to your guidance.

Witness: I have nothing to do with it.

Miss Pankhurst: You know we are asked to show cause why we should not be bound over for having incited people to commit an unlawful act? – I take it from you, Miss Pankhurst, but I don't know.

Miss Pankhurst: Yet the result of the summons being in this form is that we are denied the right of trial by jury.

The Magistrate: The witness has nothing to do with that. That is the law of the land.

Miss Pankhurst: Does it occur to you that the authorities, in choosing this form of procedure against us, deliberately wished to deprive us of the right to trial by jury?

The Magistrate: That, again, is not a question for the witness.

Miss Pankhurst: May I put the question if you think it a very serious thing – this proposal to rush the House of Commons?

Witness: Oh, yes. I should have thought you would have thought that too, Miss Pankhurst.

Still, it is in the nature of a political offence? – Well, I should not like to say anything about that. In fact, I am simply here as a witness to give evidence of what I saw. I really cannot go into the political aspect of the matter.

You are aware that we argue that, as we are deprived of a share in the election of Parliamentary representatives, we are entitled to go in person to the House of Commons? – That was a point put by Mrs. Pankhurst.

Do you agree with that point of view? – I should not like to express an opinion.

The Magistrate: It is not for the witness to express an opinion.

Miss Pankhurst: I should like to put this question, Do you think that coercion is the right way of dealing with political disturbers?

The Magistrate: That, again, is not for the witness.

Miss Pankhurst: You refuse to answer?

Witness: I don't refuse to answer, but I must obey the decision of the Bench that I cannot express an opinion about things in the witness-box.

Miss Pankhurst: Am I to understand that an answer must not be given to that?

The Magistrate: No.

Miss Pankhurst: Not even if the witness would like to do so?

The Magistrate: No.

Miss Pankhurst: Well, is it likely to be a successful way of dealing with political disturbances?

The Magistrate: That, again, is not admissible.

Miss Pankhurst: But for these restrictions, your worship..! (To witness): Can you tell me whether any interference with public order took place in connection with previous movements for franchise reform? – I should have thought that was an historical fact, Miss Pankhurst.

Have you yourself taken part in any such movement? Does your mind go back to 1884?

The Magistrate: That is cross-examination. Your witness cannot go into that.

Miss Pankhurst: In a sense, he is my witness.

The Magistrate: In every sense at present.

Mr. Lloyd George's Encouragement

Miss Pankhurst: Have we not received encouragement from you, or, if not from you, from your colleagues, to take action of this kind?

Witness: I should be very much surprised to hear that, Miss Pankhurst.

You would be surprised to hear that? – Very.

You deny that we have been encouraged by Liberal statesmen to take action of this kind? – I simply express astonishment at the statement.

Miss Pankhurst: Have you ever heard these words spoken by us at Trafalgar-square or by any Liberal statesman? 'I am sorry to say that if no instructions had ever been addressed in political crises to the people of this country, except to remember to hate violence and love order and exercise patience, the liberties of this country would never have been attained' – have you heard these words before? – I cannot call them to mind.

Miss Pankhurst: These were the words of William Ewart Gladstone. – I accept your statement, Miss Pankhurst.

Miss Pankhurst: Is not that encouragement to such actions as we have taken? – You ask me a question of opinion again. I am not competent to express an opinion in the witness-box.

Were you present in the House of Commons when Mr. Herbert Gladstone gave advice to the women of this movement, while addressing the House on women's suffrage? – No, Miss Pankhurst.

Miss Pankhurst: You were not present. – When was it?

In this present Parliament? – I don't remember.

You don't know, then, that he encouraged us to action of this kind?

The Magistrate: He says he doesn't remember.

Witness: I don't think I heard him on the subject. I was probably attending to the duties of my department.

Miss Pankhurst: Is it not a fact that you yourself have set us an example of revolt?

The Magistrate: You need not answer that question.

Miss Pankhurst: Well, your worship, my point of view was –

The Magistrate: You must not attack your own witness.

Miss Pankhurst: My point of view was that, when it comes to the moment when you make your decision, you will inquire a little into the motive.

The Magistrate: Yes, but you must not attack your own witness.

Mr. Lloyd George: I certainly never incited a crowd to violence.

Miss Pankhurst: Not in the Welsh graveyard case? – No.

You did not tell them to break down the wall and disinter a body? – I gave advice which was found by the Court of Appeal to be sound legal advice.

Miss Pankhurst: We think we are giving sound legal advice, too. Are you aware that in planning the action of the 13th we were carrying out literally the advice given by Liberal statesmen? – Oh, I could not tell you.

You don't know that John Bright advised the people to take a precisely similar course? – No, Miss Pankhurst.

Are you aware that Mr. Chamberlain in 1884 threatened precisely the same action? – I did not know.

You don't know that he threatened to march 100,000 men on London?

The Magistrate: He has answered the question – he never heard of it.

Miss Pankhurst: Do you know what action was taken against him by the Liberal Government? Was he prosecuted?

Witness: Miss Pankhurst, I have already said that I do not remember the incident you refer to.

You might remember Mr. Chamberlain being in the dock? – I don't know.

You don't know what action the House of Commons took? Your mind is a blank upon the subject? – Since you put it to me, I don't believe Mr. Chamberlain ever threatened to use violence and break the law.

I must refer you to the pages of Hansard. – Certainly.

Do you know what advice another eminent statesman gave? Do you know that Lord Randolph Churchill urged the men of Ulster to fight, and said they would be right? He advised them to use the arbitrament of force? – Yes.

Did he ever stand in the dock? Was he prosecuted? Yet are you not of opinion that he incited to violence more than we have done? – Well, I think I have already told you, Miss Pankhurst, I cannot express opinions here in the witness-box.

Miss Pankhurst again quoted from 'Taylor on Evidence' as to the discretion of the magistrate in allowing questions to be put to a witness who obviously appeared to be hostile or interested for the other party.

The Magistrate: I have seen neither one nor the other.

Miss Pankhurst. Or unwilling to give evidence.

The Magistrate: I think the witness is giving his evidence most fairly.

Miss Pankhurst: I think I need not trouble him with any further questions.

Questions by Mrs. Pankhurst

Mrs. Pankhurst: I should like to ask Mr. Lloyd George one further question about his being present with his little girl. You remember you told my daughter that you anticipated no danger for your little girl, and that you were rather amused?

Mr. Lloyd George: I said the little girl was amused.

You took her out to be amused by the sight of the crowd? – She wanted to see the crowd, and I took her out.

Don't you think that from that fact we might gather that probably if it had been less possible for your little girl to go out to be amused that the people with whom you are associated would have taken the thing a great deal more seriously? That the very self-restraint which allowed your little daughter to go out and be amused – I am not sure as to the question you are putting, but I think you are asking me for an opinion again. I am here to give evidence as to facts.

I want to ask you a question about what you heard me say on Sunday. Did I ask the crowd to help the women get into the House of Commons because it was the people's House of Commons; women formed part of the people, and they had as much right to be represented there as men? – Yes, that seemed to be the argument.

Then perhaps you remember I said that since women were not in the position of men, and could not send representatives to press their claim on the Government, they had a constitutional right to go there themselves? – Now that you remind me, I remember your saying that.

And that they were unlawfully shut out from the House of Commons? – Yes, that was the argument.

Mrs Pankhurst: Now, I put it to you, Mr. Lloyd George, to show cause why we should not be bound over.

Mr. Lloyd George: Well, you have asked me to come here and go into the witness-box to say what I have seen, that is all.

The Magistrate: Yes, that is the only thing a witness can do.

Mrs. Pankhurst: I want to ask you whether we can ask Mr. Lloyd George some questions –

The Magistrate: You have asked him a great many.

Mrs. Pankhurst (to the magistrate): Questions which would show you cause why we should not be bound over?

The Magistrate: No, that is for me.

Mrs. Pankhurst: My point is that the evidence he would give would assist you.

The Magistrate: Well, the evidence he has given will assist me.

Mrs. Pankhurst: But we want him to give more. I want to ask him some further questions about what he and other Liberal statesmen have advised people to do.

The Magistrate: We have had a great deal of that from your daughter. Do you wish to have it again?

Mrs. Pankhurst: I want to ask you whether, in your opinion, the whole of this agitation which women are carrying on, very much against the grain, would not be immediately stopped if women got their constitutional rights conceded to them? – I should think that is very likely.

I want to ask you whether, in your opinion, the women who are in the dock here to-day are women who are ordinary lawbreakers, or who would have occasion to come into this Court for any other than political reasons? – No, of course not.

Questions by Mrs. Drummond

Mrs. Drummond: When you received the bill in Trafalgar-square, did you say anything to the lady who gave it you? – No; I took it from her.

Did you not consider it would rather be your duty to draw attention to the bill to the lady who gave it to you? – It is not my business. Certainly not.

Mrs. Drummond: Well, I am asking you as a responsible

member of the public. – Well, the Commissioner of Police would be the person to attend to that.

Mrs. Drummond: Did you draw the attention of the police to the bill? – No.

Mrs. Drummond: I should like to ask Mr. Lloyd George this question. Many times he has refused to answer me. When do you intend to put a stop to these things by giving us the vote?

The Magistrate: That is not a question.

Mrs. Drummond: Perhaps he cannot answer me; but there is one thing, he cannot run away. You refuse to answer?

The Magistrate: You cannot ask it.

Mrs Drummond: You and your colleagues are more to blame for this agitation.

The Magistrate: You must not make a statement.

Mrs. Drummond: You see, we ladies don't get a chance.

Mr. Lloyd George (smiling): Indeed, you do.

Mr. Muskett did not cross-examine the Chancellor of the Exchequer.

Miss Brackenbury and Mr. Horace Smith

Mr. Curtis Bennett at this point wished Miss Pankhurst to call Mr. Herbert Gladstone, but Miss Pankhurst asked leave to call one other witness first. The magistrate demurred, and Miss Pankhurst said: 'I have only one question to put to this lady.'

The Magistrate: Very well, then, *one* question.

Miss Marie Brackenbury, in reply to Miss Pankhurst, said she had suffered six weeks' imprisonment in connection with the votes for women agitation.

Miss Pankhurst: Did Mr. Horace Smith tell you that in sentencing you to that term he was doing what he was told?

'You must not put that question,' said the magistrate; but the witness had already replied, 'He did.'

Miss Pankhurst: The witness has said 'Yes' upon oath.

Mr. Gladstone's Evidence

Mr. Herbert Gladstone, the Home Secretary, was next called, and questioned by Miss Pankhurst.

By virtue of your office as Home Secretary have you not immediate control over the Metropolitan police? – No, not exactly immediate control.

Then who has immediate control? – The Commissioner.

And he is responsible to you? – To me.

You also appoint the police-magistrates in the metropolis, and the regulation of the business of their courts is entirely in your hands?

The Magistrate: You must not go into questions of State, you know. That is clearly laid down.

Miss Pankhurst: You are, therefore, ultimately responsible for the proceedings which have been taken against us? – The responsible department.

Did you not, as a matter of fact, instruct the Commissioner of Police to take the present proceedings?

Mr. Muskett: I object to that.

The Magistrate: That question cannot be answered.

Miss Pankhurst: Are the Government as a whole responsible for these proceedings?

Mr. Muskett: I object to that.

The Magistrate: That, again, you cannot put.

Miss Pankhurst: Did you instruct Mr. Horace Smith to decide against Miss Brackenbury and give her six weeks?

The Magistrate: You cannot put that question either.

Miss Pankhurst: It is a pity that the public interest should suffer on that account. (To witness): Did you ever give any instructions to Mr. Horace Smith?

Mr. Muskett: I object to this. It is contempt of Court to continue putting these questions.

Miss Pankhurst: The public will answer them. (To witness): What do you suggest is the meaning of what Mr. Horace Smith has said?

The Magistrate: The same ruling applies. This witness is here to answer any question you have got to ask him about what he saw when he was in Parliament-square on the day in question.

Miss Pankhurst: Is this question permissible? Did you see a copy of the bill issued by us inviting the public to the House of Commons? – I have seen it.

The Magistrate: If it was shown to you in your official capacity it is not admissible.

Witness: I am under your ruling, sir.

Miss Pankhurst: Was it given to you as an ordinary member of the public in the street? – No, certainly not.

Can you define the word 'rush'? What impression has it made on your mind? – I can hardly give any definition of it, but a rush implies force.

Do you deny that it implies speed rather than force? – Speed generally involves force.

Miss Pankhurst: Suppose I am standing near the door of the House, and I run up the steps – I have rushed the House of

Commons – Yes, but I should say you must exert a considerable amount of force to do that.

Energy, perhaps, but I should not offer any force to anybody or anything? – I hope not.

I suggest that it is possible to rush the House without attacking anybody or hurting anybody? – If you ask me that, I don't think it is possible.

Miss Pankhurst: Not according to present regulations, perhaps. There are so many people in one's way. We did not know what amount of force would be directed against us.

Mr. Muskett: Put questions, please.

Miss Pankhurst: I think it is important we should ascertain how this is understood.

The Magistrate: He has told you he thought it meant force. You must take the answer.

Miss Pankhurst: Were you anticipating you would be in bodily danger as a consequence of the issue of this bill? – I didn't think of it at all. I didn't think whether the possibility existed or not.

You are like us. You are above those considerations. You were not in fear? – No, not at all.

Did you think public property was in danger as a consequence of this bill having been issued? – Do you mean on the 13th?

Yes, as a consequence of this bill. – I thought it was quite possible.

You thought the public would be violent? – I thought there would be danger from the crowds.

Then you were agreeably disappointed on the morning of the 14th, when you found no harm had been done? – No, I was not. The police measures were sufficient to stop any serious accident or danger.

You were in the street on the 13th? – Yes.

Did you see the public make any attack on anybody? Do you think that, but for the action of the police, they would have assaulted you? – I was in the street for a very short time.

During the time did you form the impression that, but for the protection of the police, your life would have been in danger? – Not my life. Certainly the situation required very strong and careful action by the police.

You were in the street on the 13th. Did you see the public make any attack on anybody? – I was only in the street for a short while.

Do you assert that the crowd showed a hostile spirit? – I was only in one or two places.

But you can speak for that portion of the crowd that you did see? – I saw a certain crowd at six o'clock when I went out.

Was their demeanour violent or hostile? Did you feel that but for the line of police protecting you they would have rushed upon you and attacked you? – The police were not protecting me.

Had it not been for the presence of the police, do you think you would have been attacked by the crowd? – I don't know what object the crowd would have in attacking me. I didn't consider it.

You didn't feel in fear? – I felt no personal fear.

Did any other person seem in danger of attack? – The police gave them very little chance.

What made you think them a dangerous or hostile crowd? – Of course, I am quite accustomed to seeing these crowds, and I know what has happened before.

What has happened? – Disorderly scenes.

You mean in connection with our demonstrations? – It is not for me to connect disorder with your demonstrations. I am referring to crowds which have assembled during the last two years.

What harm have they done? – Very little, as it happened.

What harm have they attempted to do? – That is not for me to answer.

Have they attempted to do more than secure an interview with the Prime Minister?

The Magistrate: That is not a question for him to answer.

Miss Pankhurst: We will get back to the 13th. Do you think anyone was obstructed in their passage to the House? – I cannot speak for other people.

You saw no attempt to waylay members or Ministers?

The Magistrate: He hasn't said he did. You must not cross-examine your own witness.

Miss Pankhurst: Well, but for the presence of the police do you think you would have been attacked by the crowd? – I do not know what object the crowd would have had in attacking me.

Did you see the crowd do any harm whatever? – I did not.

Now you saw a portion of the crowd. Did you see them attack property? – No, certainly not.

Did you see them attack any person? – Not where I was.

Did you see them do any harm whatsoever? – No, I did not.

What were these people doing? – There was a great crowd.

But a great crowd assembles when the King goes to open Parliament. – Presumably they were waiting to rush the House of Commons.

Did you see any women whom you identified as Suffragists? – I didn't see many women.

Did you see any women wearing our colours, purple, white, and green? – I did not notice any.

Did you see any arrests? – I saw no arrests.

Did you see anyone injured? – No.

Did you hear of anyone being injured? – I have seen it stated that certain police-constables were injured.

You did not hear that ten people were received in hospital, but discharged? – I know nothing about that.

Will you tell me what harm has resulted from what took place? – All I can say is that there were thirty-seven arrests and over forty complaints of losses of purses and watches.

Comparing that with the net result of a Lord Mayor's Show crowd, or any sort of procession, really less harm resulted? – I could not say that.

I suppose I may not ask how many policemen were on duty?

The Magistrate: I don't suppose the Home Secretary knows that.

Miss Pankhurst: I suppose I may not ask these questions either. This would have been more suitable to the other witness (Mr. Lloyd George). What has been the cost to the country?

The Magistrate: We cannot go into these questions.

Miss Pankhurst: Will you tell me why we were not charged with unlawful assembly? – I cannot tell you.

You know the consequence to be that we are deprived of trial by jury? – You tell me. I am not acquainted with the particular part of the law you are referring to.

If I say that the reason is that the Government are afraid to send us to a jury . . . (Continuing) What have you to say with regard to our contention that the offence with which we are charged is a political offence?

The Magistrate: You must not put that question.

Miss Pankhurst: How do you define political offence? – I wish you would give me a good definition. I am often asked that question in the House of Commons.

Well, with the Magistrate's permission, I will. A political offence is one committed in connection with political disturbances and with a political motive. – I don't think that a sufficient explanation.

If I am at liberty after this day's proceedings are over, I shall have pleasure in sending you a fuller account. Do you recollect that when a deputation of women went to the House of Commons, instead of being allowed to enter they were arrested? – I have no immediate knowledge of that. I have a general recollection.

Do you remember that when a deputation went to the House of Commons to see the Prime Minister instead of being allowed to enter they were arrested?

The Magistrate: That does not arise on the issue.

Miss Pankhurst: It throws a little light on it.

The Magistrate: Please do obey, otherwise I shall have to stop it altogether. I have given you much more licence than I should give counsel.

Miss Pankhurst: In the action we took on the 13th, is it within your knowledge that in taking that action we were acting on advice given by yourself? – I wish you would take my advice.

We are trying to take it. What did you mean when you said men had used *force majeure* in demanding the vote? – If you hand me the speech I daresay I can tell you.

I have a copy of the speech.

The Magistrate: How is this material as to what Mr. Gladstone saw? You are cross-examining your own witness, Miss Pankhurst, and you must not do that.

Miss Pankhurst: May I not ask any explanation whatever as to the counsel given to us?

The Magistrate: No, you may not.

Miss Pankhurst: We never have any other opportunity. May I ask whether he made certain statements? (To witness): Did you say it was impossible not to sympathise with the eagerness and passion which have actuated so many women on this subject? – Yes.

Did you say you were entirely in favour of the principle of women's suffrage? – Yes.

Did you say men had had to struggle for centuries for their political rights? – Yes.

Did you say that they had to fight from the time of Cromwell, and for the last 130 years the warfare had been perpetual? – Yes.

Did you say that on this question experience showed that predominance of argument alone – and you believed that had been attained – was not enough to win the political day? Did you say that? – Yes.

Predominance of argument alone will not win the political day. Did you say that we are in the stage of what is called 'academic discussion,' which serves for ventilation of pious opinions, and is accompanied, you admit, by no effective action on the part of the Government, or of political parties, or of voters throughout the country? – Yes.

Did you say that members of the House of Commons reflect the opinion of the country, not only in regard to the number of people outside, but in regard to the intensity of the feeling in support of a movement, and that the Government must necessarily be a reflex of the party which brought it into being? – Yes.

Did you say this, 'There comes a time when political dynamics are far more important than political arguments'? You said that? – Yes.

And that 'Men had learned this lesson'? – Yes.

And that they know the necessity for demonstrating that *force majeure* which actuates and arms a Government for effective work? – Yes. I think it a most excellent speech. (Laughter.)

I agree with you. Did you say that that was the task before the supporters of this great movement? – Yes.

Did you speak of people assembling in tens of thousands in the 'thirties, 'sixties, and 'eighties, and do you know that we have done it on Woodhouse Moor and in Hyde Park? – Yes.

Why don't you give us the vote then? (Laughter.) Are you aware of the words your distinguished father spoke on the matter? – I heard the quotation.

Do you assent to the proposition he laid down? – Yes.

Then you cannot condemn our methods any more? – That is hardly a matter for my opinion.

It is a very interesting question, though. I think I need not trouble you further.

Questions by Mrs. Pankhurst

Mrs. Pankhurst: I want to ask Mr. Gladstone if he is aware that the consequence of our being ordered to be bound over is that we cannot consent and we shall go to prison?

The Magistrate: That is a matter of law, not for the witness.

Mrs. Pankhurst: If that happens to us, if we go to prison, I hope Mr. Gladstone will see that we go as political prisoners.

The Magistrate: That you must not ask.

Mrs. Pankhurst: But may I ask Mr. Gladstone this – if he is aware that in the City-square in Leeds on last Friday night 10,000 people, at six hours' notice, assembled, and carried, with two dissentients, a resolution calling upon the Government to pass Mr. Stanger's Bill during this session?

Mr. Muskett: That is not a question for Mr. Gladstone.

Mrs. Pankhurst: Well, Mr. Gladstone has answered some other political questions, sir.

(Continuing) I should like to ask Mr. Gladstone whether he recognises this morning that this is a political agitation? – I suppose it is a political agitation to get the franchise for women.

Do you think we should be likely to break the criminal law if we had the same means of representation as men? – I am sure your motive is excellent. It is a hypothetical question which I cannot answer.

Mrs. Pankhurst: I will ask Mr. Gladstone whether in his opinion he thinks we should be treated as ordinary criminals – searched, stripped, and put into the cells, as though we were drunkards or pickpockets?

The Magistrate: You must not put that question.

This concluded Mr. Gladstone's evidence, and as he and Mr. Lloyd George were about to leave the Court Miss Pankhurst said: May we tender our warm thanks to these two gentlemen who have done us the favour of coming forward as witnesses?

Miss Pankhurst proceeded to quote numerous authorities in support of her contention that the charge should have been one of unlawful assembly, and that the magistrate had no power to bind the defendants over.

Mr. Curtis Bennett said he would give his decision later.

A Succession of Witnesses

Miss Pankhurst then produced a great number of witnesses in support of her contention that the crowd on the night of the 13th was an orderly one, and that no violence was done.

Colonel Percy H. H. Massy stated that he was in Victoria-street on the evening of October 13, and in his opinion the crowd was perfectly orderly. He saw nobody attacked or injured.

Lady Constance Lytton said she considered the crowd was remarkably well-behaved and respectable.

Miss Annie Moor stated that she had been more roughly treated at society weddings than she was in this crowd. She was in the crowd on the occasion of Mr. Winston Churchill's marriage, and was much more jostled than on the evening of the 13th.

Mr. Henry Wood Nevinson and Dr. Louisa Garrett Anderson both agreed that the crowds sympathised with the suffragists, and that there was no disorder.

In cross-examination, Dr. Anderson, after some hesitation, said she approved of the bill containing the invitation to 'rush' the House.

Mrs. May, replying to Mr. Muskett, said she worked as actively as possible for the cause, but she did not speak or organise. She compared the use of the word 'rush' with that of 'dash' in a 'dash to the Pole.'

Spiritual Force

Miss Sylvia Pankhurst said the suffragists' instructions were to meet physical force with spiritual force.

After the luncheon adjournment several witnesses testified that there was never any intention to make use of violence, and that the demeanour of the crowds which collected was perfectly orderly. It was also frequently stated that the people appeared to sympathise with the women more than they had done upon any previous occasion.

Miss Evelyn Sharp, the well-known writer, said she regarded the bill as an invitation to go to the House of Commons, and if possible not to turn back. Witness herself 'doubled,' and got past the biggest policeman she ever saw. She was, however, afterwards caught by an inspector, and sent back. It was like a rush at hockey.

Albert Rettick said he looked upon the bill as an invitation to the public to support the women in going to the House, and possibly to see fair play.

Miss Florence Elizabeth Macaulay gave historical instances of women going to the House of Commons for the purpose of presenting petitions.

Miss Pankhurst: It appears that we were within our constitutional rights in going to the House?

Witness: I have been a student of history for many years, and I think you were only reviving an ancient custom.

Mrs. Celia M. McKenzie thought the common sense of Mr. Asquith would have caused him to receive a deputation of thirteen quiet ladies.

Sidney Dillon Shallard, a journalist, said the police made a desert of about a quarter of a mile round the House of Commons.

Miss Pankhurst: They made a desert, and called it peace.

At seven o'clock the magistrate, who had constantly refused up to this point to allow any adjournment, agreed to allow an interval of ten minutes. Miss Pankhurst then recalled Superintendent Wells, who admitted considerable police precautions were taken on Monday, October 12, though no Suffragist 'rush' was anticipated. At 7.20 the magistrate asked how many more witnesses there were for the defence.

Miss Pankhurst: About fifty. We are sorry to take up the time of the Court, but we are fighting for our liberty.

The hearing was then adjourned until Saturday, the defendants being released on the same bail as before.

The Case Resumed

Upon the three ladies being brought into Court on Saturday, October 24, the magistrate said: I have carefully considered what steps should be taken by me to prevent the conduct of this case being so continued as to become a serious obstacle in the administration of justice at this Court. I may at once state that simple repetition of the same class of evidence given by the last twenty-four witnesses will not affect my judgment, and therefore I must refuse to hear a continuation of that class of evidence. If you wish me to hear any particular person or persons on even the same lines of evidence as that already given I will consent now to hear them, but not more than two or three of such witnesses. If the defendants have evidence of a different nature which they wish me to hear I am quite willing to do so, provided it is limited to what is absolutely relevant to the matter before me, and is admissible in point of law. As this may take you a little by surprise I give you half an hour to consider what further evidence you may desire me to hear.

Miss Pankhurst: Would you kindly give us some definition of what evidence you think admissible?

The magistrate repeated that he was not going to take the same class of evidence as that of the witnesses he had already heard. He was willing to hear witnesses who could speak to a different state of facts, if their evidence was relevant.

Mrs. Pankhurst: Would you say what evidence you consider relevant?

The Magistrate: I cannot say more than I have done.

James Murray, M.P.

The case was then put back for a while. Upon resuming, Miss Pankhurst said the first witness they wished to call was Mr. James Murray, M.P. for East Aberdeen. That gentleman went into the witness-box, and was asked by Miss Pankhurst whether he was present at the Suffragists' meeting in Trafalgar-square on the 11th inst.

Witness: I was going into the National Gallery, and saw a congregation of well-dressed people in the square. I think your mother was speaking, but I could not hear anything. What struck me was that the crowd listening to her was composed of exactly the type of men and women who go to Church on Sunday in Scotland.

Miss Pankhurst: Then they must have been very respectable. Did you get a copy of the bill? – No.

I dare say you saw it in the papers? – I saw a statement in the paper.

How did you understand the word 'rush'? – I didn't take the matter seriously at all.

The Magistrate: That really is for me, Miss Pankhurst, as I have told you.

Miss Pankhurst: Did you resolve to act on the invitation? – I could not very well, you see, because I was inside the citadel.

The Magistrate: He has the right of entry.

Miss Pankhurst: Were you near Westminster on the 13th? – I was in the House, and sitting down to dinner when I got a telegram sent from the neighbourhood of Bow-street from your mother, asking me to come across here.

The Magistrate: This cannot be relevant.

Witness: In coming here I drove in a hansom up Parliament-street. The whole place was like a besieged city, except that we had police-officers instead of soldiers. A little beyond Dover House the crowd was held back by a cordon, but I had not the slightest difficulty in getting through in a hansom. Afterwards I returned to the House by the Strand and the Embankment, and had very little difficulty in getting back.

Miss Pankhurst: Was it a disorderly crowd? – No; I should think you could say an ordinary London crowd.

Mrs. Pankhurst: Did you come to the conclusion that the persons who had called the meeting desired to incite the crowd to disorder or damage? – No. I thought if it was for any purpose at all it was simply to advertise the cause.

Mrs. Pankhurst: You know something of the women who are conducting this agitation?

Witness: Yes; and I have the highest admiration for them for their earnestness of purpose, ability, and general management of the whole scheme. I don't say I approve of everything they do, but most of it I approve of.

You know they have tried every other political method? – Yes; and if they had been men instead of women they would not have been in the dock now, judging by the past.

Mrs. Pankhurst: Do you agree with Mr. Lloyd George when he said that if the Government would give us what we were asking for this agitation would cease? – I have no doubt it would. I go further than Mr. Lloyd George, and say you are entitled to it.

The Remaining Witnesses

Dr Miller McGuire stated that he was at the Trafalgar-square meeting, and heard nothing that anyone could object to. He spent most of the 13th looking at the 'performance.' There was nothing remotely approaching disorder of any kind.

Miss Agnes Murphy, of Hampstead, said the crowd in Victoria-street was the most orderly she had ever seen. She attributed this to the goodwill of the people towards the women, who had been ill-treated and grossly misrepresented in the Press.

The Magistrate: Those are three witnesses on exactly the same lines as the others.

Miss Pankhurst: We shall be delighted to follow other lines, with your permission.

The Magistrate: If you have any witnesses on different lines I will hear them.

Miss Pankhurst: I can call witnesses on different lines, but I don't know that the lines will be admissible. We can call witnesses to show that in taking this course we are taking the only possible course.

The Magistrate: That will not do.

Miss Pankhurst: We can call witnesses to show that we have been incited to this kind of action by our political opponents, the members of the Government.

The Magistrate: No; that you must not.

Miss Pankhurst: We can call witnesses to testify to our good character.

The Magistrate: That has not been raised in issue.

Miss Pankhurst: Then, if you will permit us to call no further evidence, I will proceed to address the Court.

The luncheon adjournment was then taken, and afterwards Miss Pankhurst stated that some fresh witnesses were forthcoming. One lady had travelled 50 miles to give evidence.

The Magistrate: Is it on the same lines?

Miss Pankhurst: I think that will appear when she is in the box.

The Magistrate: No; I will not hear it.

Miss Pankhurst: I have now to ask you to state a special case.

The Magistrate: Not at present.

Miss Pankhurst then applied for an adjournment, in order that she and her companions might be in a position to do themselves full justice when they addressed the Court.

The Magistrate: You have had a long time to take this matter into consideration. I think you must either address me now or not at all.

Miss Pankhurst: I can only do it under protest, and I want to point out that you are rushing this case through the Court. (Laughter.) You are not setting us at all a good example. I want again to insist upon our right to call further witnesses.

The Magistrate: I have decided that point once and for all. Are you going to address me or not?

The three prisoners then delivered their speeches from the dock.

These speeches, which roused great feeling in the Court, are reported verbatim above.

At the close of the speeches, Mr. Muskett, in reply to the magistrate, said Mrs Drummond had been convicted twice, and the other two defendants had each been dealt with once.

The Magistrate's Decision

Mr Curtis Bennett said there could be no doubt that it was for that Court, and that Court alone, to deal with the offence for which the defendants were in the first place summoned. The case of Wise *v.* Dunning, argued in the King's Bench Division on November 19 and 20, 1901, absolutely decided the point, to his mind, as to whether these proceedings were right or wrong. As to the facts, the defendants admitted that they were responsible for the distribution of this handbill, and although they were warned of the danger and difficulty which might arise in consequence of it, they persisted in going on. He had heard the very able speeches of the defendants, but he did not wish to make any further observations upon them, because it was not for him to discuss political matters. He was simply there for the purpose of endeavouring to carry out the law in order to preserve the peace and well-being of the metropolis, and there could be no question that that handbill, which was circulated, was by its contents liable to cause something to occur which might and probably would end in a breach of the peace. The Chief Commissioner of Police was bound to keep Parliament-square and the vicinity free and open, and he felt that it would be impossible to do that if crowds assembled together in order to help and see the women rush the House of Commons.

Between 5,000 and 6,000 police were required to keep order in consequence of this circular. Ten persons were taken to hospitals, seven policemen were placed on the sick-list, thirty-seven persons were charged at that court the following morning, and it was reported that no fewer than thirty watches were stolen. Could it for one instant be said that that circular asking the public to rush the House of Commons was not liable to create breaches of the peace? Therefore, as to the law there could be no question. To call a number of people to assemble together for that avowed object must bring the persons who called that meeting within the limits of this section, namely, they were doing something which was calculated to bring about a breach of the peace. Each of the two elder defendants would be bound over in their own recognisances of £100, and they must find two sureties in £50 each to keep the peace for twelve months; in default, three months' imprisonment.

In the case of the younger defendant, her own recognisances would be £50, with two sureties of £25 each, the alternative being ten weeks' imprisonment.

Miss Pankhurst: I ask you to state a case on a point of law, namely, the construction of the leaflet.

The Magistrate: I shall not state a case.

Miss Pankhurst: I ask you to suspend judgment until after the return of a writ of certiorari.

The magistrate refused.

The prisoners refused to be bound over, and were removed to Holloway Gaol and placed in the second division.

Christabel Pankhurst

Votes for Women in 1908. A Reply to Mr Lloyd George

(1908)

The Women's Social and Political Union call upon the Government to grant the Parliamentary Franchise to women on the same terms as to men during the Session of 1908. We have been told by at least one Cabinet Minister that the Government cannot constitutionally take this step until the opinion of the country has been taken at a General Election.

We refuse to accept this excuse for delay. We notice that the present Government are quite willing to make, without any appeal to the country, other constitutional changes which are, from a purely legal point of view, quite as revolutionary as that of Woman Suffrage. Not only did they introduce a Plural Voting Bill (a proposal that was not before the country at the General Election), but the Prime Minister, Mr Haldane, and other members of the Cabinet have announced that before the next General Election a Bill modifying the relationship between the two Houses of Parliament will, after passing through the House of Commons, be presented to the House of Lords. Only in the event of the House of Lords rejecting this measure do the Government intend to submit the question to the electors. Providing the consent of the Peers can be obtained, the position of the House of Lords is to be altered without the consent of the electors being asked.

It is plain, therefore, that it is merely for the purpose of evading the just claims of women to the Franchise that the present Government become such sticklers for constitutional propriety.

Consulting the Country

Those who contend that the country must be consulted before votes are granted to women, apparently overlook the fact that at a General Election it is not the country as a whole, but the men electors only, whose opinion is asked. To expect women to wait for votes until the men have endorsed their demand is no more reasonable than it would have been to expect men to wait for their votes until the women had given their consent to the enfranchisement of men. Since men are in possession of their own political rights it is difficult to see what claim they have to hinder or obstruct women in their hard struggle with the Government for political power. For women to admit that their right to vote depends upon the consent of the male sex would be inconsistent with the very principle upon which their claim to the franchise is based.

As a matter of fact, a General Election cannot and never will be fought on the question of Woman Suffrage. The reason is that immediately upon the adoption of Woman Suffrage as a fighting plank in the platform of, for example, the Unionist Party. Sir Henry Campbell-Bannerman will be compelled to adopt, as a matter of expediency, the same attitude, and the Labour Party will follow suit. Accordingly, whichever party was returned to power would be committed to Woman Suffrage, and the electors would therefore have no opportunity of assenting to or dissenting from the proposal to enfranchise women.

The Mandate of Women

There are many who cling to the theory that the Government, at a General Election, receive a series of direct mandates to legislate upon particular questions. These persons hearing our demand that the existing Government shall grant Woman Suffrage, protest that the Government has had no mandate to deal with this matter.

Such a point of view is the result of an entire failure to understand that a mandate may be delivered to the Government by voteless women as well as by enfranchised men. A Parliamentary vote gives to men a more effective way of expressing their wishes, but their mandate, though more easily and effectively delivered, has no higher authority than the mandate delivered by women.

The mandate of the educated, thoughtful, and responsible women of the country is that the Government shall grant the vote without delay, and they are, if need be, prepared to enforce obedience to that mandate by the methods of revolt to which the oppressed and disenfranchised have had to resort in all ages and in all lands.

Militant Methods

(c. 1909)

The militant methods of the Women's Social and Political Union were first adopted in 1905 after a 40 years' campaign of persuasion and appeal to which politicians have turned a deaf ear. These militant methods consist – (1) In opposing the Government at elections by canvassing and speaking against their nominee. (2) In protests made for the purpose of showing that women do not give their consent to a system of government in which they have no share. This second form of militant action has aroused special criticism, for **it is alleged that Suffragette protests are violent and lawless**.

The first of these methods is in regular use to-day by associations of men; it therefore needs no explanation. The second is only necessary in the case of those who are voteless, and therefore to an explanation of this second method this leaflet is devoted.

In the first place, we point out that it was the Government who first resorted to violence by causing women who asked questions about Woman's Suffrage to be thrown out of their meetings. Also, the violence used by the Government is much greater in degree than any used by the women. For example, it is the Suffragettes and not members of the Government who have been arrested and sent to prison as common criminals; it is the Suffragettes and not Members of the Government who have been assaulted by the stomach tube to the injury of their health and at the risk of their life.

In the second place, no violence of any kind was used by the Suffragettes until the Government, by refusing to see deputations and by excluding women from public meetings, had taken from them every peaceful method of agitation.

The Example Set by Men

In the third place, we are able to show that men have found the use of militant methods necessary in order to win reform. In our own country, from the time when the Barons forced King John, at the point of the sword, to sign Magna Carta, until now, men have resorted to violence of a kind undreamed of by Suffragettes. Violent measures were used in winning votes for men. Thus when men were agitating for the vote at Bristol, in a single day, between the hours of 6 o'clock and 12 o'clock, the new gaol, the toll-houses, the Bishop's Palace, two sides of Queen's Square, including the Mansion House, the Custom House, the Excise Office, warehouses, and other property to the amount of upwards of £100,000 were totally destroyed. The opponents of men's enfranchisement were subjected to fierce and dangerous attack; thus the Bishop of Lichfield was nearly killed, and the Archbishop of Canterbury was insulted, spat upon, and with great difficulty rescued, amidst the yells and execrations of a violent and angry mob. The Bristol men were so menacing in their attitude towards Sir Charles Wetherell because of his opposition to reform, that the Riot Act was read, and he had to leave the house, making his escape over the roofs.

Fourthly, we say that according to a recognised legal principle force may be used in order to preserve property, to save life or to vindicate a right. Thus, a few days ago Judge Rentoul decided that because the driver of a motor bus ran into and damaged a house in order to avoid running over a cyclist, the owner of the house could not recover for the damage done to his property. It is well known that a man may abate a nuisance which he finds upon his land, although in doing so violence has to be used. He may also forcibly eject a trespasser providing the violence used is not unnecessarily great. A public right-of-way is frequently asserted by forcible means. On this same principle, those who are claiming the vote are clearly entitled to use such force as is necessary to vindicate this supreme right of citizenship.

Fifthly, we would remind Liberals that Liberal Statesmen have defended the use of militant methods such as ours.

The Rt. Hon. W. E. Gladstone said:

'I am sorry to say that if no instructions had ever been addressed in political crises to the people of this country, except to remember to hate violence and love order and exercise patience, the liberties of this country would never have been attained.'

Sir William Harcourt, discussing the methods of the Irish, declared that:

'In judging of a system of government, we know no test by which to distinguish good government from bad, except this – that good government is government which is conducted and founded upon the assent and consent of the governed. If a Government is alien to the sympathies, the wishes and the wants of a people, that Government breeds discontent, and of that discontent there is inevitably born illegal conduct and illegitimate proceedings. . . .'

Mr Asquith has rejoiced at the militant methods adopted by the men of Turkey and Persia in order to win political rights.

Mr Lloyd George is an enthusiastic defender of militancy. Speaking recently at Carnarvon, he said:

'Freedom does not descend like manna from heaven. It has been won step by step, by tramping the wilderness, fighting enemies, crossing Jordan, and clearing the Jebusites out of the land. I do not regret that we cannot obtain these blessings except by fighting. The common people have taken no step that was worth taking without effort, sacrifice, and suffering.'

On another occasion *Mr Lloyd George* declared that 'the kingdom of politics is like the Kingdom of Heaven, it suffereth violence, and the violent take it by force.'

The Women's Social and Political Union, believing that 'rebellion to tyrants is obedience to GOD,' intend to continue their campaign of protest, using just so much force, and no more, as is necessitated by the action of the Government.

Atrocities in an English Prison

(1910)

Two Englishwomen, unconvicted prisoners on remand in an English prison (Walton Gaol, Liverpool), have been assaulted, knocked down, gagged, fed by force, kept for consecutive days and nights in irons. One of them has been **frog-marched**. Frog-marched! What does that mean? Read the story.

The Facts

On December 20th Miss Selina Martin and Miss Leslie Hall were arrested in Liverpool, and were remanded for one week, **bail being refused**.

Accordingly, while **still unconvicted prisoners**, they were sent to Walton Gaol, Liverpool. There, contrary to regulations, intercourse with their friends was denied to them. As unconvicted prisoners they refused to submit to the prison discipline or to take the prison food. Forcible feeding was threatened and Miss Martin therefore barricaded her cell. The officials, however, effected an entrance, fell upon her and handcuffed her, dragged her to a punishment cell and flung her on the floor, with her hands tightly fastened together behind her back.

Frog-Marched

All that night she was **kept in irons**. Next day her cell was entered, she was seized, thrown down, rolled over with her face upon the floor. In this position, face downwards, her arms and legs were dragged up behind her till she was lifted from the

120

ground. Her hair was seized by another wardress. In this way she was 'frog-marched' up the steps to the doctor's room, **her head bumping on the stone stairs**. In the doctor's room the operation of forcible feeding was performed – causing intense suffering – and then this tortured girl, in a terrible state of physical and mental distress, was handcuffed again, flung down the steps and pushed and dragged back into her cell. Her companion, Leslie Hall, was kept in irons for two and a half consecutive days and nights.

What was the Charge against Miss Martin?

What terrible crime had Miss Martin done? She had dared to protest against the political slavery of her sex; against the refusal of the Prime Minister to receive any Deputation from women; and against the exclusion of women from political meetings. The charge against Miss Martin was that she had thrown an empty ginger-beer bottle at an empty motor-car – the car that had taken Mr Asquith to the meeting. But when she was treated in this terribly cruel way these charges had not been proved, she was 'on remand,' and by the theory of English law presumed innocent. Bail had been offered, she was ready to give an undertaking that no disturbance should take place during the week for which the case was remanded. **Bail was arbitrarily refused** in spite of the fact that though there have been hundreds of Suffragette prisoners, they have never attempted to escheat their bail.
The frog march, and the other assaults and cruelties, the brutal feeding by force, were resorted to during this week of remand, **while she was an unconvicted prisoner**. Prison officials, encouraged by the Government, have cast aside both law and humanity in dealing with women political prisoners.

Is this England?

If such deeds were done in Russia there would be an outcry in this country. Are they to be tolerated here?

Electors! You and you only can put a stop to this terrible injustice. These two women are in prison **now**. Miss Martin is sentenced to two months' hard labour and Miss Hall to one month.

Electors! assert your will. Secure the release of these women who have already suffered such horrible torture. It can be done by voting against the Government which is responsible for this cruelty. The prison authorities are the tools of the Government, and act as they are bidden by the Home Office. Because women are making their cry heard for that political freedom which Liberals profess to hold so dear in the case of men, the Liberal Government is persecuting them with unheard of violence and cruelty.

Electors, vote against the Liberal Candidate in your Constituency, for if returned he will go into Parliament to support Mr Asquith and his Government, who are the torturers of women.

Vote against the Government and keep the Liberal out!

Broken Windows

(1912)

'I lay down this proposition – democracy has never been a menace to property. I will tell you what has been a menace to property. When power was witheld from the democracy, when they had no voice in the Government, when they were oppressed, and when they had no means of securing redress except by violence – then property has many times been swept away.' – MR LLOYD GEORGE AT BATH, November 24, 1911.

In these words, more valuable than all his unprofitable remarks on Women Suffrage, Mr Lloyd George, without perhaps intending it, explained and justified the action taken by militant Suffragists on March 1st. We hold that militant Suffragists themselves are under no obligation to give justification of that action. They are answerable to their conscience, and they are answerable to the law. Their conscience approves, indeed, commands the action taken on March 1st, and the law has pronounced sentence upon them. Those well-disposed and law-abiding persons who condemn and wish to prevent a recurrence of the militant action in question have only one course open to them. It is not to remonstrate with those who took this action, but to call upon the Government to remove the cause of the trouble by introducing and carrying a Bill granting the vote to women. To argue with a revolution they will find futile indeed. As well might they argue with Nature and her laws. Militant Suffragists owe no allegiance to public opinion; our task is to alter public opinion, which, to our indignation, we have found shamefully tolerant of hideous wrongs and indignities inflicted upon women. We have taken upon ourselves the task – which falls to some few in each generation – of transforming public opinion into something higher and better than it is at present.

There are in every community people who are a law unto

themselves. These are of two classes, criminals and reformers. Both reformers and criminals are alike in that they break the established law of the land. They differ only in their motive. The criminal breaks the law to the injury of the State and for his own profit; the reformer breaks the law to his own injury, but for the salvation of the State. To restrain the criminal by rebuke and by imprisonment may be possible but when have such measures broken the spirit and purpose of reformers? Our critics are therefore simply squandering precious time in denouncing the Women's Social and Political Union, and we counsel them to devote their energies to compelling the Government to cease from provoking women to riot and destruction of property.

Emmeline Pankhurst

Defence

(Tuesday, May 21st, 1912)

May it please your lordship, gentlemen of the jury: – Before I enter into my personal defence in this matter, I would like to say a few words to you as laymen about the matter of conspiracy. Like you, I am not a lawyer, and, unlike you, I have an additional disadvantage in being a woman. It is assumed that men, by their education and training, are fitted to deal with these matters. Women have never been encouraged to think questions of law were the concerns of women; though in spite of that, a certain number of women have tried to study law and qualify themselves. But the law does not admit women; and women to-day are not in a position to call upon members of their own sex, trained in law, to plead for them, defend them, or to put their case. And so, when I speak of this charge of conspiracy brought against us, I can only speak to you as a lay woman to whom, presumably, the same advantages as yours are not given; but I do wish, having paid some attention to these matters and having been much interested in public affairs, to say a few words about the word conspiracy. I know the legal interpretation and legal meaning of the word conspiracy is not our meaning of the word.

The Word 'Conspiracy'

In the public mind the word conspiracy contains some suggestion of secrecy and intrigue. We naturally think it means something done by people who are ashamed of what they are doing – people who think that it is essential that they should preserve secrecy and intrigue to make their conspiracy successful. I am sure that you came into that jury-box with the idea that you were going to hear of some disgraceful conspiracy, some conspiracy in which the parties did things of which they were ashamed, and things which they wished to conceal in order to succeed. That interpretation has by this time been entirely removed from your mind. If one thing more than another has been made plain in this trial, it has been that we defendants at the bar have not behaved as people who are ashamed of what they are doing and who desire to conceal anything which they do, or desire to intrigue in any secret way. I venture to say, although I am not a lawyer, had it not been for the evidence which we ourselves have openly supplied, there would be absolutely no case to come before you to-day. Through our newspaper, through our speeches, through our acts, we have been beyond reproach so far as any disgraceful reproach can attach to us, so far as any criminal intent is concerned, and I use the word criminal in the sense which a layman attaches to the word. And so, although we must defer to the legal interpretation of the word conspiracy – both you gentlemen in the jury-box and we prisoners at the bar – although we must defer to the legal interpretation of that word, and we prisoners here may have to suffer because of that legal interpretation, I submit to you and the Judge on the bench that so far as the ordinary acceptation of the word conspiracy is concerned, the general public, thinking of conspiracy as they undoubtedly do, can and will attach a different interpretation to that word from the mere legal interpretation.

Then I want to say a word as to whether this is a political case or not. I say this because the Attorney-General said to you – I hope I am correct in my interpretation – that although you might hear a good deal about politics in the course of this trial, it really was not a political case which was being tried; that you must not regard it as being political or the offence as political. I hope I am not in any way distorting what the Attorney-General has said. Well, now, with regard to that point I want to say in the very clearest and most definite terms that if we defendants here, the accused people, are not accused of a political offence, then I can't see how we can be accused at all. Is it for a moment to be supposed that we three defendants, and my daughter who is not here, would have taken part in this agitation for any reason but for a political one? It is unthinkable to suggest for a moment that we are people who would in any way break the law for a selfish purpose, for our own interests or for our personal ends!

An Important Distinction

Now, greater people than I have laid it down that there is a very clear distinction between political and criminal offenders. It has been laid down so clearly that even the simplest of untrained women can understand it – that a political offence is one committed for an end which is not a personal one; that the breach of the law is made not for personal gain, not for personal advantage, but because the offender is satisfied in her or his own mind that it is necessary to break the law in order to get a political grievance remedied. I think it has been already clearly established – I think it was clearly established before my friend, Mr Pethick Lawrence, made his speech – that, rightly or wrongly, we persons accused here to day are persons who never would have come within the precincts of the Court or committed any breach of the law but for political purposes.

The definition of the word criminal is very different. Authorities have laid it down, and in other countries it has been generally accepted, that a criminal is a person who breaks the law for personal advancement or personal gain. In the course of these days during which the case has occupied your attention, it has not been proved, although I have felt myself that an attempt has been made to suggest, that the accused had some personal objects to serve. If that was so intended, and it seems to me intended (not so much here, but in the preliminary examinations in the police court), if that suggestion was intended it has absolutely failed. And I want, before going into my personal defence, to try to convince you and his lordship that this offence with which we are charged is a political offence. I know in other countries than ours – France, for instance – there would be no need for any prisoner to stand at the bar and plead that this was a political offence. In that country – and I wish our own country had reached the same height of civilisation – political offences are recognised and political status is accorded to political offenders even when they commit breaches of the law surpassing in seriousness the breaches of the law of which we are accused. In fact, they have gone so far in trying political prisoners in France as to lay it down that the possession of arms by the accused is not a criminal offence, but a political offence, if the person can prove that the possession of these arms is for a political purpose. That I wanted to say with regard to our status as prisoners whose guilt you are called upon to decide in the course of this trial.

The Word Militant

I would like to spend a little time in dealing with the definition of a word that has been very much used in describing this political movement for the enfranchisement of women, which is carried on by the Women's Social and Political Union to which I belong. There are several organisations for women's suffrage, but our organisation has been distinguished from others by the use of the word 'militant.' I have thought, and have been proud to think, that probably we had the word 'militant' attached to our organisation because we showed by our readiness even to suffer, and to pay heavy penalties in the course of our agitation, that we were more in earnest, more determined, than the other organisations; that we did not content ourselves merely with discussion; that we did not merely talk about our grievances, but that we were prepared even to put ourselves in the way of having great violence done to us in order to call attention to those grievances; that we were not merely content with words – because in this country everybody has a right to talk about his or her grievances – but we felt that we were distinct as a militant class even when we were a young organis-ation, which had just come into existence, determined not only to talk about our grievances but to terminate them by securing the object for which we existed. In fact, we adopted the motto, 'Deeds, not words.' There is a great deal of talk in politics, and there are a great many political gentlemen who make very strong speeches – even Members of the Government make strong speeches. Even the gentleman who is representing the Crown here to-day makes strong speeches. (Laughter.) But we women had thought in our agitation that we would never say anything if we did not feel ourselves justified in acting also, if we thought action necessary. Now, because we have taken that attitude we have been called a militant organisation. We were not called militant in the first instance because we were violent, or because we did actual deeds of violence. Had that been so I do not think the Prosecution would have limited the scope of the indictment to last November. Fortunately, we have definitions of the meaning of every word in the English language, and I want to call your attention to some of the definitions of the word 'militant.' (It is a word which is liable to be misunderstood, my lord, and I have felt, sitting in this dock in the course of this trial, that I have reason to be grateful – I think that is a curious thing to say – for the way in which this agitation has been tried; I have been grateful even in a Court of Law like this for the opportunity of putting our case, however imperfectly, to my fellow-countrymen and fellow-countrywomen.) I find in Webster's dictionary militancy defined as 'a state of being militant, warfare.' Well, that sounds like violence, doesn't it? Then I find militant, or militant in the sense of 'engaged in warfare, fighting, combating, serving as a soldier, also combating the powers militant.' Then, on reference to Milman, I find that the 'Church must become militant in its popular and its secular sense.' Then, again, it is defined as meaning 'a conflict, to fight.' In Nuttall, I find it is 'to stand opposed to, or to act in opposition.' In the Century dictionary I find a quotation from Froude which refers to a 'condition of militancy against social injustice.' Then it is described as 'being militant, a state of warfare,' and then I find 'in a state of conditional militancy,' and that is taken from a divine named Montagu. And so I could go on showing you that the word 'militant' is not necessarily interpreted to mean only violence done by those people who are militant. I want to prove to you, in the course of my defence, that although women ever since 1903 have been described as militant suffragists, never until November of last year had there been anything done by this organisation which could be in any way described as organised violence. I say that advisedly, and no one is better qualified to say that than myself. It may be said that there were isolated occasions on which stones had been thrown; but on those isolated occasions stones had been thrown by isolated individuals who might be members of the Women's Social and Political Union or might not be. But those women on their trial – and the police have always admitted it, and even gone out of their way to confirm what the women said – have never said they were instructed by the leaders of this movement; and the leaders of this movement, while they have never, as some politicians have done, repudiated their followers, have always made it clear that they did not think the time for violence had come, and they also made it clear that they hoped that the time for violence would never come. And so we have been described as militant.

History's Repetitions

I want to say a word or two as to my co-defendants. I want to say something about Mr Pethick Lawrence, and I feel this very strongly because the Attorney-General in his opening thought fit to call attention to the fact that Mr Lawrence is a member of the learned profession. Well, it is not the first time, and I am glad to think it, that members of the learned profession have helped to fight the people's battles. The Attorney-General's remarks brought to my recollection events of which my husband used to talk to me. Out of these events arose a trial in the Central Criminal Court, in the buildings on the site of which this building is, I believe, erected. At that Central Criminal Court a man – a barrister – was put upon his trial on a similar charge to ourselves. That was Ernest Jones, the Chartist. I never knew him personally, but my husband was a personal friend of his. My husband used to feel that Ernest Jones was his inspirer in the part he took in public affairs later on. That man – a man who had great expectations of wealth, a man of great learning, a man who might have risen to the highest position in his profession – chose to give it all up, chose to relinquish all opportunity of advancement in his profession, because his conscience made him espouse an unpopular cause, and he was put upon his trial in what I might term this very Court. History has a very curious way of repeating itself, and it has repeated itself in the case of Mr Lawrence. When Ernest Jones was prosecuted for his political activities, the then Attorney-General – on looking over the list of counsel engaged for the prosecution I find repeated the name of one of the counsel engaged in this case – made just the same statement about Ernest Jones that the Attorney-General has made about Mr Pethick Lawrence. He seemed to suggest that because Ernest Jones was a lawyer and a member of the learned profession he ought not to have taken the part he took. Well, I think that things more disgraceful to your great profession can be done by the members of your profession than were done by Mr Ernest Jones or are charged against Mr Pethick Lawrence. It seems to me no profession is degraded by unselfish men. It seems to me no man is unworthy of his position even if he brings himself within the grasp of the law because he has followed the dictates of his conscience, because he is generous, because he goes to the side of those he thought oppressed. And so when judgment is passed I think it will be decided that it is much better to find ignominy and to be imprisoned; it is better even to bear shame in your own generation, than to use your profession for personal advance, for personal gain, or for personal ends. And so, speaking as a woman who is at a disadvantage because she is a woman, I want to say I am grateful to Mr Pethick Lawrence because, being a member of a great and privileged profession, he has disregarded the privileges of his profession, and is in the dock by the side of women less fortunate than himself.

And then there is Mrs Pethick Lawrence. These two people are very dear, personal friends. I met them first at a stage of this agitation when it seemed just touch and go whether we could carry on the agitation any longer. They came into it when some of us who were not rich women had exhausted our means, sold our personal property and little things like jewellery dear to us, in order that we might carry on the agitation. At that critical stage these people came to our aid, and so I want to say what is due to those people. I know they would have come into the movement sooner or later, being what they are. I want to say it is due to these people, coming as they did then into the cause, that we have been able to create a great constitutional organisation – I mean a great political organisation – an organisation which has not only done much to advance the cause in this country, but throughout the whole world. It was inevitable that Mrs Pethick Lawrence should come, and she was the first to come into it. She is in it in the fuller sense of the word, because she is a woman. Mr Lawrence could never be in the organisation, because one of the essential conditions of membership is that no man can be a member. It is restricted to women, and Mr Pethick Lawrence is, therefore, I think, in a unique position in the history of politics. He would not have the glory – if there were any glory – attaching to the movement. He could not have the political recognition that he would undoubtedly have had if he had devoted himself to any of the great political parties. He has been content to play a part which I think no other man has ever played in politics: entirely to withdraw himself from the ordinary opportunity of advancement in politics to play a secondary part in the Women's Movement, because he felt we wanted some men to stand by us and help us in order to make our position secure.

Chorlton v. Lings

There is an old proverb which says that to know all is to understand all. It is impossible, gentlemen, to tell you all about this movement. We have not taken up very much time in the ordinary methods of defence in this trial. The prosecution has occupied many days. There has been a great deal of repetition; a great deal of unnecessary time has been spent in the opening of the case against the defendants, and I am sure, when you remember what this trial means to me and to my co-defendants, how it may possibly mean loss of liberty for a long time, when you, although you have been wearied by this case, will be able to go away, that you will bear with me a little. I will try to be as brief as possible. I will try to make you understand what it is that has brought a woman no longer young into this dock. My lord, I think I have already said that if one lives long enough one sees strange things happen, and I cannot forbear from reminding you that forty-two years ago next November, your father, who was not then the Lord Chief Justice, the great judge that he afterwards became, was at the bar pleading on behalf of women after the Reform Act of 1867. He was counsel for the women associated with my husband in the case of Chorlton *v.* Lings. He pleaded their cause very ably, and I want to tell the jury exactly what the case was about. After the passing of the Reform Act of 1867 women imagined – and, I think, had good reason to imagine – that that enfranchising Act would entitle women to register as Parliamentary voters. The great Reform Act of 1832, which has been referred to in this case because it was characteristic of very great violence on the part of men, enfranchised a great many men, but, at the same time, excluded women from the franchise because the word 'male' was used for the first time in history. In regard to the word 'male,' it made it impossible for the woman to be registered, and women maintained that while it was enfranchisement for men it was disenfranchisement for women. That is to say, that until that Act was passed women had the right to vote, and to a certain extent exercised that right to vote for Members of Parliament. After the Reform Act of 1867 a large number of women claimed to be put on the register, and in Lancashire alone four thousand women were put on the register in response to that claim. The overseers accepted them as qualifying voters. When the Revision Courts sat, the Revising Barristers considered the claims of the women. Some allowed the claims; others disallowed them.

Now that was the case to which I have referred just now. It was a case brought by a woman in Manchester named Chorlton against a revising barrister whose name was Lings, and by the result of the case women had to stand or fall. Sir Charles Coleridge was the leader in that case. My husband, who at the time was a confirmed Suffragist, and who was already making considerable sacrifices – because men have had to make great sacrifices in this cause, which was so long unpopular – my husband prepared the case.

Together those two lawyers argued the case. It was argued at considerable length. Evidence was given that prior to 1832 women had a vote; arguments were used against their having a vote. The case was finally decided, and, to us laymen and laywomen, it was an extraordinary decision. In effect it was this, that where it was a question of rights and privileges a woman is not a person, but where it was a question of pains and penalties woman is a person.

So, gentlemen, in this Court, Mrs Pethick Lawrence and I are persons to be punished, but we are not persons to have any voice in making the laws which we may break, and which we may be punished for breaking. That was the decision – the final decision – that we must pay our taxes, we must obey laws; but when it comes to choosing the men who impose the taxes and make the laws, we have no legal existence; we have no right to help choose these men. That was the decision. I venture to say, my lord, to you and to the jury, that had the judges of that time decided as a judge last year, decided in Portugal,* that since the women pay taxes and obey laws, they have the right to choose their tax-masters and their law-makers like men – had the judges of that day agreed with the arguments laid before them by your lordship's father and my husband, this agitation would not have been necessary, the status of women would have been established, and sex exclusion would have disappeared. It has an intimate bearing upon this question of violence on the part of the members of the Women's Social and Political Union.

The Right of Petition

The year before last I was convicted with other women for having gone to the House of Commons with a petition in my hand, insisting upon going to the door of the House of Commons, and insisting on my right to remain there until my petition was received. I argued that I had a constitutional right to do that; I argued that it is established in the Bill of Rights that every subject of the King has a right to present a petition in person, though in the case of men it was not very necessary to emphasise or insist upon that right, because that right, in the case of men, had been replaced by the Parliamentary franchise, and men could freely vote for their representatives on the floor of the House of Commons to voice their demands and claims; and I argued that, since the right of petition had not been replaced in the case of women by any other right, women still had the right to go in person to-day, not as in the old days to present their petitions to the King – the conditions have changed to-day – but to present their petitions to

* In Portugal, in 1911, it was decided in the case of Doctor Caroline Beatriz Angelo, who had applied to be placed on the register, that the word 'Portuguese' in the franchise decree could only be interpreted as applying to women as well as to men. The name of the judge was Doctor Joao Baptiste de Castro.

the King's representative, the Prime Minister. That was our case. It was very ably argued before the magistrates, and as the result of that argument a case was stated, and it was argued out before the judges in the Higher Court as to whether or not women had this right. It was decided, as in 1867, that we had not the right. That, in substance, was the decision, that we had not the right to insist upon presenting this petition. We had the right to petition, and we had the right to present petitions, but if the person to whom we wished to present them would not receive them, we could not present them. So we were acting illegally in insisting upon the right to present. I want to say here, my lord, that had these judges in 1909 decided that women had the right to petition there would have been no organised violence, there would have been no stone-throwing in this agitation. It was because the women were made to feel that they had no hope in the law – in the consciences of specious politicians – that there was no one to whom to appeal, that the women said, 'Well, this is a belated agitation; it is the twentieth century, when these things were supposed to be settled; but we have got to fight out the weary fight as women, and get this question settled somehow as best we can.' Now, this is how it all started. I do not want to go over the ground covered by Mr Pethick Lawrence. I do not want in any way to repeat what he has said; but I do want – as a woman who has taken part in the Suffrage Movement for something like thirty years – to try to make you understand how it is that things have come to where they are.

The Constitutional Agitation

When the case was argued – that case which decided that women were not persons – I was a small child. I had not grown up; but when I grew up, quite early in life, I had the great honour and privilege of joining the Suffrage Movement as it was then, under the leadership of Miss Lydia Becker, in Manchester, and under the leadership of people like Mr Jacob Bright; and at the same time I had the great happiness of being married to the man I have mentioned, who fought the women's battle in the Law Courts with your lordship's father. From that time on I took an active part in the Suffrage agitation. I was put upon the executive committee of the then Suffrage Society when I was about twenty-one years of age. I took part in the agitation of the 'eighties, right through the 'eighties – the late 'seventies and 'eighties – my connection with it began in the year 1879. From that time on until the passing of the next Reform Act, which enfranchised agricultural labourers, I took an active part in the agitation, and I say without hesitation that if constitutional methods alone could win women the vote, they would have become voters in 1884, when that Reform Act was passed. We held more meetings and greater meetings than did the agricultural labourers. You have heard from Mr Pethick Lawrence how the great towns and cities of England petitioned in support of the Conciliation Bill, which was 'torpedoed' out of existence by Mr Lloyd George, according to his own words. In those days, in the early 'eighties, the great towns and city councils petitioned in favour of the inclusion of women in the Reform Act of 1884. We filled all the great halls in the country with women, who enthusiastically passed resolutions in support of their enfranchisement; we got up monster petitions – one so huge that it had to be wheeled into St. Stephen's Hall on a trolley by several men. Members of Parliament came out and looked at it, and they smiled and went back to their places and forgot all about it. We found friendly Members of Parliament to move an amendment to that Reform Act, and that amendment had, I think – at least, we thought then that it had (we were less trained politically in those days) – we thought that it had an excellent chance of being passed into law; it certainly had a better chance of becoming law than the suggested amendment to the Manhood Suffrage Bill, because, as you remember, the Act of 1884 was not a measure like the Manhood Suffrage Bill; it insisted upon a certain qualification of residence. We thought we were going to win our enfranchisement.

What happened? The very men who introduced the amendment were told by their Parliamentary leader to throw over their amendment, because, they were told, it 'overweighted the ship.' It was even threatened by their leader, Mr Gladstone, that he would withdraw the whole measure if they persisted in the Women's Suffrage Amendment. The women had not votes to bring pressure to bear upon the Government, and women at that time did not dream of using violence or threatening violence. The result was that the agricultural labourer, who burnt some hayricks to show their impatience – the agricultural labourers, who were to be marched over a hundred thousand strong to the House of Commons by Mr Chamberlain – these men got their votes, and the women, who had been content to agitate by constitutional means, were left voteless. That was the beginning of a decline in the Woman Suffrage agitation. Many women lost heart and hope; many of us, whilst we still continued to be Suffragists, listened to men who told us that we ought to join political parties and show what good and useful work we could do in those parties in order to win the gratitude of the parties. Others told us that it was now open to us to go on Boards of Guardians and School Boards, to do useful public work, and they urged us to do that to prove that women were fit and worthy for the vote. We ought to have known, gentlemen, that that was an argument that had never been used in the case of men. It was never urged upon the agricultural labourers that they should show fitness for the vote; it was never suggested to the working men that they should show themselves fit for the vote. We listened to that argument – some of us; I was one of those women. I did join a political party, and worked very hard for it in the belief that the gentlemen who promised that when their party came into power they would deal with our grievance, would keep their pledges.

Social Work

When my children were old enough not to need my constant service, I became a member of a Board of Guardians. In this agitation there are always strange things happening, and yesterday, as I was stepping into the dock, a member of the Bar in the Court came up to me and recalled himself to my recollection. He was a member of the Board of Guardians, on which I served, with me, and I suppose I was recalled to his recollection because he is now a member of the Bar, and he was interested to see that a former colleague was being tried on what is called a criminal charge. I served about five years on that Board of Guardians. In speaking of myself, I am, in my own person, telling you what a great many other women have done. A very great many women have tried to do this useful public work to show that they were fit for the rights and responsibilities of citizenship – as fit as some drunken loafer who neglects his family, but who, because he is a man and has the necessary qualification, is entitled to decide not only his own fate and the fate of other men, but the fate of women and children as well. All this I did, and at the end of it – since there is no distinction in sex where brains are concerned – at the end of it all I was forced to the conclusion that so far as our enfranchisement was concerned, we had been wasting time. I found that men would say that you were not unfit for the vote, and that if all women were like you they would have no objection to giving you the vote. Oh! we women, who have done the dirty work of the political parties, have never had any reason to complain that our services have not been appreciated personally. But some of us came to realise that after all this appreciation we were blacklegs, as the working men call it – blacklegs to our own sex, and so some of us decided that a time had come when this became a sort of reproach to us, which we could not endure any longer.

'To Revolt against Injustice'

Now, gentlemen, I want to tell you a few of the things that led me, in 1903, when the Women's Social and Political Union was founded, to decide that the time had come when we had reached a situation, which, I think, I can best describe in the words of the Chancellor of the Exchequer, Mr Lloyd George, when he was addressing an audience in Wales a little while ago. He said: 'There comes a time in the life of a people suffering from an intolerable injustice when the only way to maintain one's self-respect is to revolt against that injustice.' That time came for me, and I am thankful to say it very soon came for a large number of other women as well; that number of women is constantly increasing. There is always something which I may describe as the last straw on the camel's back, which leads one to make up one's mind, especially when the making up of one's mind may involve the loss of friends, loss of position, loss of money – which is the least of all things, I think – and the loss of personal liberty.

I have told you that I have been a Poor Law Guardian. While I was a Poor Law Guardian I had a great deal of experience which I did not possess before of the condition of my own sex. I found that when dealing with the old people in the workhouse – and there is no work more congenial to women than this work of a Poor Law Guardian – when I found that I was dealing with the poor of my own sex, the aged poor, I found that the kind of old women who came into the workhouse were in many ways superior to the kind of old men who came into the workhouse. One could not help noticing it. They were more industrious; in fact, it was quite touching to see their industry, to see their patience, and to see the way old women over sixty or seventy years of age did most of the work of that workhouse, most of the sewing, most of the real work which kept the place clean, and which supplied the inmates with clothes. I found that the old men were different. One could not get so much work out of them. They liked to stop in the oakum-picking room, because there they were allowed to smoke; but as to real work, very little was done by these old men. I am not speaking in a prejudiced way; I am speaking from actual experience as a Poor Law Guardian. Any Poor Law Guardian could bear me out.

I began to make inquiries about these old women. I found that the majority of them were not women who had been dissolute, not women who had been criminal during their lives, but women who had lived perfectly respectable lives, either as wives and mothers, or as single women earning their own living. A great many were domestic servants, or had been, who had not married, who had lost their employment, and had reached a time of life when it was impossible to get more employment. It was through no fault of their own, but simply because they had never earned enough to save, and anyone who knows anything about the wages of women knows it is impossible to earn enough to save, except in very rare instances. These women, simply because they had lived too long, were obliged to go into the workhouse. Some were married women; many of them, I found, were widows of skilled artisans who had pensions from their unions. But the pensions had died with them. These women, who had given up the power of working for themselves, and had devoted themselves to working for their husbands and children, were left penniless; there was nothing for them but to go into the workhouse. Many of them were widows of men who had served their country, women who had devoted themselves to their husbands; when the men died the pensions died, and so these women were in the workhouse. And also I found younger women – always women, doing the bulk of the work. I found there were pregnant women in that workhouse, scrubbing corridors, doing the hardest kind of work, almost, until their babies came into the world. I found many of these women were unmarried women – very, very young, mere girls. That led me to ask myself, 'How is it that these women, coming into the workhouse as they do, staying a few weeks, and going out again – how is it they occupy this position?' I found these young girls, my lord, going out of the workhouse over and over again with an infant two weeks old in their arms, without hope, without home, without money, without anywhere to go. And then, as I shall tell you later on, some awful tragedy happened – simply because of the hopeless position in which they were placed; and then there were the little children – and this is the last example I am going to give out of my experience.

Sympathy – not Deeds

For many years we Poor Law Guardians, especially the women, tried to get an Act of Parliament passed dealing with little children. We wanted an amendment of the Act of Parliament which deals with little children who are boarded out – I do not mean by the Union, but by their parents, the parent almost always being the mother. It is from that class – young servant girls – which thoughtless people always say working girls ought to be; it is from that class more than any other that these cases of illegitimacy come. These poor little servant girls, who only get out perhaps in the evening, whose minds are not very cultivated, and who find all the sentiment of their lives in novelettes, fall an easy prey to those who have designs against them. These are the people by whom the babies are put out to nurse, and the mothers have to pay for their keep. I found, as other Guardians found, when we examined that Act, that it was a very imperfect one. The children were very ill-protected. We found that if some man who had ruined the girl would pay down a lump sum of £20 when that child was boarded out, the inspectors, whom the Guardians had to appoint, had no power to enter the house where the child was to see that it was being properly cared for. We found, too, that so long as a baby-farmer took one child at a time the women inspectors, whom we made a point of appointing, could not perform their object. We tried to get this law amended. For years, as the Attorney-General knows, efforts were made to amend that Act, to reach all these illegitimate children, to make it impossible for some rich scoundrel to escape from any future liability with regard to the young child if this lump sum were paid down. Over and over again we tried, but we always failed because those who cared most were women. We could go and see heads of departments, we could tell them precisely about these things, we could talk to them and get all their sympathy. In fact, in this movement on the part of the women, we have been given a surfeit of sympathy. Sympathy? Yes, they all sympathised with us, but when it came to the women asking them to do something, either to give us power to amend the law for ourselves or to get them to do it for us, it has always stopped short at sympathy. I am not going to weary you with trying to show you the inside of my mind, trying to show you what brought me to the state of mind I was in, in 1903; but by 1903 – I was at that time a member of the Manchester Education Committee – I had come to the conclusion that the old method of getting the vote had failed – had absolutely failed – that it was impossible to get anything done; that some new means, some new methods, must be found. Well, there is another defendant, who is not here to-day, and I want to say as a woman well on in life, that perhaps, if I had not had that daughter who is not here to-day, I might never have found the courage to take the decision which I took in the course of the years 1903, 1904, and 1905.

Founding the W.S.P.U.

We founded the Women's Social and Political Union in 1903. Our first intention was to try and influence the particular political Party, which was then coming into power, to make this question of the enfranchisement of women their own question and to push it. It took some little time to convince us – and I need not weary you with the history of all that has happened – but it took some little time to convince us that that was no use; that we could not secure things in that way. Then in 1905 we faced the hard facts. We realised that there was a Press boycott against Women's Suffrage. Our speeches at public meetings were not reported, our letters to the editors were not published, even if we implored the editors; even the things relating to Women's Suffrage in Parliament were not recorded. They said the subject was not of sufficient public interest to be reported in the Press, and they were not prepared to report it. Then with regard to the men politicians in 1905: we realised how shadowy were the fine phrases about democracy, about human equality, used by the gentlemen who were then coming into power. They meant to ignore the women – there was no doubt whatever about that. For in the official documents coming from the Liberal party on the eve of the 1905 election, there were sentences like this: 'What the country wants is a simple measure of Manhood Suffrage.' There was no room for the inclusion of women. We knew perfectly well that if there was to be franchise reform at all, the Liberal party which was then coming into power did not mean Votes for Women, in spite of all the pledges of members; in spite of the fact that a majority of the House of Commons, especially on the Liberal side, was pledged to it – it did not mean that they were going to put it into practice. And so we found some way of forcing their attention to this question.

Now I come to the facts with regard to militancy. We realised that the plans we had in our minds would involve great sacrifice on our part, that it might cost us all we had. We were at that time a little organisation, composed in the main of working women, the wives and daughters of working men. And my daughters and I took a leading part, naturally, because we thought the thing out, and, to a certain extent, because we were of better social position than most of our members, and we felt a sense of responsibility. And I hope, gentlemen, you will bear with me when I tell you of two events which led me – a little worn by the world, and having children about whose interests I cared greatly – which led me to throw all else aside and go straight into this thing without regard to consequences. One evening there came to my house in Manchester a Russian lady – a lady of Polish birth, who had lived most of her life in Russia. We sat round the fire on that winter evening talking about agitations, the Suffrage, and a number of other things. And then quietly this woman said to me and to my children sitting there: 'For a great number of years of my life I have never got up in the morning without feeling that before the day closed some member of my family, some relation, some friend, might be arrested and might be torn away from us altogether.' And she said this so calmly, so sadly and so quietly, and without any feeling, that it made a very deep impression on my mind. And when she had gone my children and I – for we were quite alone – talked about it. And, of course, I, being older than they, must take the greater responsibility for what we decided that night. I don't think we ever reopened the discussion. I think it was settled once and for all. We said, 'What is there that we can sacrifice or risk compared with what that woman has spoken about?' and so we decided to go on. In the course of our discussion I said to my daughter – because we were then talking of transferring our work to London, and launching out on a larger scale – 'What is there in our power to do? We are not rich people. We are already doing without a great many of the things which we hitherto thought necessary. Few people have hitherto helped us with money. How can we expand our work?' And she said: 'Never mind, Mother, go on, and the money will come,' and when I heard that from that girl – who is not in the dock to-day, not because of any lack of courage, not because of any unwillingness to share our position, but because she has a sense of public duty – because of what that girl said I felt inspired with the courage to go on.

The First Militants

Then came the election of 1905, and the first of the acts which, my lord, can by any stretch of imagination be described as militant.

What those acts were Mr Pethick Lawrence has told you. The first act was the going to a great Liberal demonstration in the Free Trade Hall, Manchester, of two girls with a little banner, made on my dining-room table, with the inscription, 'Votes for Women,' and asking Sir Edward Grey, the speaker, not 'Are you in favour of Woman's Suffrage?' but, 'Will the Liberal Government when it takes office give women the Vote?' For asking that question, just as men would have asked it, but with more respect for order than men would have shown, because they sat patiently, and waited for their opportunity, while many men had interrupted with questions about Chinese labour, and were respectfully answered – for insisting upon an answer to that question when the speech was finished, these girls were treated with violence and flung out of the meeting; and when they held a protest meeting in the street they were arrested, and were sent to prison, one for a week as a common criminal, and the other for three days. That was the so-called militancy. I ask you, gentlemen, whether, if that had been done by men, the word militant would have borne any construction but one of determination and earnestness and insistence upon having that question answered. As long as they had a chance of putting questions, even if they were thrown out after having asked them, women were content to do nothing more. Then, these gentlemen developed a desire to catch trains; they rushed away from their meetings directly their speeches were finished, and the women got no opportunity of putting their questions. Now bear in mind that no politician of to-day can feel as deeply about any political question as women feel about their disfranchisement, having regard to the things we are out for – reforms for women, for old and for young women and for little children, who are dying through the absence from legislation of the effective influence of women.

What did they do next? (I want you to realise that no step we have taken forward has been taken until after some act of repression on the part of our enemy, the Government – because it is the Government that is our enemy; it is not the Members of Parliament, it is not the men in the country; it is the Government in power alone that can give us the vote. It is the Government alone that we regard as our enemy, and the whole of our agitation is directed to bringing just as much pressure as necessary upon those people who can deal with our grievance.) The next step the women took was to ask questions during the course of meetings, because, as I told you, these gentlemen gave them no opportunity of asking them afterwards. And then began the interjections of which we have heard, the interference with the right to hold public meetings, the interference with the right of free speech, of which we have heard, for which these women, these hooligan women, as they have been called – have been denounced. I ask you, gentlemen, to imagine the amount of courage which it needs for a woman to undertake that kind of work. When men come to interrupt women's meetings, they come in gangs, with noisy instruments, and sing and shout together, and stamp their feet. But when women have gone to Cabinet Ministers' meetings – only to interrupt Cabinet Ministers and nobody else – they have gone singly. And it has become increasingly difficult for them to get in, because as a result of the women's methods there has developed the system of admission by ticket and the exclusion of women – a thing which in my Liberal days would have been thought a very disgraceful thing at Liberal meetings. But this ticket system developed, and so the women could only get in with very great difficulty. Women have concealed themselves for thirty-six hours in dangerous positions, under the platforms, in the organs, wherever they could get a vantage point. They waited starving in the cold, sometimes on the roof exposed to a winter's night, just to get a chance of saying in the course of a Cabinet Minister's speech, 'When is the Liberal Government going to put its promises into practice?' That has been the form militancy took in its further development.

Cabinet Ministers' Insults

What happened to those women and to the men who, I am thankful to say, when they began to understand the movement, rallied to our support? You may not have heard of it. You would not read it in the papers, because it was not reported. Two Cabinet Ministers have incited women by their insults to do more serious things. The Minister for War, for instance, on one occasion when women interrupted him, said, 'Why do you content yourselves with pin-pricks? Why don't you do something serious?' Then you get Mr Lloyd George; I refer to that speech of his where he talked about human beings, who suffered an intolerable sense of injustice, revolting; and, at the very self-same meeting, after saying those eloquent words which I could not improve upon, because I agree with them entirely – directly after that, a woman got up fired by those words, and said, 'Then why don't you deal with our grievance?' and he looked on smiling and remarked, 'We shall have to order sacks for those ladies.'

And it has not been one member of the Government only. There is hardly a member of the Government who has not used those insulting words to women, and there were other insults that we have not cared to make public, because there are some things women do not like to tell about. But they have faced rough usage because they have felt it was their duty to remind the Government that there was a question which would have to be dealt with sooner or later, and I would say again, gentlemen, that I welcome this trial because we have here, what I have often wished for – we have at any rate someone in close touch with the Government present, and he perhaps will convey to the Government some of the things that we women have long desired to tell them.

Leeds By-Election

When we tried to present petitions in the old days at the House of Commons, the women went unarmed, with petitions only in their hands. We always held a preliminary meeting at Caxton Hall, Westminster. Yesterday, when we had a police witness in the box, I asked him about a particular meeting, because I hoped that he was present, and I wanted to elicit something from him, and I will tell you what it was.

In 1908 there was a great by-election at Leeds, and we had been opposing the Government candidate, not because we had anything against his opinions, but because we believed by defeating him and by getting men to work against him, we should bring pressure to bear upon the Government, and make the Government realise that if they lost that election and other by-elections, there was some serious question they had neglected, that required attention. Well, upon that occasion we very much reduced the majority. The Press boycott had extended to our election work to a very large extent. We have never been able to get the facts of what we have done at elections into the Press. Little by little the facts of our work have filtered through, but the public have never been told the amount and the extent of our work at by-elections. Women have held bigger meetings and better meetings, more sympathetic and more orderly, than the candidates. On some notable occasions, when the Government candidate has sustained defeat, the papers have attributed it to, say, an increasing feeling in favour of Tariff Reform, rather than to the real cause, which was the opposition and the part played by women in the contest. Well, I had just returned from this particular election to take part in a demonstration outside the House of Commons. I was to lead one of those deputations – a small deputation of women, well within the Act of Charles II. – which defined the number of persons who can take petitions to Parliament. I was to lead that deputation, and I came straight back from this election, where I had spoken at hundreds of outdoor meetings to men and women. I remember distinctly the speech I made in Caxton Hall. It was just after Mr Herbert Gladstone had given us the advice to hold great demonstrations such as the men had in Hyde Park and elsewhere. Well, we had had in Leeds at the election a procession, a huge procession of women, the day before the election, culminating in a great open-air meeting on the moor in South Leeds. That night a great many working women came out of the factories which abound, you know, in Leeds, and where they work hard for little pay. They joined our procession. The students, who as you know are always very irresponsible – and one always wonders how the responsible sex should be so very irresponsible in the days of their youth – these students tried to break up our procession, and I was alarmed at the resentment shown by the crowd. In fact, I had to use what influence I had gained in order to save the lives of some of these students by appealing to the crowd, otherwise something serious would have happened. I returned by the night train to London, and on the following afternoon addressed that meeting in the Caxton Hall, and then, as on many other occasions, I explained why I was hoping that the Prime Minister would receive us. I said there comes a time when movements may outgrow the people who start them. There comes a time when people who desire that everything shall be orderly, suddenly may fail, and I felt so seriously that day that that time was rapidly coming, my lord, that I earnestly hoped, and I put it in my speech, that members of the Government, although we were only women, would see us, would hear us, and would look for themselves, and not merely look to the columns of the newspapers which excluded all references to the magnitude of this agitation.

Armed with Lilies

What was the result? I only got a few yards from the Caxton Hall when I was arrested. I had a petition in one hand; I had a little bunch of lilies in the other hand. And the other women who were with me were no more armed than I was. We were arrested. Next day we were taken before the magistrate, and in consequence of that act I suffered my first imprisonment of six weeks in Holloway

Gaol. Now on the floor of the House of Commons, in describing these so-called raids, even Home Secretaries – more than one – had talked about the women scratching, and biting policemen and using hatpins. These things were said not merely by the sensational Press, nor by irresponsible members of the Liberal Party. These gentlemen, Cabinet Ministers, have thought fit to attack women who, they knew, had very little opportunity of answering, because even the columns of the Press were closed to us – these gentlemen have thought fit to say these things about the women, although not one tittle of evidence has ever been produced to substantiate these charges which have been made. Now, I ask you, gentlemen, if you could put yourselves into the place of women so maligned, would you not feel some sense of resentment against such an injustice? We say in this country that everybody at least is entitled to justice, but in the police courts, whatever the women said was disregarded. The police evidence was beyond all contradiction. It has not been until quite recently, when we have got out of the atmosphere of the police court – an atmosphere in which this movement ought never to have been kept so long – at least a little light has been let in upon the character of the women engaged in this agitation, because when these women whose actions have been mentioned in the course of this case came before Mr Wallace at the Sessions, and contested the evidence against them, he said he was prepared to take the word of those women, for from his experience of them he knew that their word – whether he approved I cannot say, I am quoting roughly – that whatever they might do they were honourable people whose word was to be trusted. Well, that is something gained. If you gentlemen had as much experience of this movement as I have, you would know that is a great deal gained – to be admitted as persons of ordinary truthfulness; because every method has been taken to traduce this agitation, to misrepresent it, to pour contempt on the women engaged in it, and to crush it.

Two Months for 2s. 3d.

Now it has been stated in this Court that it is not the Women's Social and Political Union that is in the Court, but that it is certain defendants. The action of the Government, gentlemen, is certainly against the defendants who are before you here to-day, but it is also against the Women's Social and Political Union. The intention is to crush that organisation. And this intention apparently was arrived at after I had been sent to prison for two months for breaking a pane of glass worth, I am told, 2s. 3d., the punishment which I accepted because I was a leader of this movement, though it was an extraordinary punishment to inflict for so small an act of damage as I had committed. I accepted it as the punishment for a leader of an agitation disagreeable to the Government; and while I was there this prosecution started. They thought they would make a clean sweep of the people who they considered were the political brains of the movement. We have got many false friends in the Cabinet – people who by their words appear to be well-meaning towards the cause of Women's Suffrage. And they thought that if they could get the leaders of the Union out of the way, it would result in the indefinite postponement and settlement of the question in this country. Well, they have not succeeded in their design, and even if they had got all the so-called leaders of this movement out of their way they would not have succeeded even then. Now why have they not put the Union in the dock? We have a democratic Government, so-called. This Women's Social and Political Union is not a collection of hysterical and unimportant wild women, as has been suggested to you, but it is an important organisation, which numbers amongst its member-ship very important people. It is composed of women of all classes of the community, women who have influence in their particular organisations as working women; women who have influence in professional organisations as professional women; women of social importance; women even of Royal rank are amongst the members of this organisation, and so it would not pay a democratic Govern-ment to deal with this organisation as a whole.

They hoped that by taking away the people that they thought guided the political fortunes of the organisation they would break the organisation down. They thought that if they put out of the way the influential members of the organisation they, as one member of the Cabinet, I believe, said, would crush the movement and get it 'on the run.' Well, Governments have many times been mistaken, gentlemen, and I venture to suggest to you that Governments are mistaken again. I think the answer to the Govern-ment was given at the Albert Hall meeting held immediately after our arrest. Within a few minutes, without the eloquence of Mrs Pethick Lawrence, without the appeals of the people who have been called the leaders of this movement, in a very few minutes ten thousand pounds was subscribed for the carrying on of this movement.

Emmeline Pankhurst

A World-wide Movement

Now a movement like that, supported like that, is not a wild, hysterical movement. It is not a movement of misguided people. It is a very, very serious movement. Women, I submit, like our members, and women, I venture to say, like the two women and like the man who are in the dock to-day, are not people to undertake a thing like this lightly. May I just try to make you feel what it is that has made this movement the gigantic size it is from the very small beginnings it had? It is one of the biggest movements of modern times. A movement which is not only an influence, perhaps not yet recognised, in this country, but is influencing the woman's movement all over the world. Is there anything more marvellous in modern times than the kind of spontaneous outburst in every country of this woman's movement? Even in China – and I think it is somewhat of a disgrace to Englishmen – even in China women have won the vote, as the outcome of a successful revolution, with which, I daresay, members of His Majesty's Government sympathise – a bloody revolution. One word more on that point. When I was in prison the second time, for three months, as a common criminal – because we women have gone through all that; we have been searched, we have been stripped, dressed in prison clothes and subjected to all the restrictions of a prison system which needs amendment – when I was in prison the second time, for no greater offence than the issue of a handbill – less inflammatory in its terms than some of the speeches of members of the Government who prosecute us here – during that time, through the efforts of a Member of Parliament, there was secured for me permission to have the daily paper in prison, which had hitherto been denied me, and the first thing I read in the daily Press was this: that the Government was at that moment fêting the members of the Young Turkish Revolutionary Party, gentlemen who had invaded the privacy of the Sultan's home – we used to hear a great deal about invading the privacy of Mr Asquith's residence when we ventured to ring his door bell – gentlemen who had killed and slain, and had been successful in their revolution, while we women had never thrown a stone – for none of us was imprisoned for stone-throwing, but merely for taking the part we had then taken in this organisation. There we were imprisoned while these political murderers were being fêted by the very Government who imprisoned us, and being congratulated on the success of their revolution. Now, I ask you, was it to be wondered at that women said to themselves – Perhaps it is that we have not done enough;

148

perhaps it is that these gentlemen do not understand womenfolk; perhaps they do not realise women's ways, and because we have not done the things that men have done, they may think we are not in earnest.

Incitement by Statesmen

And then we come down to this last business of all, when we have responsible statesmen like Mr Hobhouse saying that there had never been any sentimental uprising, no expression of feeling like that which led to the burning down of Nottingham Castle. Can you wonder then, that we decided we should have to nerve ourselves to do more, and can you understand why we cast about to find a way, as women will, that would not involve loss of human life and the maiming of human beings, because women care more about human life than men, and I think it is quite natural that we should, for we know what life costs. We risk our lives when men are born. Now, I want to say this deliberately as a leader of this movement. We have tried to hold it back, we have tried to keep if from going beyond bounds, and I have never felt a prouder woman than I did one night when a police constable said to me, after one of these demonstrations, 'Had this been a man's demonstration, there would have been bloodshed long ago.' Well, my lord, there has not been any bloodshed except on the part of the women themselves – these so-called militant women. Violence has been done to us, and I who stand before you in this dock have lost a dear sister in the course of this agitation. She died within three days of coming out of prison, a little more than a year ago. These are things which, wherever we are, we do not say very much about. We cannot keep cheery, we cannot keep cheerful, we cannot keep the right kind of spirit, which means success, if we dwell too much upon the hard part of our agitation. But I do say this, gentlemen, that whatever in future you may think of us, you will say this about us, that whatever our enemies may say, we have always put up an honourable fight, and taken no unfair means of defeating our opponents, although they have not always been people who have acted so honourably towards us.

We have assaulted no one; we have done no hurt to anyone; and it was not until 'Black Friday' – and what happened on 'Black Friday' is that we had a new Home Secretary, and there appeared to be new orders given to the police, because the police on that occasion showed a kind of ferocity in dealing with the women that they had never done before, and the women came to us and said: 'We cannot bear this' – it was not until then we felt this new form of repression should compel us to take another step. That is the question of 'Black Friday,' and I want to say here and now that every effort was made after 'Black Friday' to get an open public judicial inquiry into the doings of 'Black Friday,' as to the instructions given to the police. That inquiry was refused; but an informal inquiry was held by a man, whose name will carry conviction as to his status and moral integrity on the one side of the great political parties, and a man of equal standing on the Liberal side. These two men were Lord Robert Cecil and Mr Ellis Griffith. They held a private inquiry, had women before them, took their evidence, examined that evidence, and after hearing it said that they believed what the women had told them was substantially true, and that they thought there was good cause for that inquiry to be held. That was embodied in a report. To show you our difficulties, Lord Robert Cecil, in a speech at the Criterion Restaurant, spoke on this question. He called upon the Government to hold this inquiry, and not one word of that speech was reported in any morning paper. That is the sort of thing we have had to face, and I welcome standing here, if only for the purpose of getting these facts out, and I challenge the Attorney-General to institute an inquiry into these proceedings – not that kind of inquiry of sending their inspectors to Holloway and accepting what they are told by the officials – but to open a public inquiry, with a jury, if he likes, to deal with our grievances against the Government and the methods of this agitation.

The Government's Conspiracy

I say it is not the defendants who have conspired, but the Government who have conspired against us to crush this agitation; but however the matter may be decided, we are content to abide by the verdict of posterity. We are not the kind of people who like to brag a lot; we are not the kind of people who would bring ourselves into this position unless we were convinced it was the only way. I have tried – all my life I have worked for this question – I have tried argument, I have tried persuasion. I have addressed a greater number of public meetings, perhaps, than any person in this Court, and I have never addressed one meeting where, substantially, the opinion of the meeting – not a ticket meeting, but an open meeting, for I have never addressed any other kind of meeting – has not been that where women bear burdens and share responsibilities like men they should be given the privileges men enjoy. I am convinced that public opinion is with us – that it has been stifled – wilfully stifled – so that in a public Court of Justice one is glad of being allowed to speak on this question.

Then, your lordship, because if we are found guilty I shall not say why sentence should not be pronounced – I want to say a word in connection with our status. Twice I have been in prison as a common criminal. I know what it is – you and the gentlemen of the jury, I hope, do not know what it is – to lose one's liberty and be sent to prison. I want you to understand what it is. God knows it is hard enough for the ordinary criminal, living a degraded life, to face all that prison means; it is doubly hard for those who have not been accustomed to that kind of life. But I am not pleading with your lordship because of the hardships – I am not pleading with your lordship because of the sense of the indignity which self-respecting women feel when those indignities are imposed upon them – but I am pleading with your lordship because I want to see my country raised to the level of every other civilised country in the world. Where political crime is concerned, I think it is a disgrace to this country that we should be so far behind. There was a time in this country when the ordinary criminal was treated with more severity than to-day. We have improved – we have become more humane since those days, and though much remains to be done with regard to the ordinary criminal, it cannot be said that their lot is as bad. But it is different with the status of political offenders. If we are convicted, our feeling very deeply on this question of our status, I assure you, is not so much for ourselves, it is because we want it to be established by you, with the great legal traditions of your position – we want it to be established that the political prisoner should not be degraded to the status of the lowest criminal; that his or her offence is not characterised by criminal tendencies, and therefore ought not to be degraded and stigmatised as disgraceful.

Summing up

I may, as a woman, say one word more. We say in England that every man is tried by his peers. I might have been justified as a woman, if at the opening of this case I had said you are not entitled to try me for this offence. What right have you, as men, to judge women? Who gave you that right, women having no voice in deciding the legal system of this country, no voice in saying what is a crime and what is not a crime? But in this Court I have not made that plea, and I have consented to be tried by this Court, and I think you will agree with me that the right of judgment of a Court depends upon consent. I have consented, and consented merely because I believe this trial marks the last in this hard struggle women are making for recognition. I feel that women, who have now, as they always have had, to perform the ordinary duties of citizenship, are now going to win some power to fix the condition of their sex and decide their duties, and I feel it all the more because this Government, which has instituted proceedings against us, is a Government dealing more with the lives of mankind than any Government which ever ruled this country. Year by year, and month by month, the fate of women is decided. How they are to live, their relationships with children, the marriage laws under which they are joined in union and pledge their affections – these great questions are being settled, and also will be settled. And so, my lord, I feel it is a great advantage, though it is at the risk of our liberty, that we are undergoing this trial. And referring, gentlemen, to what I said about your right to try me, I might tell you of a case – and that is my last word – of a young girl who was put on her trial for her life before a great Irish judge not long ago. And the judge said to those who were responsible for her being there, Where was the man? There was nothing in the law to make the father of that child responsible for the murder of the child for which the girl was being tried. But the judge said: 'I will not try that child till the participator of her guilt is in the dock with her,' and that case was never tried by that jury at all; but was adjourned till the father of the child also stood in the dock. If we are guilty of this offence, this conspiracy, other people, some of the members of His Majesty's Government, should be in the dock by our side. But I do not ask you to say that you will not sentence us until they are by our side, though I do suggest that members of His Majesty's Government and Opposition have used language at least as inflammatory and dangerous as ourselves, and I think in justice, while these people set us such an example, the verdict of this Court in our case should be one of Not Guilty.

Why We Are Militant

(A Speech Delivered in NEW YORK
OCTOBER 21st, 1913)

I know that in your minds there are questions like these; you are saying, 'Woman Suffrage is sure to come; the emancipation of humanity is an evolutionary process, and how is it that some women, instead of trusting to that evolution, instead of educating the masses of people of their country, instead of educating their own sex to prepare them for citizenship, how is it that these militant women are using violence and upsetting the business arrangements of the country in their undue impatience to attain their end?'

Let me try to explain to you the situation.

Although we have a so-called democracy, and so called representative government there, England is the most conservative country on earth. Why, your forefathers found that out a great many years ago! If you had passed your life in England as I have, you would know that there are certain words which certainly, during the last two generations, certainly till about ten years ago, aroused a feeling of horror and fear in the minds of the mass of the people. The word revolution, for instance, was identified in England with all kind of horrible ideas. The idea of change, the idea of unsettling the established order of things was repugnant.

Now, in America it is the proud boast of some of the most conservative men and women that I have met, that they are descended from the heroes of the Revolution. You have an organisation, I believe, called the Daughters of the Revolution, whose members put an interpretation upon the word revolution which is quite different from the interpretation given to it in Great Britain. Perhaps that will help you to realise how extremely difficult it is in Great Britain to get anything done. All my life I have heard people talking in advocacy of reforms which it was self-evident would be for the food of the people, and yet it has all ended in talk; they are still talking about these reforms, and unless something happens of a volcanic nature they will go on talking about them until the end of time. Nothing ever has been got out of the British Parliament without something very nearly approaching a revolution. You need something dynamic in order to force legislation through the House of Commons; in fact, the whole machinery of government in England may almost be said to be an elaborate arrangement for not doing anything.

The extensions of the franchise to the men of my country have been preceded by very great violence, by something like a revolution, by something like civil war. In 1832, you know we were on the edge of a civil war and on the edge of revolution, and it was at the point of the sword – no, not at the point of the sword – it was after the practice of arson on so large a scale that half the city of Bristol was burned down in a single night, it was because more and greater violence and arson were feared that the Reform Bill of 1832 was allowed to pass into law. In 1867, John Bright urged the people of London to crowd the approaches to the Houses of Parliament in order to show their determination, and he said that if they did that no Parliament, however obdurate, could resist their just demands. Rioting went on all over the country, and as the result of that rioting, as the result of that unrest, which resulted in the pulling down of the Hyde Park railings, as a result of the fear of more rioting and violence the Reform Act of 1867 was put upon the statute books.

In 1884 came the turn of the agricultural labourer. Joseph Chamberlain, who afterwards became a very conservative person, threatened that, unless the vote was given to the agricultural labourer, he would march 100,000 men from Birmingham to know the reason why. Rioting was threatened and feared, and so the agricultural labourers got the vote.

Meanwhile, during the '80's, women, like men, were asking for the franchise. Appeals, larger and more numerous than for any other reform, were presented in support of Woman's Suffrage. Meetings of the great corporations, great town councils, and city councils, passed resolutions asking that women should have the vote. More meetings were held, and larger, for Woman Suffrage than were held for votes for men, and yet the women did not get it. Men got the vote because they were and would be violent. The women did not get it because they were constitutional and law-abiding. Why, is it not evident to everyone that people who are patient where mis-government is concerned may go on being patient! Why should anyone trouble to help them? I take to myself some shame that through all those years, at any rate from the early

'80's, when I first came into the Suffrage movement, I did not learn my political lessons.

I believed, as many women still in England believe, that women could get their way in some mysterious manner, by purely peaceful methods. We have been so accustomed, we women, to accept one standard for men and another standard for women, that we have even applied that variation of standard to the injury of our political welfare.

Having had better opportunities of education, and having had some training in politics, having in political life come so near to the 'superior' being as to see that he was not altogether such a fount of wisdom as they had supposed, that he had his human weaknesses as we had, the twentieth century women began to say to themselves. 'Is it not time, since our methods have failed and the men's have succeeded, that we should take a leaf out of their political book?'

We were led to that conclusion, we older women, by the advice of the young – you know there is a French proverb which says, 'If youth knew; if age could,' but I think that when you can bring together youth and age, as we have done, and get them to adopt the same methods and take the same point of view, then you are on the high road to success.

Well, we in Great Britain, on the eve of the General Election of 1905, a mere handful of us – why, you could almost count us on the fingers of both hands – set out on the wonderful adventure of forcing the strongest Government of modern times to give the women the vote. Only a few in number; we were not strong in influence, and we had hardly any money, and yet we quite gaily made our little banners with the words 'Votes for Women' upon them, and we set out to win the enfranchisement of the women of our country.

The Suffrage movement was almost dead. The women had lost heart. You could not get a Suffrage meeting that was attended by members of the general public. We used to have about 24 adherents in the front row. We carried our resolutions and heard no more about them.

Two women changed that in a twinkling of an eye at a great Liberal demonstration in Manchester, where a Liberal leader, Sir Edward Grey, was explaining the programme to be carried out during the Liberals' next turn of office. The two women put the fateful question, 'When are you going to give votes to women?' and refused to sit down until they had been answered. These two women were sent to gaol, and from that day to this the women's movement, both militant and constitutional, has never looked back. We had little more than one moribund society for Woman Suffrage in those days. Now we have nearly 50 societies for Woman Suffrage, and they are large in membership, they are rich in money, and their ranks are swelling every day that passes. That is how militancy has put back the clock of Woman Suffrage in Great Britain.

Now, some of you have said how wicked it is (the immigration commissioners told me that on Saturday afternoon), how wicked it is to attack the property of private individuals who have done us no harm. Well, you know there is a proverb which says that you cannot make omelettes without breaking eggs. I wish we could.

I want to say here and now that the only justification for violence, the only justification for damage to property, the only justification for risk to the comfort of other human beings is the fact that you have tried all other available means and have failed to secure justice, and as a law-abiding person – and I am by nature a law-abiding person, as one hating violence, hating disorder – I want to say that from the moment we began our militant agitation to this day I have felt absolutely guiltless in this matter.

I tell you that in Great Britain there is no other way. We can show intolerable grievances. The Chancellor of the Exchequer, Mr Lloyd George, who is no friend of the woman's movement, although a professed one, said a very true thing when speaking of the grievances of his own country, of Wales. He said that there comes a time in the life of human beings suffering from intolerable grievances when the only way to maintain their self respect is to revolt against that injustice.

Well, I say the time is long past when it became necessary for women to revolt in order to maintain their self respect in Great Britain. The women who are waging this war are women who would fight, if it were only for the idea of liberty – if it were only that they might be free citizens of a free country – I myself would fight for that idea alone. But we have, in addition to this love of freedom, intolerable grievances to redress.

We do not feel the weight of those grievances in our own persons. I think it is very true that people who are crushed by personal wrongs are not the right people to fight for reform. The people who can fight best are the people who have happy lives themselves, the fortunate ones. At any rate, in our revolution it is the happy women, the fortunate women, the women who have drawn prizes in the lucky bag of life, in the shape of good fathers, good husbands and good brothers, they are the women who are fighting this battle. They are fighting it for the sake of others more helpless than themselves, and it is of the grievances of those helpless ones that I want to say a few words to-night to make you understand the meaning of our militant campaign.

Those grievances are so pressing that, so far from it being a duty to be patient and to wait for evolution, in thinking of those grievances the idea of patience is intolerable. We feel that patience is something akin to crime when our patience involves continued suffering on the part of the oppressed.

We are fighting to get the power to alter bad laws; but some people say to us, 'Go to the representatives in the House of Commons, point out to them that these laws are bad, and you will find them quite ready to alter them.'

Ladies and gentlemen, there are women in my country who have spent long and useful lives trying to get reforms, and because of their voteless condition, they are unable even to get the ear of Members of Parliament, much less are they able to secure those reforms.

Our marriage and divorce laws are a disgrace to civilisation. I sometimes wonder, looking back from the serenity of past middle age, at the courage of women. I wonder that women have the courage to take upon themselves the responsibilities of marriage and motherhood when I see how little protection the law of my country affords them. I wonder that a woman will face the ordeal of childbirth with the knowledge that after she has risked her life to bring a child into the world she has absolutely no parental rights over the future of that child. Think what trust women have in men when a woman will marry a man, knowing, if she has knowledge of the law, that if that man is not all she in her love for him thinks him, he may even bring a strange woman into the house, bring his mistress into the house to live with her, and she cannot get legal relief from such a marriage as that.

How often is women's trust misplaced, and yet how wholehearted and how touching that trust must be when a woman, in order to get love and companionship will run such terrible risks in entering into marriage! Yet women have done it, and as we get to know more of life we militant Suffragists have nerved ourselves and forced ourselves to learn something of how other people live. As we get that knowledge we realise how political power, how political influence, which would enable us to get better laws, would make it possible for thousands upon thousands of unhappy women to live happier lives.

Well, you may say, the laws may be inadequate, the laws may be bad, but human nature, after all, is not much influenced by laws, and upon the whole, people are fairly happy. Now, for those who are fortunate it is very comfortable to have that idea, but if you will really look at life as we see it in our centralised civilisation in Europe, you will find that after all the law is a great educator, and if men are brought up to think the law allows them to behave badly to those who should be nearest and dearest to them, the worst kind of man is very apt to take full advantage of all the laxity of the law.

What have we been hearing of so much during the last few years! It is a very remarkable thing, ladies, and gentlemen, that along with this woman's movement, along with this woman's revolt, you are having a great uncovering of social sores. We are having light let into dark places, whether it is in the United States or whether it is in the old countries of Europe, you find the social ills from which humanity suffers, are very much the same. Every civilised country has been discussing how to deal with that most awful slavery, the white slave traffic.

When I was a very tiny child the great American people were divided into hostile sections on the question of whether it was right that one set of human beings of one colour should buy and sell human beings of another colour, and you had a bloody war to settle that question. I tell you that throughout the civilised world to-day there is a slavery more awful than negro slavery in its worst form ever was. It is called prostitution, but in that awful slavery there are slaves of every shade and colour, and they are all of one sex.

Well, in my country we have been having legislation to deal with it. We have now a White Slave Act, and in that Act of Parliament they have put a flogging clause. Certain men are to be flogged if they are convicted and found guilty under that Act of Parliament, and the British House of Commons, composed of men of varying moral standard, waxed highly eloquent on the need of flogging these tigers of the human race, men engaged in the white slave traffic.

Well, we women looked on and we read their speeches, but in our hearts we said, 'Why don't they decide to go to the people for whom the white slave traffic exists? What is the use of dealing with the emissaries, with the slave hunters, with the purveyors? Why don't they go to the very foundation of the evil; why don't they attack the customers? If there was no demand there would be no traffic, because business does not exist if there is no demand for it?' And so we women said, 'It's no use, gentlemen, trying to put us off with sentimental legislation on the white slave traffic. We don't trust you to settle it; we want to have a hand in settling it ourselves, because we think we know how.' And we have a right to distrust that legislation. They passed the Act very, very quickly; they put it on the Statute Book, and we have seen it in operation, and we know that the time of Parliament and the time of the nation was wasted on a piece of legislation which I fear was never intended to be taken very seriously; something to keep the women quiet, something to lull us into a sense of security, something to make us believe that now, at least, the Government were really grappling with the situation.

And so we attacked this great evil. We said, 'How can we expect real legislation to deal with the white slave traffic on a small scale when the Government of the country is the biggest white slave trading firm that we have got?'

And it is true, because you know, although we have suppressed such regulation of vice in England, we have got it in full swing in the great dependencies that we own all over the world, and we have only to turn to India and look to other places where our Army is stationed to find the Government, which is in no way responsible to women, actually taking part in that awful trade, in absolute cold bloodedness where native women are concerned, all, forsooth, in the name of the health of the men of our forces.

Well, we have been speaking out, ladies and gentlemen; we have been saying to our nation and the rulers of our nation, 'We will not have the health of one-half of the community, their pretended health, maintained at the expense of the degradation and sorrow and misery of the other half.'

I want to ask you whether, in all the revolutions of the past, in your own revolt against British rule, you had deeper or greater reasons for revolt than women have to-day?

Take the industrial side of the question: have men's wages for a hard day's work ever been so low and inadequate as are women's wages to-day? Have men ever had to suffer from the laws, more injustice than women suffer? Is there a single reason which men have had for demanding liberty that does not also apply to women?

Why, if you were talking to the *men* of any other nation you would not hesitate to reply in the affirmative. There is not a man in this meeting who has not felt sympathy with the uprising of the men of other lands when suffering from intolerable tyranny, when deprived of all representative rights. You are full of sympathy with men in Russia. You are full of sympathy with nations that rise against the domination of the Turk. You are full of sympathy with all struggling people striving for independence. How is it, then, that some of you have nothing but ridicule and contempt and reprobation for women who are fighting for exactly the same thing?

All my life I have tried to understand why it is that men who value their citizenship as their dearest possession seem to think citizenship ridiculous when it is to be applied to the women of their race. And I find an explanation, and it is the only one I can think of. It came to me when I was in a prison cell, remembering how I had seen men laugh at the idea of women going to prison. Why they would confess they could not bear a cell door to be shut upon themselves for a single hour without asking to be let out. A thought came to me in my prison cell, and it was this: that to men women are not human beings like themselves. Some men think we are superhuman; they put us on pedestals; they revere us; they think we are too fine and too delicate to come down into the hurly-burly of life. Other men think us sub-human; they think we are a strange species unfortunately having to exist for the perpetuation of the race. They think that we are fit for drudgery, but that in some strange way our minds are not like theirs, our love for great things is not like theirs, and so we are a sort of sub-human species.

We are neither superhuman nor are we sub-human. We are just human beings like yourselves.

Our hearts burn within us when we read the great mottoes which celebrate the liberty of your country; when we go to France and we read the words, liberty, fraternity and equality, don't you think that we appreciate the meaning of those words? And then when we wake to the knowledge that these things are not for us, they are only for our brothers, then there comes a sense of bitterness into the hearts of some women, and they say to themselves, 'Will men never understand?' But so far as we in England are concerned, we have come to the conclusion that we are not going to leave men any illusions upon the question.

When we were patient, when we believed in argument and persuasion, they said, 'You don't really want it because, if you did, you would do something unmistakable to show you were determined to have it.' And then when we did something unmistakable they said, 'You are behaving so badly that you show you are not fit for it.'

Now, gentlemen, in your heart of hearts you do not believe that. You know perfectly well that there never was a thing worth having that was not worth fighting for. You know perfectly well that if the situation were reversed, if you had no constitutional rights and we had all of them, if you had the duty of paying and obeying and trying to look as pleasant, and we were the proud citizens who could decide our fate and yours, because we knew what was good for you better than you knew yourselves, you know perfectly well that you wouldn't stand it for a single day, and you would be perfectly justified in rebelling against such intolerable conditions.

Well, in Great Britain, we have tried persuasion, we have tried the plan of showing (by going upon public bodies, where they allowed us to do work they hadn't much time to do themselves) that we are capable people. We did it in the hope that we should convince them and persuade them to do the right and proper thing. But we had all our labour for our pains, and now we are fighting for our rights, and we are growing stronger and better women in the process. We are getting more fit to use our rights because we have such difficulty in getting them.

And now may I say a word about the reason for my coming to America.

Always when human beings have been struggling for freedom they have looked to happier parts of the world for support and sympathy. In your hour of trouble you went to other peoples and asked them for help. It seems to me, looking into the past, into my recollections of history, that a great man named Benjamin Franklin went to France to ask the French people to help in the struggle for American independence. You didn't apologise for sending him, and I am sure he didn't apologise for going. There may have been people in France who said, 'Why does this pestilent, rebellious fellow come over trying to stir up people here in our peaceful country?' But, in the main, the people of France welcomed him. Their hearts thrilled at the idea of a brave and courageous struggle, and they sent money and they sent men to help to fight and win the independence of the American people.

Those who have been struggling for freedom in other lands have come to you, and I can't help remembering that right through the struggle of the Irish people they sent law-breakers to plead with you for help for law-breakers in Ireland.

Yes, and like all political law breaking done by men, the form their violence has taken has not been merely to break some shop windows or to set on fire the house of some rich plutocrat, but it has found its expression in the taking of human life, in the injury even of poor, dumb animals who could have no part in the matter. And yet you looked at that agitation in a large way. You said, 'In times of revolution and revolt you cannot curb the human spirit, you cannot bind men and women down to narrow rules of conduct which are proper and right in times of peace,' and you sent help and cheer to the Irish people in their struggle for greater freedom.

Why, then, should not I come to ask for help for British women? Whatever helps them is going to help women all over the world.

It will be the hastening of your victory. It has not as yet been necessary in the United States for women to be militant in the sense that we are, and perhaps one of the reasons why it is not necessary and why it may never be necessary is that we are doing the militant work for you. And we are glad to do that work. We are proud to do that work. If there are any men who are fighters in this hall, any men who have taken part in warfare, I tell you, gentlemen, that amongst the other good things that you, consciously or unconsciously, have kept from women, you have kept the joy of battle.

We know the joy of battle. When we have come out of the gates of Holloway at the point of death, battered, starved, forcibly fed as some of our women have been – their mouths forced open by iron gags – their bodies bruised, they have felt when the prison bars were broken and the doors have opened, even at the point of death, they have felt the joy of battle and the exultation of victory.

People have said that women could never vote, never share in the government, because government rests upon force. We have proved that is not true. Government rests not upon force; government rests upon the consent of the governed; and the weakest woman, the very poorest woman, if she withholds her consent cannot be governed.

They sent me to prison, to penal servitude for three years. I came out of prison at the end of nine days. I broke my prison bars. Four times they took me back again; four times I burst the prison door open again. And I left England openly to come and visit America, with only three or four weeks of the three years' sentence of penal servitude served. Have we not proved, then, that they cannot govern human beings who withhold their consent?

And so we are glad we have had the fighting experience, and we are glad to do all the fighting for all the women all over the world. All that we ask of you is to back us up. We ask you to show that although, perhaps, you may not mean to fight as we do, yet you understand the meaning of our fight; that you realise we are women fighting for a great idea; that we wish the betterment of the human race, and that we believe this betterment is coming through the emancipation and uplifting of women.

Letter Sent to Enquirers from 4, Clement's Inn

(1907)

The Constitution of the W.S.P.U. is not worth the paper it is written on from a legal point of view. A year ago the members of the Union who were then very few indeed, were called together to send a Resolution to the Prime Minister and to discuss the militant plan of action on the eve of the arrest in the House of Commons on Oct. 23rd. The night before this meeting was held, a hastily drafted Constitution was put forward by a few members of the Union. The meeting consented to this Constitution as an experiment. The majority of those who attended the meeting were not delegates and some were not even members, there were hardly more than half a dozen branches in existence. It was very soon discovered that the branches could not become the pivot of the movement or support the work at Headquarters; it was as much as they could do to support their own local existence. There are now 70 branches. Many of the members have never seen the leaders of this movement. Some have been hastily formed within the past few weeks and arranged at their first meeting to send a delegate to the Conference and to amend the policy and Constitution. We have no time to do the public work and also keep the Branches in close personal touch. While we have been occupied with the work of the National Campaign and by-election, these 70 branches have been used as a happy hunting ground for intriguers whose device was to get control of the Union to modify the policy of independence and change the general methods of work. This would not matter so much in an ordinary society, for one year's experience would have taught the members that they had chosen people to lead them who were totally unfit to do so, but we are not playing experiments with representative Government. We are not a school for teaching women how to use the vote. We are a militant movement and we have to get the vote next session. The leaders of this movement are practical politicians;

they have set out to do an almost impossible task – that of creating an independent political party of women. They are fighting the strongest Government of modern times and the strongest prejudice in human nature. They cannot afford to dally with the issue. It is after all a voluntary militant movement; those who cannot follow the general must drop out of the ranks. As far as we are concerned the action which we have taken is the last word that we have to say upon the controversy. Of course we cannot expect that anyone who views the facts from the outside should understand the action that Mrs Pankhurst and those of us who support her have been compelled to take. We can only remind them that the W.S.P.U. is different from any other well known existing society. It is a militant society. We are now in the thick of the battle. This internal difficulty has been facing us for many months. The very fact that we were so extremely anxious not to split the Movement or allow any difference of opinion to be known by the public gave the opposition, in itself weak, a very strong weapon against us.

We yielded concession after concession in order to satisfy those who wanted to get power within the movement by other means than by sheer devotion and hard work, but all the power that they obtained by this concession only made them stronger to spread disaffection and disruption in the ranks. Then at last we saw clearly that nothing would satisfy them until they had the leaders of this movement completely down. Always while we were hard at work they were getting hold of the local unions and spreading suspicion and disaffection. At last we faced the whole thing. We foresaw every contingency and every possibility, and we decided to show fight and to show that we had no fear either of split or publicity or of anything else, and that we were prepared for the disloyal members within the union to do their very worst. This stand has now been taken for good and evil. It was taken with extreme forethought, with every legal precaution and with an absolute determination to see the whole thing through, no matter what it may mean. The real workers in the Union are absolutely united. We are prepared if necessary to leave everything that our hands have constructed and to go out empty to build up a new movement from the very ground. We have the energy, we have the devotion and we are prepared to sell all that we have if necessary to raise the funds. I don't think we need go empty; I don't think we need go at all. We believe that this noise is sheer bluster and it will prove to be so, but if the worst comes to the very worst we are still ready to face it with courage and good hope. Every political movement has had this crisis to face, and at such times strong leadership is essential. Apart from those whose past associations and life have been bound up with political causes that are dear to them and which they can hardly be expected at an advanced age to leave we have against us others whose motives are less pure. There are disappointed place-seekers and those who have thought that they were more capable of filling certain posts than those who have been selected. The seceding camp is made up of every dissatisfied and disappointed person and is held together by no bonds of union such as the bonds which unite the real workers.

The stand which we have taken we have taken for good or evil. It was months before we decided to do it. It cost us weeks of earnest thought and consultation. All the consequences were reckoned upon and nothing could possibly persuade us to deviate from it in the smallest degree. We are absolutely confident in ourselves and in our cause and we press on towards the goal which we have set before us.

Our Demand: What it is and What it is not

(N.W.S.P.U. leaflet, c. 1908)

From the first women suffragists have demanded neither more nor less than the abolition of the political disability of sex. They have claimed that whatever qualifies a man to vote shall qualify a woman to vote. They have asked that an Act shall be passed which shall run as follows:-

> In all Acts relating to the qualifications and registration of voters or persons entitled or claiming to be registered and to vote in the election of members of Parliament wherever words occur which import the masculine gender, the same shall be held to include women for all purposes connected with, and having reference to the right to be registered as voters.

That is our claim to-day. And this was the principle adopted in Mr Dickinson's first Bill introduced in February, 1907, and talked out on March 8th. If such a law were passed, it would mean that the principle of sex equality would be established for ever, and whatever the franchise for men precisely the same franchise would exist for women.

But this claim, reasonable as it appears to be, has been opposed by certain professing friends of women who have argued that women ought to ask for more than this simple measure of justice.

In the early stages of the present agitation, adult suffrage was urged upon women by this class of politician as the only true solution. Women should ask, it was said that all men and all women should possess the vote, and should be content with no other demand.

To-day opposition from this quarter may be disregarded, but a somewhat similar attack is being delivered by a section of Liberal politicians, who claim that our demand is "undemocratic." Their views were embodied in the second Bill which Mr. Dickinson introduced on August 14th, 1907. This Bill contained clauses providing that (a) plural voting, which is legal for men, should be illegal for women, and (b) that married women should be entitled to vote on their husband's qualification as joint occupier (whereas under the existing law two men living together cannot qualify as joint occupiers).

At first sight some women may perhaps be inclined to applaud this measure because it seems to promise more to women than what we are asking for. But if they consider it carefully they will see that it is thoroughly bad.

In the first place it is totally wrong in principle to make one franchise for men and another, different, franchise for women. The removal of the disability of sex is the only logical and safe solution.

In the second place the introduction of this measure is bad tactics. It tends to divide our friends into two camps, while leaving our enemies united. The original simple proposal is supported by 420 out of 670 members of the House of Commons, but this new proposal would find only a very few supporters. Moreover, it introduces into the question of women's suffrage other highly contentious proposals which would put out of account any possibility of carrying it into law next Session.

This new Bill is nothing but another attempt on the part of Liberal politicians to side-track the women's movement, and is prompted by enemies to women masquerading under the guide of friends.

Lest we be charged with undue suspicion in taking this line, we quote, in furtherance of our view from a source which cannot be charged with bias against Government. In a leading article on October 26th, The *Manchester Guardian* said:

"Women simply ask that they shall be allowed to vote on the same terms as men. This is the principle which was embodied in Mr. Dickinson's Bill of last Session [March 8]. and it was certainly a surprise to the meeting yesterday, and not a pleasant one, when he proceeded to disclaim it, and to plead for something quite different because he thinks it more 'democratic.' We can conceive some women present should say 'Be hanged to your democracy. We ask for justice, and by justice we understand equal treatment for our sex.' Mr. Dickinson has, of course, a perfect right to his opinion, and he no doubt felt it is his duty to express it; but he will get no support from the women who are working hardest for the suffrage, though he may get a good deal from nominal friends of the movement who see quite clearly that the awkwardness of the present demand lies in its moderation, and that the bigger you can make it the longer you may put it off."

Women who want votes must turn their back deliberately upon this insidious proposal: they must refuse to fall into the trap laid for them by the Liberal Government, and must continue to urge their demand for the possession of the vote **on the same terms as it is or may be granted for men.**

Why We Oppose The Liberal Government

(N.W.S.P.U. leaflet, c. 1908–9)

Why do Women fight against the Liberal Government?

This is the question asked by many ardent Liberals, who, though not opposed to Women's Suffrage, have many Social Reforms at heart, and believe that the Liberal Party is the Party essentially pledged to Social Reform.

Our reply is, that the quarrel between the National Women's Social and Political Union and the Liberal Government is not a quarrel of our making. We did not begin it, neither do we wish to continue it for a day longer. It was begun on October 13th, 1905, by the foolish policy of **throwing out of a Liberal meeting two Delegates of the Women's Social and Political Union, who asked a question at the proper time and in a perfectly correct manner**, and by the subsequent arrest and imprisonment of the two questioners.

We are quite prepared to let bygones be bygones. We have no grudge against the Liberal Party; we have no resentment and no bitterness against it. We wish for peace, and we are prepared to make peace to-day. But it must be peace with honour, for to women honour is as indispensable as it is to men.

Our demand is a perfectly reasonable, constitutional and logical one. It is simply that Taxation and Representation shall go together – that women who pay the taxes shall be represented in the legislation.

We submit first, that we are not asking for anything which is contrary to the essential principles of Liberalism. If we were asking something which was against Liberal principles, then we should admire the Government for standing out against our demand and refusing to yield to any pressure. But what is the case? We find that our Watchwords are the very Watchwords of the Liberal Party itself.

'A strong Government is one that trusts the people.' Then why does not the Liberal Government trust the women of the country?

'The Will of the People must prevail.' Then why refuse to half the people the elementary right of expressing their will?

'A Government can only rest upon the consent of the Governed.' Women are governed by the laws of the country, why not secure their consent?

'Taxation without Representation is Tyranny.' Then, as women are taxed, they must have representation. A Government that refuses this is self-convicted of tyranny; and when was tyranny considered an attribute of the Liberal Party?

This question should have been settled in 1832. It is more than 60 years too late. We are not content to wait for it any longer. We ask for no generosity. We ask for no special favour to be given to women, but we ask that barest justice shall be done immediately, and that women who are qualified as men are qualified shall become voters at once.

Just as we are asking for nothing which is against the principles of the Liberal Party, so also we are asking for nothing that is not expedient; for nothing that it would be difficult for the Liberal Government to grant at once. The Liberal Government holds the key to the position. The House of Commons, by passing the second reading of Mr Stanger's Enfranchisement Bill by a large majority (179) on February 28th, 1908, placed upon the Government the onus of its refusal to proceed further with the question, but the Government failed to take advantage of the opportunity thus afforded it, of adopting the Bill as a Government measure, thereby ensuring its becoming law.

Why, then, does the Liberal Party continue its foolish quarrel with the women of the country? If it will withdraw its opposition to a Reform which is based upon one of the root principles of Liberalism, we shall be only too glad for our part to withdraw our opposition to the Liberal Government both at by-elections and on all other occasions.

Liberal Men and Women! Use what influence you have, and do what you can to induce your Party to conform to its past traditions and to carry out the principles of Justice, Freedom, and Democracy by giving Votes to Women; for these are the only principles which will preserve the honour of the great Liberal Party.

What Women Demand

(N.W.S.P.U. leaflet, c. 1908–9)

The Women's Social and Political Union are asking for votes for women on the *same terms* as they are possessed by men.

They are not asking for the vote for every woman, but that a woman shall not be refused a vote simply because she is a woman.

At present men who pay rates and taxes, who are owners, occupiers, lodgers, or have the service or university franchise possess the Parliamentary vote. The Women's Social and Political Union claim that women who fulfil the same conditions shall also enjoy the franchise. This means that those women who pay taxes, and bear the responsibilities imposed upon men voters, will have the same political rights. Married women will obtain the vote, provided they possess the necessary qualifications; thus, where a married woman, and not her husband, is the householder, or where a woman is in business on her own account, she will become a voter.

It is estimated that when this claim has been conceded about a million and a-quarter women will possess the vote, in addition to the seven and a-half million men who are at present enfranchised.

The Women's Social and Political Union claim that the following simple measure, giving the vote to women on these terms, shall be passed this Session:

Women's Enfranchisement Bill.

That in all Acts relating to the qualification and registration of voters or persons entitled or claiming to be registered and to vote in the election of Members of Parliament, wherever words occur which import the masculine gender the same shall be held to include women for all purposes connected

**with and having reference to the right to be registered as
voters, and to vote in such election, any law or usage to the
contrary notwithstanding.**

Votes for Women. The Conciliation Bill Explained

(N.W.S.P.U. leaflet, 1911)

What is the Conciliation Bill?

An attempt to bring all political parties together in support of a **moderate and practical** plan for giving votes to women. The Bill was drafted by a committee of fifty M.P.'s representing all four parties in the House, with the Earl of Lytton as its chairman.

It succeeded so well that in 1910 it was carried on the second reading **by a majority of 110.** In May, 1911, when Sir George Kemp introduced it, it was once more read a second time, and secured a majority of **167.**

Among those who have voted for it are:

Mr Birrell	Mr Lyttelton	Mr Snowden
Mr John Burns	Mr Wyndham	Mr Devlin
Sir Edward Grey	Mr Barnes	Mr Healy
Mr Runciman	Mr Keir Hardie	Mr Swift MacNeill
Mr Balfour	Mr Ramsay MacDonald	Mr W. Redmond
Mr Bonar Law		

Will it give Votes to all Women?

No! It will give votes only to **women who pay rates and taxes** (whether directly or as part of the rent). These women already have a vote for Town and County Councils. There is no dangerous innovation here. It is common sense that a woman who can choose a County Councillor can also choose an M.P.

What Women will get the vote?

Women Householders. A Householder is a woman who inhabits a dwelling-house, or part of a house over which she has full control, however small it may be, and **however low its value**. A duchess may get a vote for her palace, and a charwoman for her cottage, or (if she has full control) **even for a single room**. The household franchise is fair to all classes.

Why are these Women chosen?

Because they are **heads of households** which at present are unrepresented. Every man who is the head of a house may qualify as a voter. These women have the same responsibilities as men householders. **More than half of them are widows**, and many have children dependent on them. The rest are chiefly single women earning their own living.

What about Married Women?

A wife will not get the vote unless the house is rented in her name. But a woman will not be disqualified simply because she is married. This means that a sailor, a fisherman, or a commercial traveller who is often away from home when the election comes on may arrange to register his house in his wife's name, and so give her the vote. Thus **every household will be represented**. In Dundee, a seaport town, it has been ascertained that 370 married women will get the vote under this clause.

How many Women will get the Vote?

About **One Million** in the three Kingdoms.

Will it stop there?

That depends on men. They will still be the vast majority of the electors. There are seven and a-half millions of men voters.

Is the Bill fair to the working classes?

Well, the Labour Party thinks so. **Mr Shackleton** introduced it in 1910. Thirty-four Labour members voted or paired for it in 1911, and none against it.

Look at these figures which were reached (February 1911) by a systematic house-to-house inquiry, supervised in each town by committees of leading citizens of all parties.

In Dundee out of 3,866 women householders on the municipal roll it was found that 2,177, or **more than half, live in one or two roomed dwellings**. Some 1,178 women live in three or four roomed dwellings. Only 511 live in houses of five or more rooms.

In Dundee **89 per cent** of these women householders are either weekly wage-earners or working-class housewives. In Carnarvon and Bangor (small residential towns with no industry) **75 per cent.** of the women householders are either wage-earners or working-class housewives who keep no servant. On the average fully **eight out of every ten** women voters will belong to the working class. **Surely this is democratic enough.**

Does the Country approve of the Bill?

No less than **90 City, Town and County Councils,** and 30 District Councils have petitioned or passed resolutions urging that the Bill may become law. These include the City Councils of:

Birmingham	Dublin	Leeds	Newcastle
Bradford	Edinburgh	Liverpool	Nottingham
Cardiff	Glasgow	Manchester	Sheffield.

What is the Government's Attitude?

It has promised **to give facilities** for the passage of the Conciliation Bill into law in the session of **1912**. This is to be (in Sir Edward Grey's words) ' **a real opportunity,**' and the Prime Minister has pledged himself that this promise shall be fulfilled 'not only in the letter, but in the spirit.'

Electors! Tell your member

that you expect him to vote for the Bill, to resist obstruction and defeat wrecking amendments. Tell him to vote straight and follow the lead of the Conciliation Committee. Tell him that women must be voters at the next General Election.

Support the Bill

Because it is **just, moderate** and **democratic**.

Because women have **the same need of the vote** as men, to protect them against unjust laws and unfair taxes.

Because honest men are tired of seeing the question played with.

Because the women have earned success by their **pluck and perseverance**.

Here is the Text of the Bill

, which was slightly modified in 19113, so as to remove any reasonable fear of **plural** or **faggot voting**.

1. Every woman possessed of a household qualification within the meaning of the Representation of the People Act (1884) shall be entitled to be registered as a voter, and when registered to vote for the county or borough in which the qualifying premises are situate.

2. For the purposes of this Act, a woman shall not be disqualified by marriage for being registered as a voter, provided that a husband and wife shall not both be registered as voters in the same Parliamentary Borough or County Division.

Suffragist Prisoners are Political Offenders. Therefore They should be treated as First-class Misdemeanants

(N.W.S.P.U. leaflet, c.1911–12)

What is a Political Offence?

'Crimes become political offences when incidental to and forming part of political disturbances.' This was the decision of Justice Denman at the Divisional Court, comprising three judges, when they decided in 1890 that Castioni, a Swiss subject, arrested at the request of the Swiss Government on a charge of murder, was not subject to the extradition laws, as he was a political offender.

What is the difference between a Common Criminal and a Political Offender?

A Common Criminal is a person who breaks the Law to satisfy personal spite, or to gain some personal end.

A Political Offender breaks the Law from unselfish motives; he wishes to bring about reform in the Government of the country in which he lives.

Have Prisoners in this country ever received first-class treatment because they were Political Offenders?

Yes. The Chartist leader, **Fergus O'Connor**, indicted for seditious conspiracy and language, was allowed his own clothes and food, and no restrictions were placed upon the visitors, books and letters he received. In short, he received full political treatment.

In 1868, **the Irish prisoners** sentenced for 'seditious libel' were given first-class treatment.

In 1885, **Mr W. T. Stead** was convicted of felony, but, because his action was taken in order to secure the passing of the Criminal Law Amendment Act, he was treated while in prison as a first-class misdemeanant.

In 1896, **Dr Jameson** was sentenced to 15 months' imprisonment in the second division, but, under instructions received from the Home Office, he was transferred within three days to the first division. Many other instances could be given.

How are Political Offenders treated in other civilised Countries?

Professor George Sigerson, M.D. (Member of the Royal Commission on Prisons, 1884), in a recent article, tells us that the practice on the Continent is for those convicted of political offences to be held in 'Custodia Honesta,' or honourable custody, which means that, except for the fact that they are not allowed to leave the prison, they live the life of an ordinary citizen.

Opinions of Politicians of all parties on the Treatment of Political Offenders.

Lord Beaconsfield, House of Commons, July 10, 1840, said, 'The imprisonment of Political Offenders was only for the safety of the State, not for infliction of punishment.'

Mr Asquith, protesting against the punishment of Mr O'Brien, said, 'They had assembled for the purpose of denouncing the treatment of political and industrial agitators on the same footing as ordinary criminals.' 'He would rather,' he continued, 'find himself face to face with the brutal despotism of Russia than see the present prostitution of constitutional forms which at the same time was dishonest, ineffectual, and demoralising' (Birmingham, Feb. 11th 1889).

The late **W. E. Gladstone**, referring to the same incident, solemnly warned the Tory Government in these words: 'a prison under the rule of the present Government is fast becoming a temple of honour.'

Surely all British people, for the honour of their country,

will do everything in their power to secure for British political prisoners the rights accorded to them in this country in the past, and to-day by all other civilised countries in the world.

A Message from the W.S.P.U.

(leaflet, c. 1911–12)

We want you to read the words that are written here, for they will appeal to *you*. It does not matter if you are old or young, rich or poor, loved or lonely, clever or simple – if you are a woman, these words are written for you.

No matter in what circumstances you are placed, it is in your power to give the greatest gifts in the world – sympathy and a helping hand – to the helpless and oppressed. All humanity has a claim on us for these gifts, but who can have a closer claim or to whom can you give them with a more understanding sympathy than to members of your own sex, who share the same joys and dangers, on whose shoulders rest the same responsibilities and duties?

You may be safe or resting in security on someone who is trustworthy, but there are hundreds of thousands of women who are dependent upon the mercy and good behaviour of others, not only for their happiness, but even for the very means of their existence.

The man who works gains for himself rights thereby, but the woman who works at the highest and most self-sacrificing of all callings – that of wife and mother – is stripped of even such rights as she may have enjoyed as a single woman and placed in a position of helplessness and subjection.

The workman can demand a definite wage from his employer, but the wife and mother has no legal claim to a definite portion of her husband's wages or income. Neither has she the right to help select her home, nor to say how it shall be conducted, nor has she even equal rights in the children that she has to care for and bear in risk and danger, whether she wants them or not, no matter if they are more or less than she wants, or if she is able or not.

Women – no matter how gifted and capable – have been, and

are, excluded from choosing and following such work as they have an aptitude for. Such work as they are permitted to do is often underpaid and unrecognised.

It is given to the influence of women to upraise and purify humanity. But if we are to develop this power at its highest, we must first be free women. How shall we enjoin others to be true and honest while we are not true to our own selves – while we are forced to disown our own personalities and become shadows of another's mind? How shall we influence others to be tender and merciful if we ourselves cannot be tender and merciful to our own sex? How can any woman call herself tender-hearted and self-respecting who can view with indifference the horrors of sweating, of child labour, of the suffering of innocent babes, upon whom are visited the consequences of their parents' vice and intemperance, of the ignoble bondage which law and convention put it into the power of the wicked and unprincipled to make of marriage?

We want to help women. We want to gain for them self-respect and such freedom as is consistent with our duty to others; we want to gain for them all the rights and protection that laws can give them. And, above all, we want the good influence of women to tell to its greatest extent in the social and moral questions of the time. But we cannot do this unless we have the vote and are recognised as citizens and voices to be listened to.

If you yourself are free, is that a reason why you should not feel for the fettered? If you are tenderly loved and protected, if you are happily married, if you are healthy and hopeful, are these reasons that you should leave the fates of other women to the same chance that has placed you upon the way of happiness, but which might just as easily have set your feet upon a hard and thorny path? Would it not be better if the happiness of women rested on a securer basis than that of the lucky chance of being born to good parents or being loved by a good man?

For fifty years we have believed and laboured in silence, but now we have realised that the day is past for silence, and that deeds and sacrifices must be the order of the day. We want reform. The Greatest of all Reformers said, 'I came not to send peace, but a sword.'

We are not fighting against men, but *for* women. Help us if you can, but if you cannot actively help, at least do not oppose us. Reflect that every word spoken against us and the enfranchisement for which we are fighting is a word spoken against the relief of the wretched, the uplifting of the bedraggled and ignorant, the raising of fair and honourable ideals and standards, and the progress of humanity.

Help us if you can, and remember that our first and greatest rule is – to be good to other women, and that, even if you cannot actively help us, you can learn and practise this rule, and thus do honour to womanhood and its cause by your example and your actions.

Remember that the facts about the Woman's Movement are steadily misrepresented in the Press. If you want to know the truth about it read the paper 'Votes for Women,' 1d. weekly, which not only gives an account of everything that is done for the movement, but explains the reason for every step taken.

Window Breaking: To One Who Has Suffered

(W.S.P.U. leaflet, c.1912–13)

Dear Sir,

You, a prosperous shopkeeper, have had your windows broken and your business interfered with, you are very angry about it, and no wonder. But you are angry with the wrong people. You are angry with the women who broke your windows, whereas you ought really to be angry with the people who drove them to it. Those people are the members of the present Government.

You know as well as I do that the Suffragettes bear no grudge against you personally, though perhaps they have some reason to do so. On the contrary, the women are good friends to you, and without them and their support what would become of that flourishing business of yours?

The people the Suffragettes are angry with, and the people you must blame for your broken windows, are, as I have said, the present Liberal Government. They are robbing women of their just right to vote for the Members of Parliament who levy taxes upon them and make laws for them. What is worse, the Government are constantly cheating and deluding the women who demand the Vote.

How would you like it yourself if you were treated in that fashion, and what would you do to get your rights? We know what men did a few years ago in South Africa for the sake of votes. It was not a question of a few broken windows then; it was a question of thousands of lives and millions of money.

'Well,' you may say, 'I sympathise with the women, but what have I got to do with it? Why should my windows be broken because Cabinet Ministers are a pack of rogues and tricksters?'

My dear Sir, you have got everything to do with it. You

are a voter, and, therefore, the Members of the Government are your servants, and if they do wrong, you are really responsible for it. That is why your windows have been broken – to make you realise your responsibility in the matter.

Let me remind you again that women are your best supporters. You can get on very well without Mr Asquith and Mr Lloyd George, but you can't get on without the women who are your good friends in business. Surely one good turn deserves another! The women have been having a very hard time in this Votes for Women fight. **What have you done, what are you doing, and what are you going to do to help them?**

You as voters and as business men have got enormous influence. Last time there was window breaking, some people clamoured for severe punishment for the women. What good did that do? Long sentences of imprisonment, hunger strikes, forcible feeding, which, as the Recorder in a recent trial admitted, is torture! What man likes to think of women going through all that, even if his window *has* been broken?

Don't let it happen again. Put a stop to window breaking, and put a stop to the sufferings and sacrifices of the women, by telling the Liberal Government that you will **stand no more of it and that women must have the Vote**.

Believe me, the women will never give in, and you would think the less of them if they did. It is the politicians who must give in, and you and your fellow electors can make them do it.

The day will come when you will be as proud as can be of your broken windows, and of the orders you delivered to the Government to give women the vote.

I am, Sir,
Yours faithfully,
A SYMPATHISER

The Outragettes

(N.W.S.P.U. Leaflet, reprinted from 'THE WEEKLY DISPATCH,' April 13th 1913)

A new kind of woman has been created by the present Government, and the sooner she disappears the better for law and order and national dignity. This new woman is the Outragette. She began simply as one asking that women should have votes. Later she became a Suffragette and then a Militant, and finally, exasperated by the pettifogging evasions which are possible under our so-called system of representative government, she became an Outragette, a window-smasher, a rioter, wrecker and incendiary.

The Outragettes are now a formidable, though small, section of the women's movement, and not the least element of their strength is that they have in Mrs Pankhurst a leader capable of heroism and martyrdom. No one who followed her trial the other day at the Central Criminal Court will ever forget the burning passion of her defence, the high resolution which she proclaimed, just as have all those men and women who in the past have fought and suffered for our liberties. No one can condone an organised attack on society, but dull would we be of mind if we could not thrill at the spectacle of a brave woman defying the whole force of government and law.

Mrs Pankhurst was never intended to be a law-breaker. Surely her qualities of devotion to the good of her fellow-women marked her out to be a law-maker. Yet the Government, led by men whose chief cleverness lies in evasion and their ability to play tricks with parliamentary procedure, have made Mrs Pankhurst a law-breaker, have called into existence this wild tumult of Outragettes, women only in name and form, so completely have they been transformed into furies.

If we believe in democracy, in the moral truth that every human being is an end in itself, and does not exist to serve another's purpose, there is not and cannot be a single sound argument against admitting women to the full right of citizenship. The democrat is not going to be put off by the disgusting nonsense which has been put forward in the name of medical science, by such hopelessly confused arguments as were some time ago stated with a great parade of learned jargon by Sir Almroth Wright. Votes for Women is no more a question to be settled by physiologists than by lawyers or political intriguers.

The Liberal Party have always been ready to raise an outcry on behalf of oppressed peoples; and yet they refuse, through their leader, Mr Asquith, to apply their own principles in the cause of the liberation of the millions of women who are the mothers, wives and daughters of the world's greatest nation. Never was the utter insincerity of Liberalism made clearer, and never has its lip-loyalty to democracy had worse consequences than the transformation of decent Englishwomen into the wild tribe of Outragettes. The smallest gleam of political insight would show our muddle-minded politicians that the cause of Votes for Women is irresistible despite the excesses of a section of its supporters. In the name of common sense and national honour, we ask the Government to try for once to put its belief in democracy to the test and confer on the women the full rights of citizenship.

Christabel Pankhurst

The Great Scourge and How to End It

(1913)

Contents

Introduction
Why This Book Was Written

This book deals with what is commonly described as the Hidden
Scourge, and is written with the intention that this scourge shall
be hidden no longer, for if it were to remain hidden, then there
would be no hope of abolishing it.

Men writers for the most part refuse to tell what the Hidden
Scourge is, and so it becomes the duty of women to do it.

The Hidden Scourge is sexual disease, which takes two chief
forms – syphilis and gonorrhœa. These diseases are due to prostitution – they are due, that is to say, to sexual immorality. But

they are not confined to those who are immoral. Being contagious, they are communicated to the innocent, and especially to wives. The infection of innocent wives in marriage is justly declared by a man doctor to be 'the crowning infamy of our social life.'

Generally speaking, wives who are thus infected are quite ignorant of what is the matter with them. The men who would think it indelicate to utter in their hearing the words syphilis and gonorrhœa, seem not to think it indelicate to infect them with the terrible diseases which bear these names.

The sexual diseases are the great cause of physical, mental, and moral degeneracy, and of race suicide. As they are very widespread (from 75 to 80 per cent. of men being infected by gonorrhoeœa, and a considerable percentage, difficult to ascertain precisely, being infected with syphilis), the problem is one of appalling magnitude.

To discuss an evil, and then to run away from it without suggesting how it may be cured, is not the way of Suffragettes, and in the following pages will be found a proposed cure for the great evil in question. That cure, briefly stated, is Votes for Women and Chastity for Men. Quotations and opinions from eminent medical men are given, and these show that chastity for men is healthful for themselves and is imperative in the interests of the race.

The use of remedies, such as mercury and '606,' is no substitute for the *prevention* of sexual disease. Drugs and medical concoctions will not wash away the mental and moral injury sustained by the men who practise immorality, nor are they adequate as a cure for the body. The sexual diseases are particularly intractable to cure, and it is never possible to prove that a cure has been effected, so that the disease, while apparently cured, is often only hidden and ready to break out again.

Regulation of vice and enforced medical inspection of the White Slaves is equally futile, and gives a false appearance of security which is fatal. Chastity for men – or, in other words, their observance of the same moral standard as is observed by women – is therefore indispensable.

Votes for Women will strike at the Great Scourge in many ways. When they are citizens women will feel a greater respect for themselves, and will be more respected by men. They will have the power to secure the enactment of laws for their protection, and to strengthen their economic position.

The facts contained in this book constitute an overwhelming case for Votes for Women. They afford reasons more urgent and of greater human importance than any other, that women should have the Vote.

The knowledge of what the Hidden Scourge really is, and of how multitudes of women are the victims of it, will put a new and great passion into the movement for political en-franchisement. It will make that movement more than ever akin to all previous wars against slavery.

The facts contained in this book are not without their bearing upon the question of militancy. There has been vigorous criticism of the policy of destroying property for the sake of Votes for Women. That criticism is silenced by the retort that men have destroyed, and are destroying, the health and life of women in the pursuit of vice.

One of the chief objects of the book is to enlighten women as to the true reason why there is opposition to giving them the vote. That reason is sexual vice.

The opponents of votes for women know that women, when they are politically free and economically strong, will not be purchasable for the base uses of vice.

Those who want to have women as slaves, obviously do not want women to become voters.

All the high-sounding arguments against giving votes for women are a sham – a mere attempt to cover up the real argument against this reform, which argument, we repeat, is sexual vice.

It is said by hypocritical opponents of Votes for Women that women must not vote because men protect them already. Women will not listen to that excuse any longer, now that they know what men's protection means.

It is in the interests of the nation that these same hypocritical opponents profess to resist votes for women. How hollow that argument is seen to be when it is realised that men are constantly infecting and re-infecting the race with vile disease, and so bringing about the downfall of the nation!

Decidedly, women's knowledge of the Great Scourge will do more than anything else to bring Votes for Women nearer.

Every young woman who reads these pages will be warned of a great danger, whose existence she may not until now have suspected. It is because of the need that young girls shall have timely warning of this danger that the question is here dis-cussed in very plain and definite terms.

It remains to be said that the ensuing chapters have appeared in the pages of the *Suffragette*, and are now published as a book in consequence of many urgent requests that they might be available in a more permanent form.

The End of a Conspiracy

Forty of the most prominent doctors recently signed a manifesto demanding the appointment of a Royal Commission to inquire into the subject of venereal disease – the disease, that is to say, which is caused by sexual vice.

The Government have since appointed a Royal Commission, but out of fifteen of its members, only three are women. Nor has re-presentation been given to the Woman's Movement in its more modern aspect. It is an intolerable insult that women should be in a minority on such a Commission. They ought to have at least equal representation with men. The secret nature of this inquiry is also to be condemned.

The doctors point out that tuberculosis, insanity, scarlet fever, typhoid, cancer, and other diseases are being fought by State and private enterprise, but, they continue, 'in all this organised effort there is one note-worthy omission: there has always been a conspiracy of silence as regards venereal disease.'

The Suffragettes are, according to the judges, not unacquainted with conspiracy of one sort, but we would point out that it is long since they refused to be a party to the conspiracy of silence regarding venereal disease. For a long time they have been clamouring for something to be done to stamp out this frightful plague.

The time has come, say the doctors, when it is a national duty to face facts and to bring them prominently to the notice of the public. They state as follows the terrible problem with which the public has to deal:

> 'The worst form of venereal disease is highly contagious, and dire in its effects. It claims its victims not only from those who have themselves to blame for contracting it. It is one of those diseases that may be transmitted from parent to child, so that the off-spring of a sufferer is born with the virus actually in its tissues, to cause, it may be, hideous deformity, or blindness, or deafness, or idiocy, ending often in premature, though not untimely death.'

Truth to tell, further inquiry is hardly necessary, though a Royal Commission ought to be the means of enlightening women as to the nature and extent of this terrible evil. Men already know a great deal, and doctors know most of all. No Royal Commission is needed to discover the cause of venereal disease. Its cause is perfectly well known. As one writer has well expressed it, 'the breeding-place of all venereal diseases without exception is in the social institution called prostitution, or sexual promiscuity; in the debasement and degradation of what should be the highest of physical powers – those involved in the act of generation.'

The doctors urge that both the cure and prevention of venereal disease shall be considered. Women will lay stress upon prevention, because even if cure were possible in the physical sense, it is impossible in the moral sense. A community which tolerates prostitution is a community which is morally diseased. The man prostitute (for why should we give this name only to the woman partner in immorality?) has his soul infected as well as his body.

We repeat that where these terrible diseases are concerned prevention is better than cure. It is not only better than cure, but it is the only cure, for whether these diseases are curable even in the narrowest sense of the term is very doubtful, and even when cured they can be contracted again. Everybody admits that one attack of gonorrhoea does not give immunity against subsequent attacks, and the idea that one attack of syphilis gives immunity from other attacks is not very seriously entertained by experts. As one authority says:

> 'The reason why so few cases of reinfection are seen is because so few cases are really cured, *i.e.*, they are syphilitic and cannot be reinfected.'

As the hope of curing venereal diseases is so illusory, prevention is obviously the true policy. No individual can hope to avoid these diseases except by abstaining from immoral sexual intercourse, and similarly a nation cannot remain unaffected so long as prostitution exists.

Therefore prostitution must go! At this shrieks of protest will be raised. We shall hear the usual balderdash about 'human nature' and 'injury to man's health.' Human nature is a very wide term, and it covers a multitude of sins and vices which are not on that account any the more to be tolerated. It is human nature to rob and to kill. Cannibalism itself is in the nature of certain human beings. Robbing, killing, and cannibalism are nevertheless all forbidden, and the people who venture to let go their 'human nature' in these directions are comparatively few!

Why is human nature to have full scope only in the one direction of sexual vice? The answer to that question is that men have got all the power in the State, and therefore make not only the laws of the State, but also its morality.

According to man-made morality, a woman who is immoral is a 'fallen' woman and is unfit for respectable society, while an immoral man is simply obeying the dictates of his human nature, and is not even to be regarded as immoral. According to man-made law, a wife who is even once unfaithful to her husband has done him an injury which entitles him to divorce her. She can raise no plea of 'human nature' in her defence. On the other hand, a man who consorts with prostitutes, and does this over and over again throughout his married life, has, according to man-made law, been acting only in accordance with human nature, and nobody can punish him for that.

One is forced to the conclusion, if one accepts men's account of themselves, that women's human nature is something very much cleaner, stronger, and higher than the human nature of men. But Suffragists, at any rate, hope that this is not really true. They have more faith in men than men have in themselves, and they believe that a man can live as pure and moral a life as a woman can. The woman's ideal is to keep herself untouched until she finds her real mate. Let that be the man's ideal, too!

Men's health can be preserved only at the price of prostitution – such is the ridiculous and wicked theory advanced by many men and some doctors. The truth is, that prostitution is the greatest of all dangers to the health of men. In the first place there is the risk amounting to certainty of infection by the terrible disease we are considering. Not only so, but prostitution involves a futile and wasteful expenditure of men's energy – energy which they greatly need to enable them to hold their own in science, art, athletics, industry, and commerce.

And what of women's health? No longer will they accept the theory that their health and dignity are to be sacrificed to the health of the other sex. Merely to state the proposition that women should suffer physically and spiritually for the benefit of men is to show its falsity. Nature certainly never intended so monstrous a thing! Indeed, it is very plain to anyone with the smallest intelligence that the ruin of women means the ultimate ruin of men.

It did not need the doctors' manifesto to warn the more instructed amongst women that prostitution and the diseases caused by it are a menace to themselves and their children. But vast numbers of women are still without this knowledge. Innocent wives are infected by their husbands. They suffer torment; their health is ruined; their power to become mothers is destroyed, or else they become the mothers of diseased, crippled, blind, or insane children. But they are not told the reason of all this. Their doctor and their husband keep them in ignorance, so that they cannot even protect themselves from future danger.

Healthy girls enter into marriage without the smallest idea of the risk they are incurring. Nobody tells them, as Dr John W.

Barrett tells us in his article in the *Bedrock,* the scientific review, that 'we know, from very careful insurance medical records, that the great majority of men put themselves in the way of infection before marriage.'

Those who read this statement will have their minds prepared to receive the further appalling statement, widely accepted by medical authorities, that 75 per cent. to 80 per cent. of men have before marriage been infected with one form of venereal disease. Some of these men may seem to be cured, but we have seen how little cure in this connection means. Very sad cases are on record of men who marry when apparently cured, and yet infect their wife. It is therefore hardly too much to say that out of every four men there is only one who can marry without risk to his bride. Such facts are terrible indeed, and the sooner they are grasped the better for the individual and for the race.

Even after marriage, danger arises over and over again unless the husband abstains from immoral acts. In future chapters we shall show more fully what venereal disease means to a woman.

We may point out in passing that prostitution and its evils are largely a medical question, and must be dealt with by medical men. Prison doctors administer medicine which keeps under control the 'human nature' of men prisoners who have no natural self-control. Apart from that, to instruct men in sex hygiene is the doctors' primary duty.

It would indeed be an extraordinary thing if the medical profession, which has discovered means of regulating every other bodily function, should be unable to tell men how to regulate the sex function, and to prevent that excessive sex activity which, as they themselves admit, is fatal to the health of the race.

We look to the medical profession, therefore, to come to the rescue of men whose will-power fails them; to come to the rescue of wives whose life will otherwise be blighted by disease; to come to the rescue of children yet unborn, who, unless help is forthcoming, will enter into a cruel inheritance. A high privilege it will be to rid humanity of a most awful scourge.

A Woman's Question

The Prime Minister has been heard eloquently discussing the prevention of tuberculosis. A most desirable thing, but it is even more desirable that the Prime Minister shall talk about another and even more terrible form of disease, and that he shall try to prevent it – that he shall strike at the cause of sexual disease.

The cause of sexual disease is the subjection of women. Therefore to destroy the one we must destroy the other. Viewed in the light of that fact, Mr Asquith's opposition to votes for women is seen to be an over-whelming public danger.

As we have said, sexual disease – or venereal disease, as it is commonly called – is more to be dreaded than even tuberculosis. It must first be remembered that the whole truth about the effects, direct and indirect, of venereal disease is not yet known. New discoveries are being made every day, and each discovery reveals fresh reason for the belief that venereal disease is humanity's greatest enemy.

As everybody knows, the more serious forms of venereal disease are two, namely, syphilis and gonorrhœa. One authority says that among the causes of death syphilis comes next to tuberculosis in frequency. This statement must be supplemented by others before we can realise the full gravity of the matter.

Firstly, owing to the campaign of silence now breaking down, medical certificates for the cause of death are often so arranged as to conceal the part played by syphilis, and therefore the available statistics do not fully represent the facts.

Secondly, the syphilitic character of various ailments formerly supposed to be non-syphilitic is now being recognised. Various other ailments are coming under suspicion, and this suspicion that they are syphilitic is only too likely to be established by further medical research.

Thirdly, syphilis, by diminishing the power of resistance of the organism, renders the effect of all illnesses and accidents more serious.

There is also this to be noted in drawing the comparison between tuberculosis and syphilis. Syphilis is a powerful predisposing cause to tuberculosis. Moreover, there is also a form of consumption which is definitely syphilitic. We may also add that syphilis is now recognised as being a strong predisposing cause to cancer.

Even in the present imperfect state of knowledge, it is safe to say that syphilis, which is one only of the venereal diseases, ousts tuberculosis as the most potent single cause of physical degeneracy and of mortality.

For women the question of venereal disease has a special and a tragic interest. It strikes at them in their own person and through their children. A woman infected by syphilis not only suffers humiliation and illness which may eventually take the most revolting form, but is in danger of becoming the mother of deformed, diseased, or idiot children. Why are such children born into the world? women have often cried in despair. The answer is – Syphilis! Miscarriage is frequently caused by the same disease. Indeed nothing, as one doctor says, is so murderous to the offspring as syphilis.

Rather different, though hardly less terrible where women are concerned, is the effect of gonorrhœa. In future chapters we deal more fully with this matter. Here we may say that gonorrhœœa is one of the most prevalent of all diseases. It is acquired before marriage by 75 per cent. or 80 per cent. of men, and it is very often contracted after marriage by such men as are not entirely faithful to their wives. To men the disease gives comparatively little trouble, and in the old days the doctors made very light of it.

But to women, owing to their physiological structure, it is one of the gravest of all diseases. , A very large number of married women are infected by their husbands with gonorrhœa. The common result is sterility, which prevents the birth of any child, or may prevent the birth of more than one child. Race Suicide!

Generally speaking, the female ailments which are urged by some ignoble men as a reason against the enfranchisement of women are not due to natural weakness, but – to gonorrhœa. Women – and there are so many of them – who 'have never been well since they married,' are victims of gonorrhœa.

An enormous percentage of the operations upon women are necessitated by this disease, which in many cases so affects the organs of maternity as to necessitate their complete removal. Race Suicide again.

These are awful truths, so awful that the woman's instinct is to keep them hidden, until she realises that only by making these truths known can this appalling state of affairs be brought to an end.

Women have suffered too much from the conspiracy of silence to allow that conspiracy to last one minute longer. It has been an established and admitted rule in the medical profession to keep a wife in ignorance of the fact that she has become the victim of venereal disease. A bride struck down by illness within a few days, or within a few weeks, of her wedding day is told by her husband and the doctor that she is suffering from appendicitis, and under cover of this lie her sex organs are removed without her knowledge. Women whose husbands contract syphilis, and are in turn infected, are kept in ignorance of this, and are thus unable to protect themselves and to do their duty by the future.

Here we have the woman question in perhaps its most urgent

and acute form. Have the Anti-Suffragist women any idea of what the wrongs of women really are? We beg them to realise that so long as the subjection of women endures and is confirmed by law and custom, so long will the race be injured and degraded, and women be victimised.

Sexual disease, we say again, is due to the subjection of women. It is due, in other words, to the doctrine that woman is sex and beyond that nothing. Sometimes this doctrine is dressed up in the saying that women are mothers and beyond that nothing. What a man who says that really means is that women are created primarily for the sex gratification of men, and secondarily, for the bearing of children if he happens to want them, but of no more children than he wants.

As the result of this belief the relation between man and woman has centred in the physical. What is more, the relation between man and woman has been that of an owner and his property – of a master and his slave – not the relation of two equals.

From that evil has sprung another. The man is not satisfied to be in relation with only one slave; he must be in relation with many. That is to say, sex promiscuity has arisen, and from that has in its turn come disease.

And so at the beginning of this twentieth century in civilised Britain we have the doctors breaking through the secrecies and traditions of long years, and sounding the note of alarm. This canker of venereal disease is eating away the vitals of the nation, and the only cure is Votes for Women, which is to say the recognition of the freedom and human equality of women.

The effect of women's enfranchisement will, where this question of redeeming the race is concerned, be manifold. There are three sets of people mainly responsible for dealing with the problem – the ordinary man, the ordinary woman, and the medical profession. The medical profession has until now viewed the question of venereal disease chiefly from the standpoint of the man. As woman's influence increases, her interests and the interests of her children – in a word, the interests of the race – begin to take their due place in medical consideration. This process will not be complete until the equality of women is recognised and enacted by the law. Then we shall have doctors taking the sound, balanced view that the moral and physical health of the race transcends their 'obligation' to foolish individuals who, for the sake of indulgences of which they themselves are ashamed, would wreck the lives of themselves, their wife, and their children. We shall have doctors applying themselves to the task of helping men, if need be by medicinal means, to live as befits a highly-evolved and self-respecting human being.

The outcome of enfranchisement will be to make women hate more than anything else in the world the very thought of selling themselves into slavery as under the conditions of the present day so many of them do sell themselves. The weapon of the vote will enable them to break down existing barriers to honest livelihood.

Upon men the effect of women's enfranchisement will be to teach them that women are their human equals, and not the sub-human species that so many men now think them; not slaves to be bought, soiled, and degraded and then cast away.

We know to what bodily and spiritual corruption the subjection of woman has brought humanity. Let us now see to what cleanness and nobility we can arrive through her emancipation!

How to Cure the Great Pestilence

The re-education of men upon sexual matters is one of the most urgent needs of the day. At present their minds are chokeful of ignorant and unclean superstition as to their own sex nature, and they entertain beliefs on this question which are directly contrary to medical opinion, and produce the most deplorable results so far as themselves, women, and the race are concerned. Although doctors affirm that a pure and continent life is never the cause of disease, whereas immorality is the greatest of all foes to health, still the opposite theory is maintained by millions of men.

It is because of men's ignorance and superstition that prostitution is so widely thought to be inevitable. Immoral intercourse with prostitutes men are pleased to term 'the exercise of their natural functions,' and now that a determined crusade is being waged against prostitution, those who wage that crusade are accused of defying Nature. Nature, indeed! As though Nature had not decreed a punishment for sexual immorality such as she imposes in respect of no other sin.

The horrible disease against which doctors are crying out at the present day is the direct outcome of prostitution, which must henceforward be classed with the other unnatural vices.

What every woman believes, who is not diseased or else morally corrupted by acute poverty on the one hand or excessive luxury and irresponsibility on the other, is this: sexual intercourse where there exists no bond of love and spiritual sympathy is beneath human dignity. That such intercourse is forbidden by Nature herself, and more strictly forbidden and more harshly punished than any other sin, we have already said. Until men in general accept the views on the sex question held by all normal women, and until they live as cleanly as normal women do, the race will be poisoned, as it is to-day, by foul disease.

Very reluctant are men to receive and act upon this truth. Always they want to sin and escape the consequences. To persist in sexual immorality and to remain free from sexual disease is their impossible deal. Even now, when the health and sanity of our race are at stake, men are trifling with a great peril, and are pretending that immorality can be made safe.

In the first place, they proclaim that they have found at last the cure for which they have been seeking throughout the centuries. A cure for sexual disease, which is of all diseases the most incurable! – as though Nature had not willed that there should be no way of escape from this scourge except one, and that one way the way of purity. This boasted new cure is called Salvarsan, and men are speaking of this supposed remedy as though its discovery were a licence to them to go and sin in safety.

But what is the truth of the matter? This cure is by no means proved to be a cure. The doctors are disagreeing about it, and with the best will in the world to believe that Salvarsan will cure syphilis, they cannot shut their eyes to the very ominous facts which manifest themselves in connection with the use of this remedy. Quite recently an inquest was held in London upon a man of forty-two, who died after an injection of Salvarsan. Dr Willcox, the expert in poisons, who was called to give evidence, expressed the opinion that death was due to delayed poisoning caused by the arsenic in injection. But a little while ago, he said, a woman died in a similar way. A French medical expert, M. Hallopeau, in a treatise on the eradication of syphilis, says:

> 'Salvarsan is not without serious drawbacks. In the first place, its efficacy is far from being absolute. In a number of cases, which vary according to the statistics from one-tenth to a quarter, the disease is not cured, and at the end of a few months new symptoms appear. In the second place, the remedy is not harmless when administered, for one has seen up to the present a large number of cases of death admittedly due to its action, and this figure must necessarily be smaller than the number of deaths that actually occur, for these intimate dramas have only two witnesses – the patient and the doctor, and if the patient disappears it is so much to the

doctor's interest to be silent that he must almost necessarily succumb to this temptation.'

Dr Marshall, surgeon to the British Skin Hospital, at a conference held some months ago, refused to admit that the curative power of Salvarsan has been proved, because, as he said, 'In such a disease as syphilis the value of a new drug cannot be estimated till it has been tried for at least ten years. The chief tests of the efficacy of such a drug are its powers in preventing tertiary or parasyphilitic manifestations and the transmission of disease to the offspring. This remedy,' added Dr Marshall, 'appears to be liable to cause severe toxic effects, sometimes ending fatally. No doubt many of the deaths after Salvarsan were due to faulty technique and like causes, but a certain number are difficult to explain, except by arsenical poisoning.'

These opinions concerning Salvarsan are entertained by many other medical authorities; even the discoverer of Salvarsan, Dr Ehrlich, now claims no more for it than that it is 'a valuable adjunct to treatment.' It is obvious, even to the lay mind, that a remedy whose advocates allege that it can swiftly destroy one of the most virulent and prolonged of maladies, must be itself a dangerous substance – a veritable two-edged sword. In fact we are brought back again to the obvious truth that the only certain cure of sexual disease is prevention.

The next method by which men hope to secure immunity from the consequences of ill-doing is that of the State regulation and recognition of vice. Some would disguise this system by calling it by another name. But one man, at any rate, has had the courage of his convictions. He is Major French, of the Royal Army Medical Corps. Whether or not as a representative of the Government is as yet unascertained, he read a paper before the International Medical Congress. He recommends that the State should assume 'the effectual control of openly-practised prostitution by the localisation of irreclaimable women into certain areas or streets.' These women would be periodically inspected, perhaps once or twice a week, in order to see whether they were diseased, and if diseased they would be isolated and treated, and then men would again begin the task of making them diseased.

Anticipating the objection that the maintenance and medical treatment of these women victims of immorality would involve a very heavy charge upon the public funds, Major French makes the extraordinary and mendacious statement that prolonged treatment is only necessary in the case of syphilis, and that one or two months' adequate treatment and isolation would be sufficient in the case of gonorrhoea. Considering that persons apparently cured of gonorrhœa have three or four years later been known to infect another healthy person, the dangerous character of Major French's false statement will be seen.

There is, according to Major French's scheme, to be no compulsory medical inspection of men, because, he says, 'men infected with venereal disease are not so dangerous as women, because a woman practising prostitution usually associates with numerous men, and a man could not and does not associate with a like number of women.'

We maintain that, on the contrary, a diseased man is far more dangerous than a diseased prostitute, because every man is free to abstain, and knowing the dangers involved he is a fool if he does not abstain, from intercourse with a prostitute, whereas the man who is diseased can, and in innumerable cases does, communicate his disease to his unsuspecting wife and to his children.

The plea for State regulation of vice is, according to Major French, based on 'the cardinal fact that prostitution has always existed, and unfortunately must continue to do so for all time.' What this means, put into other words, is that men will always sacrifice their own self-respect, and the health of their wife and family, on the altar of immorality. We think better of men than this, provided that the necessary work of education and reform is done amongst them. Major French must really speak for himself, and not for other men!

It is contended that since the system of regulated vice was established in connection with the Indian Army the percentage of the cases of syphilis in that army has been reduced. Major French in saying this ignores the fact that of late years those at the head of the Indian Army have enjoined upon the soldiers the possibility and the necessity, from the health point of view, of a moral life. Thus Lord Kitchener issued a memorandum to every soldier, in which he said: 'It is necessary that those who are serving their country in India should exert to the utmost those powers of self-restraint with which every man is provided, in order that he may exercise a proper control over his appetites.'

Lord Kitchener further declared 'that every man can by self-control restrain the indulgence of those imprudent and reckless impulses that so often lead men astray.' Sir George White and Lord Wolseley have issued statements to soldiers on the same lines. The soldiers who become infected by disease are punished by loss of promotion, forfeiture of first-class pay, and in other ways, and this has obviously a salutary effect.

It is to be noticed, too, that a decline in venereal disease has also taken place in the Home Army, although there is no State regulation of vice where the Home Army is concerned.

Another point to be noticed is that, in spite of the regulation of vice in Berlin, a high medical authority is of the opinion that in that city every man who reaches the age of thirty has, on an average, had gonorrhœa twice, and every fourth or fifth man has had syphilis! State regulation of vice has been tried in many countries, and always it has failed – its failure being now almost universally admitted by medical men.

But it is not the opinion of medical men or the opinion of women which will necessarily prevail, if things are left to take their course, and there is danger that an attempt may be made, under cover of what will be called 'notification of disease,' to establish some form of State regulation of vice and State control of women of a certain class.

Against any such system women will fight to the very death. No woman-slavery of that kind can be tolerated at this time of day. If men venture to re-establish in this country a system according to which certain women will be segregated, controlled, and medically examined for the purposes of vice, that will mean the establishment of a sex war. It will mean that women in general, not only for the sake of the slave women but for their own sake, will regard men as contemptible and degraded beings.

Even though, by the degradation of a slave class of women, men could keep their bodies clean, they could not keep their minds clean, and the modern woman, emancipated as she already is spiritually, and as she soon will be politically, will have nothing to do with men who are foul in mind.

The great pestilence, this sexual disease which is ravaging the community, makes a problem that has got to be solved. And now that we all know what is wrong, none of us can rest until it is put right. But the quackery of regulated vice must be put aside once and for all. Also, while medical treatment will, and ought to be, fully available to those diseased, there can be no reliance upon remedies as a substitute for clean living.

The real cure of the great plague is a two-fold one – Votes for Women, which will give to women more self-reliance and a stronger economic position, and chastity for men.

Plain Facts About a Great Evil

As might be expected, the statements that we make as to sexual disease and its causes evoke a good deal of comment on the part of men. Some men say that they completely endorse our statements of fact, and that they agree with us that Votes for Women and chastity for men are the sole cures for sexual disease. Other men offer criticism.

These critics say, in the first place, that our statements as to the prevalence of sexual disease amongst men are exaggerated. In the second place, they say that the reason of men's vice is an economic one, and that if men could afford to marry they would no longer have intercourse with prostitutes. It is, of course, principally Socialist men who adopt this second line of argument.

There is a complete answer to both these objections. Firstly, as to the denial of our assertion that 75 per cent. to 80 per cent. of men contract gonorrhœa. Men's favourite method of arguing against women is to deny their statements of fact. But as it happens, the assertion in question is not made upon our own authority, but upon that of medical men.

This is what great medical authorities say as to the percentage of men who contract gonorrhœa – the malady which is so dangerous to the wives, who in thousands are infected by a diseased husband.

Noeggerath says that in New York, out of 1000 married men, 800 have had gonorrhœa, and that 90 per cent. of these have not been healed and can infect their wives.

Ricord also says that 80 per cent. of men contract gonorrhœa, and says further: 'When anyone has once acquired gonorrhœa God only knows when he will get well again.'

Neisser, who discovered the gonococcus, said: 'The statement that of the adult male population inhabiting large towns, *only an insignificant proportion escapes gonorrhœal infection is not at all exaggerated.*'

Dr A. Prince Morrow, author of *Social Diseases and Marriage*, says: 'Gonorrhœa is the most widespread and universal of all diseases in the adult male population, embracing 75 per cent. or more.'

Taylor, in his book on venereal diseases, says: 'We are certainly warranted in asserting that gonorrhœa, taken as a whole, is one of the most formidable and far-reaching infections by which the human race is attacked.'

Finger, the great German authority on gonorrhœa, says: 'Gonorrhœa of the male urethra is probably the most frequent disease with which the practical physician has to deal. With it he usually begins his early practice, and until the end it causes him many anxious hours. Frequent as is the disease, it is equally ungrateful as regards a positive and radical cure.'

Dr Douglas White, M.D., and Dr C. H. Melville, of the Royal Army Medical Corps, who jointly prepared a paper on venereal disease read at the Annual Congress of the Royal Institute of Public Health, said: 'The majority of all young men get gonorrhœa before the age of thirty.'

These statements of fact may be supplemented by two further statements. One is that, as James Foster Scott, M.D., expresses it, 'In every case where a woman is infected with gonorrhœa, she is in danger not only of being rendered a permanent invalid and barren, but also of losing her life from peritonitis and septicæmia.' In mild cases a woman suffers from that 'poor health' that is falsely supposed to be Nature's gift to women. In severe cases the sex organs have to be removed by the surgeon's knife.

Dr Prince Morrow says: 'All modern writers on the diseases of women recognise that *gonorrhœa is the chief determining cause of the inflammatory diseases peculiar to women.*'

A further point to be noticed is that it is to all intents and purposes impossible for doctors to give a guarantee of cure, so that a man may marry and infect his wife, although he was apparently cured at the time of the marriage.

Dr Prince Morrow shows that a gonorrhœa which appears to be cured may really be lying latent, and he says the experience of all gynæcologists is concurrent in the conclusion that infection of the wife by latent gonorrhœa in the husband is the most prolific source of illness in married women, often leading to invalidism, unsexing (by surgical operation), or death.

Taylor says that in very many cases the infection remains dormant, latent, and unrecognised, and these cases may drag on for one or more, and even five, ten, or twenty years without giving any indication of lurking trouble, when for some reason or other the disease may break out again. The result, of course, is that the wife of the man so diseased becomes infected. Other cases are seen, says James Foster Scott, that defy all measures of treatment.

Price, an American authority on the question at issue, says that out of 1000 abdominal operations on women, 950 – all save 50! – were the result of conditions due to gonorrhœa.

These few quotations from great authorities are more than enough to establish our contention that 75 per cent. to 80 per cent. of men acquire gonorrhœa; moreover, they are a warning to men to abstain from vice and a warning to women of the grave danger of marriage so long as the moral standards of men continue to be lower than their own.

And now to reply to the statement of our critics who say that the reason of sexual vice is an economic one, and that if all men could afford to marry, prostitution would disappear. That this contention is unfounded is proved by these facts. Firstly, that rich men, who can perfectly well afford to marry, are quite as immoral as poorer men. Secondly, that married men as well as unmarried men have intercourse with prostitutes.

The problem of vice is certainly an economic one in this sense, that where women are economically dependent upon men, they more readily become the victims of vice. It should be noticed that the man's instinctive endeavour is to keep the woman in a state of economic dependence. This desire to keep women in economic subjection to themselves – to have women, as it were, at their mercy – is at the root of men's opposition to the industrial and professional employment of women.

If a woman can earn an adequate living by the work of her hand or brain, then it will be much the harder to compel her to earn her living by selling her sex.

Here we have the reason why a man-made Socialism is not less dangerous to women than man-made Capitalism. So long as men have the monopoly of political power, it will be impossible to restrain their impulse to keep women in economic dependence and so sexually subservient. In this sense, as we have said, the question of White Slavery is an economic one.

But as we have also said, and say again, sexual vice is not caused by the poverty of men, because the ranks of the vicious are recruited from the ranks of the rich men, the poor men, and the men of moderate means. As we have further said, and now repeat, marriage does not deter men from vicious courses, because married men as well as unmarried men descend to such courses.

The fact is that the sex instinct of these men has become so perverted and corrupted that intercourse with virtuous women does not content them. They crave for intercourse with women whom they feel no obligation to respect. They want to resort to practices which a wife would not tolerate. Lewdness and obscenity is what these men crave, and what they get in houses of ill-fame. Marriage does not 'satisfy' them. They fly to women who will not resent foul words and acts, and will even permit unnatural abuse of the sex function.

The facts brought out by the prosecution in the Piccadilly Flat Case, scanty though these facts were, show how matters stand. No wonder decent women are loth to marry, knowing what they know to-day!

And there is another infamous thing to be told. The men, married and unmarried, who visit bad houses are not content to degrade women of full age and mature physical development. They want young girls, and, if they can get them, virgins. Bernard Shaw, in his preface to *Three Plays by Brieux*, cites Brieux's contention, and himself seems to endorse it, that no man likes to face the responsibility of tempting a girl to her first step from the beaten path. Mr Shaw is behind the times, for at the present day it is, as the White Slaves can tell us, 'a perfect craze with men' to have intercourse with the youngest possible girl, and they are especially eager to be the first to ruin her.

Where is the father instinct which should be prompting every man to defend and not to destroy youth and purity?

The fact is that it is no longer any use for men to try to preserve the illusions of the virtuous woman as to what goes on in the underworld. This men must now accept. A double standard of morality means that they will be more and more cast out by self-respecting women. Until men accept the same moral standard as women, how can it be said that they are fit companions for them?

The virtuous woman has often been condemned for shrinking from her 'fallen' sister and holding out the hand of friendship to the fallen man. Not much longer will women continue to deserve that reproach, because they have come to the conclusion that men are not worthy to associate with them who are not of clean mind and of clean life.

Chastity and the Health of Men

In urging that votes for women and chastity for men are the double cure for the sexual disease that is destroying individuals and the race, we are met by the excuse that chastity for men is dangerous to their health, and that immorality is necessary to the preservation of their health.

This excuse is in direct conflict with the highest medical opinion.

Medical testimony is that immorality not only soils and debilitates a man's body, but also contaminates his mind. Intractable to cure as is the bodily disease caused by immorality, the brain stains which it produces are even more difficult to wash away.

But since so many men rank the body higher than the mind, it is above all things important to make them understand that the physical well-being which they think, or pretend to think, that they are achieving by immorality is actually being destroyed.

That immorality causes bodily weakness as well as actual disease is obvious, because the sexual act involves a very great expenditure of a man's energy – energy which can, if it is not expended in that way, be transformed and expended in other ways, either physical or mental.

In support of our contention we may point out that when athletes are in training sexual intercourse, even in the legitimate relation of marriage and in moderation, has to be completely avoided. Considering that a man goes into training with a view to getting himself into a perfect physical condition, the fact to which we have referred is of the very greatest significance.

And now we will give, one after another, quotations from medical authorities showing the desirability, from the point of view of men's health, of an equal moral standard for men and women.

The matter is clearly expressed in the following statement by the late William Acton, M.R.C.S.:

'The argument in favour of incontinence deserves special notice, as it purports to be founded on physiology. I have been consulted by persons who feared, or who professed to fear, that if the organs were not regularly exercised they would become atrophied, or that in some way impotence might be the result of chastity. There exists no greater error than this, or one more opposed to physiological truth. I may state that I have, after many years of experience never seen an instance of atrophy of the generative organs from this cause. I have indeed met with the complaint: but in what class of cases does it occur? It arises in all instances from the exactly opposite cause – early abuse; the organs become worn out, and hence atrophy arises. Every year of voluntary chastity renders the task easier by the mere force of habit.'

Sir T. C. Allbutt, K.C.B., M.D., Regius Professor of Physics, Cambridge, says: 'Continence, so far from being harmful, is not harmful at any age.'

John Kellock Barton, M.D., says: 'Continence is possible, and not only compatible with but conducive to health.'

Lionel S. Beale says:

'No sufficient valid objections have been established upon reasonable grounds or upon facts of physiology and health to living, nay, to passing the whole life in a state of celibacy. The argument that if marriage cannot, for various reasons, be carried out, it is nevertheless necessary upon physiological grounds that a substitute of some kind should be found, is altogether erroneous, and without foundation.'

Clement Dukes, M.D., Physician of Rugby School, says:

'It is a frequent observation instilled into the young at all ages: "I am told it is very bad for me to be continent; my health will suffer from it." No greater lie was ever invented. It is simply a base invention to cover sin, and has no foundation in fact.'

Very important are the words of G. M. Humphrey, M.D., Professor of Surgery at the University of Cambridge. He says:

'*There are no organs so much under control as those of generation.* Their functions are neither directly nor indirectly in the least essential to life – *scarcely even to the well-being of the body.* The functions of the testicle, like those of the mammary gland and the uterus, may be suspended for a long period, possibly for life; and yet its structure may be sound, and capable of being roused into activity.'

Says the great surgeon, Bryant:

'Unlike other glands, the testicle does not waste or atrophy for want of use, the physical parts of man's nature being accurately adapted to the necessities of his position, and to his moral being.'

The late Sir James Paget, Sergeant-Surgeon Extraordinary to the late Queen Victoria, Consulting Surgeon to St Bartholomew's Hospital, says: 'Chastity does no harm to mind or body; its discipline is excellent.'

Sir Dyce Duckworth, M.D., Honorary Physician to the King, Treasurer and Representative on the General Medical Council of the Royal College of Physicians, says: 'The sexual organs can lie dormant for years, can be left alone, out of consideration, and forgotten, so to speak, until the time comes for matrimony.'

Sir Andrew Clarke said: 'Continence does not harm, does not interfere with development, elevates the whole nature, increases energy, and sharpens insight.'

The opinion of Sir W. R. Gowers, M.D., F.R.S., Lecturer of the Medical Society of London, is expressed as follows:

'The opinions which on grounds falsely called "physiological" suggest or permit unchastity are terribly prevalent among young men, but they are absolutely false. I assert that no man ever yet was in the slightest degree or way the worse for continence or the better for incontinence.'

The lower moral standard of men has always been a cause of offence to women, and men have sought to silence women's condemnation by assuring them that chastity involves not only injury to the health of men (with this point we have dealt), but also very great physical distress. Upon this matter also the doctors have pronounced, and in a sense destructive of men's pretensions.

The doctors inform us that the immorality to which men resort on the pretext of relieving physical distress is, on the contrary, the very cause of that distress.

'Fallen men,' says James Foster Scott, M.D., 'by continual stimulation of their sexual passions with erotic thoughts, sensual conversation and literature, and by the rehearsal of lewd stories, produce in themselves and in others who fall under their noxious influence an uncontrollable passion.' Says the same authority: 'Intercourse with different women is well known morbidly to increase desire.'

Another important statement made by Dr Scott is this:

'The proper subjugation of the sexual impulses and the conservation of the complex seminal fluid, with its wonderfully invigorating influence, develop all that is best and noblest in men.'

'It is incontinent men,' says W. J. Jacobson, Surgeon, Guy's Hospital, 'who are subject to this constant irritability of the sexual organs, and it is they who, from unshunned excitement, must suffer from an excess of seminal secretions and its results. On the other hand, it is the strictly continent men who keep themselves healthily occupied in mind and body, men who, when attacked by imperious sexual desire, simply sally out and seek in exercise a change of surroundings; to such as these the secretion of semen is soon only sufficient to be easily got rid of by an involuntary emission during sleep once or twice a month, a state of things which is perfectly natural.'

Here we have stated the fact that Nature has supplied an innocent means of relief for men, upon which they ought to depend instead of polluting the bodies of the white slaves.

A further statement on this point we take from the writings of James Foster Scott, M.D. and C.M. of Edinburgh University, and late Obstetrician to Columbia Hospital for women in Washington. He says:

'Nocturnal emissions of semen occur occasionally in all normal men as desirable physiological events which give convincing proof of virility. Silly men who gain their information from the evil publications of charlatans who are wholly mercenary in their aims, wrongly attribute these losses to some mischief in the generative functions. The emissions occur with varying frequency in different men, and in the same man at different times. If one takes little exercise, oversleeps, lives on a rich diet, uses tea, coffee, or tobacco to excess, and stimulates his mind with erotic fancies and pursuits, he will probably experience them with more frequency than the active man who directs his energies more to his brain and muscles than to his sensual nature.'

Self-control is perfectly possible. The men who profess to be at times incapable of it, should remember that in prisons men, constituted as they are, have medicine administered by the medical officers. If prostitution can thus be abolished in prisons, it can be so in the world of free men. Self-control for men who can exert it! Medical aid for those who cannot! At all costs prostitution must go and the race be saved.

To sum up! Chastity for men is not only morally imperative, but is also physiologically imperative. Incontinence on the part of men causes a waste of vital force which impoverishes their moral nature and weakens their body.

Furthermore, the incontinence of men gives rise to terrible sexual diseases, whose victims are not themselves alone and the white slaves whom they destroy, but innocent wives and children.

Chastity for men, far from causing atrophy of men's sexual organs, is the surest guarantee against atrophy. As a high medical authority says: 'No continent man need be deterred by this apocryphal fear of atrophy of the testes from living a chaste life. It is a device of the unchaste – a lame excuse for their incontinence, not founded on any physiological law. The testes will see to it that their action is not interfered with. Physiologically it is not a fact that the power of secreting semen is annihilated in well-formed adults leading a healthy life and yet remaining continent.' Sexuality ought to lie dormant until legitimate occasion arises for its use, when it will be found to exist in full natural vigour.

The sexual power of men has been given to them in trust for the perpetuation of the race, and they have not been faithful to that trust. Says a man who is a doctor: 'The secretion of the testicles is the hope of the future of the race, and yet if wrongfully used it is so potent that it may figuratively be classed with the secretions of the poison fangs of venomous reptiles.'

Although by clean thinking and healthy living men can gain control over themselves, they renounce that control, and stimulate their desires by foul thinking, by obscene words, sights, and acts, by alcohol, and even by drugs and unnatural practices.

Although by medical means they can obtain such aid as may be necessary, and although Nature herself affords an innocent means of relief, these are rejected on the plea that they are dangerous to health. By this excuse men have contrived to bar all ways save the way that conducts them to the brothel!

It is essential that women shall, for their own protection, take firm hold of these facts. Let them remember that, in the words of Sir Dyce Duckworth, M.D., Consulting Physician to St Bartholomew's Hospital, there are *no organs in a man's body that can be better controlled than the sexual organs*, and then let them say to men: 'And what of *women's* health? Why should it any longer be sacrificed, not to your health even, but to your vices?'

The Dangers of Marriage – I

Women have always known that marriage, viewed as a spiritual union, is not without its risks; that either on the man's part or the woman's part love may fail, or that the clash of temperament or opinion may threaten happiness. Hence the old saying that marriage is a lottery.

But what women have not known is that marriage as a physical union is (apart from the natural risk of childbirth, which also they foresee) a matter of appalling danger to women.

The danger of marriage is due to the low moral standard and the immoral conduct of men. Men before marriage, and often while they are married, contract sexual disease from prostitutes and give this disease to their wives.

'The infection of pure women in marriage is,' says Dr Prince Morrow, 'the crowning infamy of our social life.' He says further:

'Statistics show that the majority of men who marry have contracted disease, and that many are the bearers of contagion to the women they marry. We witness the effects in the women who suffer ill-health, sterility, mutilation of their bodies, and permanent invalidism. Society's only solicitude is that they suffer in silence. In addition, many of them are compelled to suffer the sight of their babies blinded at birth, children aborted or born with the mark of death upon them, or, if they survive, compelled to bear in their frail bodies the stigmata of degeneration and disease which are the heritage of the prostitute. . . . No one can deny that these facts, the saddest facts of human experience, are of common occurrence, and they will continue so long as society shuts its eyes to the existence of this danger to the family, and from a false sense of prudery or a fastidious nicety refuses to be enlightened.'

There we have a clear statement, and if anything, an *under-*statement, of the risks attendant upon marriage.

What women must realise is that sexual disease communicated to them by their husbands is the cause of the special ailments and the poor health by which so many women are afflicted. Women are not naturally invalids, as they have been taught to believe. They are invalids because they are the victims of the sexual diseases known as syphilis and gonorrhœa.

Let every woman not yet married remember that the vast majority of men contract sexual disease in one of its forms before they are married. Let every woman learn that to cure a man of such disease is long and difficult, and strictly speaking impossible, since no doctor can give a guarantee that his patient is cured, and will not immediately, or in years to come, infect his wife.

The unmarried woman, whereas now she is well and strong, may within one day of her marriage lose her health for ever. This is a hard saying, but it is true, and women have a right to the protection that knowledge gives.

Never again must young women enter into marriage blind-folded. From now onwards they must be warned of the fact that marriage is intensely dangerous, until such time as men's moral standards are completely changed and they become as chaste and clean-living as women.

A clear statement of the case is given by Dr Prince Morrow, when he says:

'The conditions created by the marriage relation render the wife a helpless and unresisting victim. The *vinculum matri-monii* is a chain which binds and fetters the woman completely, making her the passive recipient of the germs of any sexual disease her husband may harbour. On her wedding night she may, and often does, receive unsuspect-ingly the poison of a disease which may seriously affect her health and kill her children, or, by extinguishing her capacity for conception, may sweep away all the most cherished hopes and aspirations of married life. She is an innocent in every sense of the word. She is incapable of foreseeing, powerless to prevent, this injury. She often pays with her life for her blind confidence in the man who ignorantly or carelessly passes over to her a disease which he has received from a prostitute. The victims are for the most part young and virtuous women – the idolised daughters, the very flower of womankind.'

It is not only the men notoriously and obviously immoral who are dangerous as husbands. As Dr Morrow says:

'Who are responsible for the introduction of venereal diseases into marriage and the consequent wreckage of the lives of innocent wives and children? As a rule, men who have presented a fair exterior of regular and correct living – often the men of good business and social position – the men who, indulging in what they regard as the harmless dissipation of "sowing their wild oats," have entrapped the gonococci or the germs of syphilis. These men, believing themselves cured it may be, sometimes even with the sanction of the physician, marry innocent women, and implant in them the seeds of disease destined to bear such fearful fruit.'

In previous articles it has been shown that an overwhelming majority of men put themselves in the way of infection before marriage by having intercourse with prostitutes, and that 80 per cent. of these men become diseased. These facts give warning to women that the chances are strongly against the man who offers himself to them in marriage being healthy.

The frequency with which married women are infected by sexual disease is very great. Noeggerath, the great authority, stated that three out of five married women are infected by gonorrhœa.

Writing on Gonorrhœa and Puerperal Fever Tausig says that 'every pregnant woman should be examined with a view to detecting a latent gonorrhœa.'

A great many men claim that before marriage they are cured of the sexual disease they have contracted, but this, as we have said, is more than they can prove and more than any doctor can certify. Dominant characteristics of the sexual diseases are the length of their duration, and their tendency to become chronic, and to recur years after every symptom seems to have disappeared.

As Marshall, a great authority on the question, says: 'In syphilis contagious lesions are known to occur ten years or more after the commencement of the disease, even in cases which have been properly treated.' It must be remembered that the views which doctors take as to the time required for the treatment of gonorrhœa and syphilis become every day more pessimistic. The modern tendency is for doctors to refuse to give to those wishing to marry any guarantee that a cure of sexual disease, in either of its forms, has been effected.

In this connection Marshall says: 'The duty of the medical man ends after pointing out to his patient the possible eventualities in case of his marriage.'

The point vitally important to women to bear in mind is that unless their husbands are completely chaste and faithful to them after marriage, this same danger that they themselves will be infected arises.

'Unfortunately,' as Dr Prince Morrow says, 'in many cases it is the unfaithful husband and father who receives the poison from a prostitute in an extra-conjugal adventure, carries it home, and distributes it to his family.'

We have in the past referred in general terms to the effects produced by gonorrhœa and syphilis respectively, and now we will address ourselves to this matter in more detail.

Syphilis is the prime cause of race degeneration. Insanity, statisticians declare, is on the increase. The cause of that is syphilis. Nerve trouble is also on the increase, we are told – the rush of modern life, telephones, and motor cars being, as people fancy, the reason of it. The true cause again is syphilis.

This poison of syphilis working in the race and being over and over again reintroduced is producing results that are the despair of doctors and sociologists.

The definition of syphilis as given by Marshall is, that it is 'a contagious disease, chronic in evolution, intermittent in manifestations, and indefinite in duration, caused by a specific microbe.'

Syphilis is hereditary and can be transmitted to the offspring, being, as Marshall expresses it, 'the hereditary disease *par excellence*.' Syphilis is not so prevalent as gonorrhœa, which is contracted by 80 per cent. of men, but complete statistics are unavailable, and it is possible that as many as 20 per cent. contract it. This ailment being fiercely contagious, a syphilitic husband almost certainly infects his wife.

The disease passes through three stages – primary, secondary, and tertiary. The aim of a doctor is to prevent the disease reaching the tertiary stage. As the appearance of tertiary symptoms is sometimes delayed for many years he can have no assurance that he has been successful.

It used to be thought that syphilis was contagious only in the primary and secondary stages, but the latest opinion is that it is contagious even in its tertiary stage. Certainly it can be communicated to the offspring in the tertiary stage, and what may happen is this, that an expectant mother is infected by her unborn child, who, having inherited syphilis from its father, in turn infects its mother. Many syphilitic children fall victims to their disease before birth. If they survive birth then they are a source of contagion to nurse and to mother.

In the tertiary stages of syphilis any part of the body may be affected – nose, lips, tongue, throat, lungs, joints, digestive organs, heart, sex organs, eyes, and ears. Above all, the brain, spinal cord, and nervous system are liable to be affected. Inherited syphilis causes mental deficiency, idiocy, malformations of all kinds, and other diseased conditions.

That syphilis causes loathsome skin disease is well known. Sometimes it manifests itself in the form of ulcers resembling lupus, but more rapidly destructive in their effect. Terrible disfigurement of the face, and especially of the nose, may be caused by syphilis.

Syphilis is an important cause of anæmia, as it acts on the blood by diminishing the number and power of the red blood corpuscles, by diminishing the proportion of hæmoglobin, and by increasing the number of the white corpuscles.

Syphilis is also a very important cause of heart disease. Says Marshall: 'Syphilitic disease of the heart is more common than is generally supposed; in fact, syphilis must be regarded as the chief factor in heart disease, apart from rheumatism. It may be insidious in onset and remain latent a considerable time without giving rise to symptoms, and then cause sudden death in persons apparently in the prime of life. True Angina pectoris must in most cases be due to syphilis, since this is the most frequent cause of the disease of the coronary arteries and aorta.'

'Probably no disease is more productive of arterial degeneration than syphilis,' says Mott. The veins and the glands are particularly subject to damage by syphilis.

Syphilis sometimes produces trouble resembling gastric ulcer and disorders of the stomach. Professor Fournier regards inherited syphilis as likely to constitute a favourable soil for the development of appendicitis.

There are syphilitic forms of pneumonia and pleurisy. That syphilis is a predisposing cause to tuberculosis is now admitted.

The sex organs are naturally very subject to attack by syphilis, and much suffering is endured by women on this account. Syphilis is also the chief cause of miscarriage. Its effect in destroying and deforming the next generation is particularly great.

Syphilis is now known to be the cause of Bright's disease, diabetes, hysteria, eye trouble, producing blindness. It is also recognised as a predisposing cause of cancer. 'If the inclusion of sarcoma and carcinoma among the parasyphilitic affections seems to be transgressing the limits of pathological knowledge,' says Marshall, 'we must admit that no other satisfactory explanation of the origin of malignant tumours has yet been brought forward.'

'Syphilis,' says Fournier, 'is a veritable poison to the nervous system.' It is a cause of paralysis, neuralgia, neuritis.

'One of the principal causes of insanity is syphilis,' says Marshall. Epilepsy and idiocy are referable to the same cause.

These consequences are not only suffered by the persons who wantonly contract syphilis in the course of immoral living. They are suffered by innocent wives, and as the Bible tells us, the sins of the fathers are visited in the form of syphilitic maladies upon their children and their children's children.

In a future article we shall have more to say as to the hereditary aspect of this question, but we may here quote the opinion of Marshall that the generative effects of syphilis are frequently transmitted to the third generation, and possibly further, only to die out with eventual sterility.

Thus, apart from the women infected in marriage, there are numbers of women who have inherited from their forbears the terrible legacy of suffering – and there are men who also suffer, though they have learned so little by it that they seek in immoral intercourse new infection, which they in their turn transmit to generations yet to come.

The medical profession is constantly discovering more about syphilis, and every new discovery teaches them to dread it more as one of the worst enemies of the human race.

The knowledge we already have, as summed up in the facts given above, bears out the saying of a doctor who affirms that syphilis is the principal cause of death occurring before the natural term, and that 'If syphilis and gonorrhœa were eliminated, you would have, from the medical point of view, almost a new world to deal with.'

Syphilis and gonorrhœa can be eliminated in two ways. One is that men shall lead chaste lives. If they refuse to do this, then the only other way in which syphilis and gonorrhœa can be exterminated is by exterminating the race itself.

The Dangers of Marriage – II

Those who declare war upon sexual disease are apt to direct their whole attention to syphilis, leaving gonorrhœa more or less out of account. Thus the doctors who lately memorialised the Government asked for a Royal Commission to inquire into syphilis, and gonorrhœa they did not mention at all. Considering that, as Neisser says, 70 per cent. of the cases of sexual disease which come under the notice of medical men are gonorrhœal, the reason why gonorrhœa is thus ignored calls for some explanation.

In the old days there was a saying that gonorrhœa need be medically treated only in one way – with contempt. In the light of present medical knowledge it is seen that not only because of its greater prevalence, but because of its devastating effect upon its victims, gonorrhœa is not less terrible than syphilis itself.

Speaking of the relative gravity of syphilis and gonorrhœa Prince Morrow, M.D., says:

'Modern science has taught us that in view of its extensive prevalence, its conservation of virulence after apparent cure, and its tendency to invade the uterus and annexial organs, with results often dangerous to life and destructive to the reproductive capacity of the woman, gonorrhœa overshadows syphilis in importance as a social peril.'

Further, comparing the effects of syphilis and gonorrhœa, Dr Morrow says:

'In the case of gonococcic infection, the individual risks the wife is made to incur are much more serious than those following syphilis. The infection may invade the cavity of the uterus and ascend to the annexial organs, causing salpingitis, ovaritis, peritonitis, etc., destroying her conceptional capacity and rendering her irrevocably sterile, to say nothing of the resulting dangers to life and the frequent necessity of surgical operations to remove her tubes and ovaries.'

The author of *Gonorrhœa in Women*, Palmer Findley, M.D., says: 'I might further add in support of the statement of Morrow that the risks to the wife are greater in gonorrhœa than in syphilis, that the prospects of cure are better for syphilis.'

It used to be thought that whereas syphilis was a constitutional disease affecting the organism as a whole, gonorrhœa was a purely local disease, affecting only the sex organs. But the greatest experts are now coming to the conclusion that gonorrhœa, besides being a disease of the sex organs, must also be regarded as a constitutional malady. A statement on this point made by Dr Prince Morrow, is as follows:

'As a result of modern investigations it may be positively affirmed that the gonococcus is susceptible of being taken up by the blood-vessels and lymphatics, and that it may affect almost every organ of the body. Experiments have demonstrated its presence not only in the ovaries, tubes, and peritonial cavity, which it reaches through progressive invasion of the intermediate mucous membranes, but also in the brain and cord, the endocardium, the pleura, the liver.'

In inquiring into the reasons why this great plague of gonorrhœa is too lightly regarded, it is impossible to reject the belief that one reason is to be found in the greater severity with which gonorrhœa attacks *women* as compared with men. Gonorrhœa is in fact the great curse of women, and is the cause of most of the special ailments from which they suffer.

Owing to the ravages that gonorrhœa works upon women, womanhood itself has almost come to be looked upon as a disease.

Women have always wondered why maternity and their sex life as a whole should, for so many of them, be indistinguishable from disease. If these are natural functions, why should they be attended by so much illness and pain? Sexual disease is at the bottom of this mystery. Syphilis inherited and acquired is partly responsible for women's suffering, but gonorrhœa plays by far the bigger part.

There are medical authorities who believe that of cases of 'women's diseases' as many as 90 per cent. or even 95 per cent. are due to gonorrhœa. As one of these authorities says, 'The more the disease is studied and the greater the improvement in bacteriology, the higher is to be found the percentage.'

Even the health of unmarried women is affected as the result of the prevalence of sexual disease.

Another point to be remembered is that, gonorrhœa being highly contagious, many girl children contract it from their mother, and one eminent doctor suggests that this gonorrhœal infection in infancy is responsible for suffering in later life. Inherited syphilis, too, is responsible for many cases of weak and diseased sex organs.

There is yet another reason which we suspect is keeping the doctors silent on the subject of gonorrhœa, and this is that the problem is so awful in its magnitude and in its character that they shrink from admitting its existence.

The fact is that this is an evil absolutely incurable save by one means, namely, the chastity of men – the observance by men of the same moral standard as that accepted by virtuous women. This the medical profession can advise but do not feel themselves able to enforce.

The only people who dare face this evil of gonorrhœa and the only people who can overthrow it are women. When women acquire the necessary influence, political and social, they will have it in their power to convince men that to live cleanly or to be cast out from the society of decent women are the alternatives open to them.

As we have said, the doctors are appalled by the problem which gonorrhœa presents, and well they may be.

To begin with, there is, as we have repeatedly shown by quotations from the greatest authorities, no disease of the adult male population which approaches gonorrhœa in its prevalence – from 75 to 80 per cent. of men (and some say more than this) being infected by it before marriage. So much for the extent of the evil. Now as to the possibility of cure.

There is perhaps no disease so difficult to cure. To speak of cure, in the strict sense of the word, is indeed impossible. And when, as so very often happens, a man has, after a first attack of the disease, again exposed himself to infection and has become reinfected, the case is serious indeed.

A man who has contracted gonorrhœa may after medical treatment show no further symptoms, but that is no proof that he is cured. Palmer Findley says that he has repeatedly demonstrated the presence of the gonococcus in the urethra when there was no visible secretion. To believe that the disease is terminated when its symptomatic discharge has disappeared is, he says, 'a delusion,' and he adds:

> 'Now we are all but ready to say that Noeggerath was right when he said the gonococcus can exist in the tissues throughout the lifetime of the individual, and at any time, under favourable influences, the infection may light upon what appears to be a new and acute infection, or may transmit a virulent infection without itself becoming manifest.'

A very important statement made by this same authority is as follows:

> 'Individuals are observed to infect others, yet apparently are themselves immune to infection. The explanation lies in the presence of a gonorrhœal infection in the absence of all the clinical signs. In the first individual the gonococcus had little virulence, but when transmitted to sterile tissues it assumed an active role.'

From this statement it will be seen that a man who is apparently long cured may infect his wife, who will then suffer from gonorrhœa in an acute form, owing to the very fact that she has until then been healthy and therefore presents virgin soil upon which the deadly gonococcus can flourish.

The truth is that a man who by immoral intercourse exposes himself to infection must act on the assumption that he will infect himself for life, and that by so infecting himself he is rendering himself unfit for marriage. As James Foster Scott, M.D., says: 'No individual who expects ever to marry has any right to indulge in sexual impurity.'

To the frequence with which wives are infected in marriage we referred in our last article. We showed that, according to Noeggerath, three out of five married women suffer from gonorrhœa. We quoted the opinion expressed by another authority that every pregnant woman should be examined for sign of gonorrhœa. Yet another doctor says that he has found more than 25 per cent. of expectant mothers suffering from this disease.

The specialist, Ricord, believed that 90 per cent. of women marrying men who had contracted gonorrhœa became themselves infected with the disease either in an acute or latent form.

Gonorrhœa in women does terrible mischief. It is a cause of peritonitis. It gives rise also to disease of the bladder and kidneys. It may cause gonorrhœal rheumatism and gonorrhœal affections of the heart.

It is, however, the sex organs that are primarily open to attack by gonorrhœa. The results of such attack vary in different persons, and range from poor health and debility to very serious diseases, necessitating surgical operation. Gonorrhœa is a potent cause of sterility and miscarriage. It is held by some doctors that the abortive influence of gonorrhœa is as pronounced as that of syphilis. Some tumours are due also to gonorrhœa.

Many cases of puerperal fever are attributable to gonorrhœa. Says Palmer Findley:

> 'Every careful observer of obstetric practice of large experience is keenly aware of the frightful prevalence of gonorrhœal puerperal infections.'

Pregnancy and child-birth have, the medical authorities tell us, a most important effect on the course of gonorrhœal infection. A woman who has been infected may suffer comparatively little until she is about to become a mother, and then and more especially at the time of child-birth and after it the disease develops and spreads with alarming rapidity. A great deal of suffering experienced by women before and at the birth of their children must be due to gonorrhœa.

The following quotation from James Foster Scott, M.D., is

instructive. He says: 'In women gonorrhœa not only tends to become chronic and to invade the internal sexual organs with destructive changes, but with each occurrence of menstruation there is also a likelihood of its renewed activity and further spread; and especially does danger threaten if she become pregnant – the result not showing fully until some weeks after the full-time labour or miscarriage.'

The symptoms of gonorrhœa which medical writers describe are only too familiar to thousands of women. Valentine, an American doctor, says:

> 'How dismal is the history of many a young woman who marries with all the accompaniments of a wedding celebration. From the husband's latent gonorrhœa many of them contract conditions which alter their lives and even their characters. They suffer from backache, irregular and painful menstruation, urinary disorders, localised peritonitis, loss of their healthful beauty, lassitude, hysteria, sterility, miscarriages, or death.'

Another doctor says:

> 'The chronic or creeping form of gonorrhœa in women demands a considerable amount of attention. A healthy young woman marries, and in about a year after her marriage she finds that her health is very much impaired. Before marriage she was full of health and spirits, was buoyant and active, but she now feels weak, depressed, and irritable, and has vague pains in her body. Formerly her periods were painless and regular. Now they are painful and variable. . . . This is a typical case. The symptoms and signs of the disease may, however, vary greatly from mere vague discomfort and slight menstrual derangement to the most distressing disturbances.'

The following words taken from the writings of another eminent physician are impressive. He says:

> 'It is common to hear women who constantly suffer from uterine torture employ such words as these: "When I was a girl I was quite well. It is only since my marriage that I have become ill." And every day this confidence, this plaintive refrain, saddens the gynæcologist. It is continual and inexorable. From the discoloured and suffering faces we may guess a whole past of debility, and the origin is always marriage. The husbands have a quiet conscience. They go about their

business, or to the clubs, create fresh pleasure or new relations for themselves, and desert the mournful marriage bed. They can reckon on sympathy, for who does not pity them for having married wives with such bad health.'

Enough has surely been said to prove the dangers of marriage, to show the injury done to women by the low standards and immoral conduct prevalent amongst men.

What a cruel mockery it is that men have alleged the very weakness of which their behaviour is the cause as a reason why women should be condemned to political inferiority!

And what a prospect of emancipation from suffering and illness is opened to women by the medical facts that we lay before them! For these facts show that it is not Nature that has doomed women to suffering, to illness. These evils are preventable, and now that women have the knowledge so long denied them they can consider how to protect themselves from foul infectious disease.

The Decline of the Birth-Rate

The birth-rate is declining. Bishops, men sociologists and others are bewailing the fact. Of course, they blame the women. That, men have done since Adam. They seem to forget that the question of how many children shall be born is one for women to decide, since it is they who have to pay the price for these new lives.

Quite apart from that, there is another sense in which women are responsible for the falling birth-rate, and so far as women are concerned it will fall lower still – not only the birth-rate but the marriage-rate as well.

Marriage becomes increasingly distasteful to intelligent women – not motherhood, but marriage. There are numbers of women who long for children, but are not satisfied with the marriage laws nor with the men's standards of husbandhood and fatherhood.

In the first place, the position to which the law relegates a wife is intolerable to self-respecting women. By law, a wife is not the mother of her own child, and her wishes concerning the child may be, except in very extreme cases, entirely over-ridden, especially where religion and education are concerned.

The English law compels a wife to submit to persistent and degrading immorality on the part of a husband, though one single act of unfaithfulness on her part entitles him to divorce her. If she should wish to take the law into her own hands and leave a husband who insults her and probably infects her with disease by frequenting houses of ill-fame, her husband can force her into submission by keeping her children, so that if she leaves him she must also leave them.

Women who know what is the moral standard of those who describe themselves as the 'average man', and what is the consequence of that standard where themselves and their children are concerned, may well abstain from marriage!

The new realisation by women of the appalling prevalence of sexual disease, and the ghastly frequency with which women are infected by their husbands, will inevitably check marriage.

Love is stronger than death, the saying goes. But love will not be found stronger than disease, when that disease is caused by vice, which blasphemes love and desecrates love.

There can be no mating between the spiritually developed women of this new day and men who in thought or conduct with regard to sex matters are their inferiors.

Therefore the birth-rate will fall lower yet.

For severely practical, common-sensible, sanitary reasons women are chary of marriage. When the best-informed and most experienced medical men say that the vast majority of men expose themselves before marriage to sexual disease, and that only an 'insignificant minority', as the authority puts it – 25 per cent. at most – escape infection; when these medical authorities further say that sexual disease is difficult, if not impossible, to cure, healthy women naturally hesitate to marry. Mr Punch's 'advice to those about to marry – Don't!' has a true and terrible application to the facts of the case.

Perhaps our childless and celibate Bishops may say that it is a woman's duty, faced by the prospect, if she marries, of being infected by her husband, to sacrifice herself and to marry all the same. They must not be surprised if such advice falls upon deaf ears. 'Sacrifice yourself, sacrifice yourself,' is a cry that has lost its power over women. Why should women sacrifice themselves to no purpose save that of losing their health and happiness? Now that women have learnt to think for themselves, they discover that woman, in sacrificing herself, sacrifices the race.

If the Bishops, and the whole pack of men who delight in advising, lecturing, and preaching to women, would exhort the members of their own sex to some sacrifice of their baser impulses, it would be better for the race, better for women, and better even for men.

Women admit, therefore, that the falling birth-rate is, and will continue to be, in part due to their own deliberate intention. But it is due also in large part to causes for which women are in no way responsible. A great many women are, through no fault of their own, incapable of becoming mothers. The reason of this is that they have been infected by venereal disease, which is the great foe to the reproduction of the race.

The two forms of venereal disease operate in different ways. Gonorrhœa causes inability to bear any child at all, or, in some cases, inability to bear more than one. It also destroys the capacity for fatherhood, although this is a point which is very often wilfully ignored by those who delight to criticise women.

It is declared by Dr Prince Morrow that men are ultimately responsible for from 50 to 75 per cent. of sterile marriages – that in 20 to 25 per cent. of such cases the disease has destroyed the husband's capacity for fatherhood, and in the others the husband has infected his wife, and thus robbed her of the power of maternity.

Such being the connection between the problem of what is called 'race suicide' and the infection of women in marriage, we realise how unjustly women have suffered in the past from self-blame, and the blame of others, for failure to bring children into the world. A childless woman used to be taught that she had failed in her life's mission. If she had known the facts that women know to-day this might have shown her that she was not herself to blame.

A quotation from a doctor is very much to the point here. He says:

'In the martyrology of women there is no more pathetic sight than the woman who has been balked of her instinctive desire for children, and who goes from one physician to another in the hope, oftentimes in vain, of having her sterility cured. The instinct and craving for maternity becomes a veritable obsession. She will, at any cost of time and pain and suffering, submit to any treatment which promises relief – curetting, division of the cervix, and even more formidable operations upon her pelvic organs. And the satire of it all is that in many cases the husband, inflated with the sense of his own virility, is himself responsible for the sterility.'

These medical statements of fact provide women with a strong defence against the accusation that they are responsible for race suicide.

Another authority on this matter, Grandin, says:

'From the present standpoint, man is not the "lord of

creation, but the exterminator of the species." Kill the gonococcus by teaching man the danger to woman and to the
species, should she acquire it, and then man returns to the
condition he is pictured as having been in before Eve tempted
him with the apple, and he weakly said to his Maker, "It is
the woman's fault." '

And this wise man continues:

'As I have reiterated above, according to my light, the
solution of our problem lies in education. Prostitution, the
social evil, is responsible to the greatest extent for the
dissemination of gonorrhœa and of syphilis. In the toleration
of this evil by society, too much stress has been laid upon
woman's part in dissemination and too little on man's. As
has been customary with the latter from the beginning of the
world, he points the finger of scorn at woman; he abets
woman in the making of the prostitute the social outcast,
and yet, were it not for solicitations of the man, for his
untrammelled licentiousness, there would be few prostitutes.
It is time that there should cease to be recognised a different
code of morals for man and for woman. That which is wrong
in woman is equally wrong in man, and in face of the disease
under consideration the man is the chief offender, and the
finger of scorn should be first aimed at him. . . . The sexual
instinct is a God-given instinct, its purpose being the perpetuation of the species. Man, largely through ignorance of the
calamities following the misuse of this instinct, has converted
it into one of extermination of the species. Ignorance being
at the bottom of his folly, it follows that man, at that age
when his instinct is established, should be educated in reference to its purposes, and also in regard to the consequences
if the instinct is misused.'

Syphilis is a second factor in race suicide. This disease produces
miscarriages, often many times repeated in the case of the same
woman. It causes the birth of dead children, and of children who
survive birth only for a few hours, weeks, or months. Syphilis is
in fact the prime reason of a high infantile mortality. Mental deficiency, dwarfism, every kind of physical deformity, even the birth
of beings hardly human, are to be found as the result of syphilis.
We say again that it is for those who have inherited from Adam
the inclination to blame women for all that goes wrong in the
world, now to admit the true facts connected with the falling birth-
rate – facts that have so long been kept hidden from women.

What Women Think

For generations women have been very silent, but they have thought the more, and the time has come to put their thoughts into words.

It is now the turn of men who have hitherto done all the talking to listen to what women have to say about life and its problems.

In a world peopled with men and women, the question of the relationship between the sexes is naturally one which occupies a large place in the minds of women as well as of men.

One of the thoughts of women which has now come to the point of expression is – that prostitution must go! They will be told, they *are* told, that such a thing is impossible. But in answer to that they say again, with the utmost firmness – prostitution must go.

They are assured that in the past attempts have been made over and over again to get rid of prostitution, and that such attempts have failed, and always will fail, so long as the world lasts.

Women have a very simple answer to that argument, and it is: 'You have never tried to abolish prostitution, and so, of course, you have not succeeded.'

Certainly, efforts have been made to cover up all outward trace of the existence of this loathsome thing, but the real cure for it has never been applied. Beneath all the surface appearance of attacking prostitution, men have cherished the belief that prostitution is necessary, and that immorality and incontinence are legitimate for them.

The true cure for prostitution consists in this – the strengthening of women, and the education of men.

To strengthen women means, in the first place, to fill them with a higher sense of their own importance as the transmitters of life. Nature, in giving to women the chief share in continuing the race, has singled them out for special honour. It is certainly not the less developed and less powerful sex to whom the great task of maternity has been entrusted.

Their capacity for maternity is, therefore, an evidence of woman's vitality and special human worth. If only for this reason, women must feel a special pride in being women. They must, and they do, condemn every law and custom which belittles and condemns to social and political inferiority the mother sex to which they belong.

In short, the disfranchisement of women is an insult to motherhood, which can no longer be tolerated. Prostitution is to be condemned on the same grounds. This is so, not only because prostitution makes slaves and outcasts of the women slaves used for purposes of vice, and degrades their high sex function, but also because the further effect of prostitution is to poison men's idea of the sex-relationship, even where all the other women are concerned.

And again, as we have so often pointed out, in prostitution is bred the sexual disease which is communicated to wives, whose health and power of maternity are in consequence injured or destroyed. When maternity holds its rightful place in the world's regard prostitution will exist no more. But that day will not come until women are valued as individuals and as human beings, and not merely as sex beings.

The idea that women exist only for race and sex purposes is held by a great many men who wish to be considered as having in view the interests of women and of the race, but it is an idea that is very largely responsible for prostitution and vice. 'If women are sex beings and nothing more,' argue the immoral men, 'then those women who are not occupied with child-bearing are fit for nothing more than to satisfy our vices.'

What men, including eugenists and social reformers of all kinds, must realise, is this: The power of maternity is something which women have in addition to their other powers. The power of maternity corresponds with the power of paternity, and not to some other power or quality in men. It is true that to give birth to a child makes a great demand upon the vitality of women, but the answer to that is that the vitality is hers, given to her by Nature to meet the need of that vitality.

The belief that women are naturally weak is the greatest of all delusions. It is true that many women's strength is now, owing to artificial causes, less than it ought naturally to be, but these artificial causes must be done away with. One of them is, as we have already shown, the great prevalence of sexual disease, which directly attacks the sexual health and vitality of women. Want of exercise, unhygienic dress, and other such circumstances contribute to make a great many women weaker than they are by nature.

Yet, even as things are to-day, we find women, in addition to bringing children into the world, doing some of the hardest and most unremitting toil. It is only when the question of wage-earning arises, or when women claim the right to be active in the higher fields of human activity, that it is aruged that maternity unfits them for equality with men.

We repeat, then, that for women to establish their freedom and equality with men, apart from any question of maternity and sex, is a necessary step towards the abolition of prostitution. It is largely because men have been too much persuaded of women's unlikeness to themselves, that they have wanted to put and keep them in subjection and exploit them for purposes of vice. For the abolition of prostitution, it is necessary that men shall hold women in honour, not only as mothers, but as human beings, who are like and equal unto themselves.

Another aspect of the problem is economic. More and more women are becoming persuaded of the fact that, both in marriage and out of it, they must be economically independent, and that there must be no question of living by the sale of sex. For sex is degraded by any hint of sale or barter.

As regards the unmarried woman, there must be a security that she can live by selling the work of her hand or brain. It is notorious that an enormous percentage of white slaves are forced into slavery by economic pressure, by the impossibility of earning more than a starvation wage, or by the impossibility of earning anything at all. Women's right to work and to live by their work is, therefore, one of the chief points in their charter of liberty.

Nor are things different where the married woman is concerned. The fact that a wife depends upon her husband for the necessities of life leads, as everybody knows, to a great deal of unhappiness in marriage. Social reformers, who attach so great an importance to the economic side of every problem, ought to be the first to realise that in the reforming of social conditions it is not enough to put the husband in possession of larger means; and that to every adult individual – man or woman, wife or maid – must be secured economic independence. And yet it is often they who uphold the reactionary theory that married women ought not to be economically independent.

The system under which a married woman must derive her livelihood from her husband – must eat out of his hand, as it were – is a great bulwark of sex-subjection, and is a great reinforcement to prostitution. People are led to reason thus: a woman who is a wife is one who has made a permanent sex-bargain for her maintenance; the woman who is not married must therefore make a temporary bargain of the same kind.

It is not as though a married woman does not earn her keep by the work she does. Here are some of the avocations which married women pursue: cooking, laundry-work, dressmaking, marketing, mending, scrubbing and cleaning; bathing, dressing, and general care of infants, house-management, sick nursing, social enter-taining, husband's career-making. This varied work, if done by married women, has a money value. It is right, therefore, that a married woman shall get the same monetary payment for her work as is received for the work done by the rest of the community. Nor is it enough, to solve the problem at issue, for a wife to have a legal claim upon a share of her husband's earnings. That may work well enough in practice where the husband is possessed of large means, but in the vast majority of cases something more than that is needed. Merely to give a woman half her husband's earnings is to make one person's wage or salary meet the needs of two persons, and perhaps of a family into the bargain. By way of illustration, we may take the case of husband and wife who are both doctors, or actors, or industrial workers. Each earns an independent income, and both should contribute equally to the maintenance of the family. If, on the other hand, the wife is earning nothing, then the family circumstances are greatly reduced, and the wife can never be in the same sense economically independent. Co-operative housekeeping, which not only lightens women's work by organising it and scientifically directing it, but also brings wage-earning within the reach of every wife without impairing domestic comfort, is a system to be heartily encouraged by those who desire the full emancipation of women. Of course, married people will always be free to make such arrangements as suit their own case, but the type of marriage will in days to come be one in which the wife is economically independent.

More important than everything else as a means of strengthening women's position is, of course, the gain of the Parliamentary vote. The vote is the symbol of freedom and equality. Any class which is denied the vote is branded as an inferior class. Women's disfranchisement is to them a perpetual lesson in servility, and to men it teaches arrogance and injustice where their dealings with women are concerned. The inferiority of women is a hideous lie which has been enforced by law and woven into the British Constitution, and it is quite hopeless to expect reform between the relationship of the sexes until women are politically enfranchised.

Apart from the deplorable moral effect of the fact that women are voteless, there is this to be noticed – that the law of the land, as made and administered by men, protects and encourages the immorality of men and the sex exploitation of women. As an illustration of this, we have only to refer to the Piccadilly Flat Case, in which male offenders were screened from punishment, and the woman who had ministered to their vice was punished so much more leniently than are women who destroy property for the sake of the vote. As a further illustration, we may point to the bastardy laws, which make it shamefully easy for a man to escape due responsibility for his children born out of marriage, and the fact that the law does not protect young girls after the age of sixteen, and not even up to that age, if a male offender against a girl pleads that he thought her to be over the age of consent. The unequal divorce laws are another illustration of the way in which a Parliament elected only by men protects the immorality of men. The scandalous leniency shown in regard to assaults upon infant girls provides another example of the evil caused by the outlawry of women.

There are speeches, pamphlets, and books by the hundred on 'motherhood,' 'mothercraft,' the 'ignorance of mothers,' and so forth. What women think is that the public attention ought now to be directed less to the education of women than to the education of men. Fatherhood, father-craft, and the duties and responsibilities of paternity are, or rather ought to be, the question of the day.

There are men who urge that almost before she herself leaves the cradle, a girl should be put in training for motherhood. When, and in what way, a girl's mind should be directed towards motherhood can best be decided by women themselves. What men ought now to do is to train the young of their own sex. As things are at present women are certainly more fit for maternity than men are for paternity.

We have already said that if men were conscious of their paternal duty prostitution would be at an end, because by intercourse with prostitutes a man endangers his own power to became a father, endangers the health of his wife, and endangers the health and sanity of his offspring. There is no doubt whatever that boys at a very early age ought to be taught their responsibility to the next generation. It is quite futile for women to prepare themselves for motherhood unless men at the same time are preparing themselves for fatherhood. To have wise and healthy mothers avails nothing if there are not also wise and healthy fathers.

One of the lessons that men have to learn is that their sex powers are given to them as a trust to be used, not for the purpose of immorality and debauchery, but to be used, reverently and in a union based on love, for the purpose of carrying on the race.

The rightness and possibility, and the imperative necessity of an equal moral standard for men and women, is what every man should be taught from youth upwards. This women think, and upon this women will more and more insist.

They will be told, of course, as they have always been told in the past, that an equal moral standard for men and women is an impossible dream. Such statements have lost all their power to deceive women, who have by this time taken care to arm themselves with the necessary medical knowledge. Women know that, as one doctor has expressed it, man's physical nature is accurately adapted to the needs of his moral being, and that the rule of chastity observed by women can also be observed by men to their great advantage in point of health and vigour. In a previous chapter, called 'Chastity and the Health of Men,' there appears the testimony of many medical men, which testimony gives overwhelming proof that prostitution and immorality are not in accordance with Nature, but are a violation of Nature's laws. Chastity and continence for men are natural and healthful; it is unchastity and incontinence which destroy men morally and physically.

Now that women are aware of these facts, they treat with contempt the gross cant about men's sexual needs, by which it is sought to excuse prostitution and vice. The truth is that the desires of men are inflamed to an unnatural degree by impure thought and action, by excess in the way of meat and drink, and by physical and mental indolence.

Sexual disease is also responsible for exaggerated sexual desire. It is most important that men and women shall have a knowledge of this fact, which is brought out very clearly in the following quotation from the writings of James Foster Scott, M.D.:

> 'It is well to remember that at certain stages of gonorrhœa the voluptuous desires of some patients are inordinately intensified. The point of importance in this connection is that a most dangerous class of diseased men, with abnormally strong sexual appetites, are going about without conscience, supervision, or legal restraint, and using these very women whom so many men feel safe in patronising. . . . Diseased men get reckless in the indulgence of their passions. Not only have they lost their *morale*, strong in the belief that there is little more for them to acquire, but also the inflammation in the deep urethra morbidly stimulates their passions, so that these men are most highly dangerous to human society, being in fact poisonous men seeking to poison others. Excessively lustful, and governed by no moral restraint, they actively seek to gratify their passions at the expense of any available woman's health and life, and at the expense of those foolish men who follow in their tracks.'

When it is reflected that from 75 to 80 per cent. of men contract gonorrhœa, the part which this disease plays in connection with the problem of vice is obviously a very large one.

The truth is that, owing to disease and other causes, the sex desire in men is stronger than is warranted by the interests of society. When some aspiration towards greater liberty and towards self-development on the spiritual plane is concerned, women are often, quite unreasonably, exhorted to sacrifice themselves to the supposed interests of society as a whole. Now, with great reason, men are called upon, in the interests of themselves and of women and of society as a whole, to keep their desires under due control.

The excuses offered by men for not doing this are many and various. Thus, one man makes his protest in the name of art, and asks indignantly, 'Do you think that any artistic manifestation could come out of chastity and normality?' Now it is very natural that inspiration should come through a union which is one of love, but that vice and uncleanness are a way to inspiration, is a fallacy with which M. Jean Finot deals very trenchantly in his *Problems of the Sexes*. He says: 'How many great minds, irremediably destroyed by misguided voluptuousness, are cut down before having expended for the human race one-tenth of their knowledge'; and he quotes Sainte-Beuve, as follows:

> 'Who shall say how, in a great city, at certain hours of the evening and the night, there are periodically exhausted treasures of genius, of beautiful and beneficent works, of fruitful fancies? One in whom, under rigid continence, a sublime creation of mind was about to unfold, will miss the hour, the passage of the star, the kindling moment which will nevermore be found. Another, inclined by nature to kindness, to charity, and to a charming tenderness, will become cowardly, inert, or even unfeeling. This character, which was almost fixed, will be dissipated and volatile.'

Art is creative. Sexual excess is a waste of man's creative energy.

Another grotesque idea which men have entertained, is that by immoral life they excite the admiration of women, and that women think immoral conduct 'manly.' On the contrary, women think it altogether unmanly and contemptible. Strength and cleanliness and self-control – and even more than self-control, a mind which is too big and fine to harbour immoral ideas and intentions – are what women admire in men. Women are in agreement with Forel, who says: 'Sexual intercourse which is bought and sold has no relation to love. As a mode of gratifying the sex instinct it stands even lower in the moral scale than the habit of self-abuse. Prostitution is a hot-bed of sexual vice and abnormal practices. By its means, the sexual instinct is perverted and led astray into every imaginable bypath, while women are degraded in the basest of all slaveries.'

Women are aware that excessive sexuality, as manifested in prostitution, is unnatural, and that it leads inevitably to other unnatural practices. Far from regarding immorality as manly, women regard it as a terrible blemish upon character – as a disqualification for fatherhood, a disqualification for husbandhood.

The normal woman regards the sex act as the final pledge of her faith and her love. The idea that her husband may take a lower view of it is repulsive to her. The thought that, before or after his marriage, prostitution can enter his mind as an alternative to marriage, is intolerable. A woman's knowledge of psychology tells her that a man who is, or has been, immoral inevitably has his sex ideals tainted, and cannot therefore regard marriage as she herself regards it. Thus the black cloud of prostitution necessarily darkens the legitimate sex union.

Another of women's thoughts born of the more developed sense of comradeship among women, is that so long as there exists a huge class of slave women, the more fortunate women cannot live peaceably and contentedly as though all were well. If some women are corrupted and outcasts, and sacrificed to immorality, this concerns all women, and those who are responsible must be called to account. Besides, as we have seen, womanhood as a whole suffers in health and happiness as the result of the maltreatment of the slave class.

It would seem that certain men are alarmed by the dangers of prostitution, and, of course, they find it expensive. At any rate, we detect a tendency in many quarters to preach to women the observance of a looser code of morals than that they have observed hitherto. 'You are asking for political freedom,' women are told. 'More important to you is sex freedom. Votes for women should be accompanied, if not preceded, by wild oats for women. The thing to be done is not to raise the moral standard of men, but to lower the moral standard of women.' To this proposal the women reply by a firm and unqualified negative. Votes they certainly intend to have, and that quickly, but they know too well what is the harvest of wild oats, and having that knowledge, they refuse to sow any.

When women have the vote, they will be more and not less opposed than now to making a plaything of sex and of entering casually into the sex relationship.

In the opinion of the Suffragettes sex is too big and too sacred a thing to be treated lightly. Moreover, both the physical and spiritual consequences of a sex union are so important, so far-reaching, and so lasting, that intelligent and independent women will enter into such union only after deep consideration, and only when a great love and a great confidence are present.

And here we may, perhaps, deal with the statement made by

some men, that women suffer who are not mated with men, and that what they are pleased to term 'the unsatisfied desires' of women are a problem. Now, in the old days when marriage was the only career open to women, those who did not marry regarded themselves, and were regarded, as failures – just as a lawyer might who never got a brief, as a doctor might who never got a patient, as a baker might who never got a customer. But nowadays the unmarried women have a life full of joy and interest. They are not mothers of children of their flesh, but they can serve humanity, they can do work that is useful or beautiful. Therefore their life is complete. If they find a man worthy of them, a man fit physically and morally to be their husband, then they are ready to marry, but they will not let desire, apart from love and reason, dominate their life or dictate their action.

It is very often said to women that their ideas of chastity are the result of past subjection. Supposing that were so, then women have the satisfaction of knowing that their subjection has brought them at least one great gain – a gain they will not surrender when the days of their subjection are over. The mastery of self and sex, which either by nature or by training women have, they will not yield up.

Warned by the evils which the tyranny of sex has produced where men are concerned, women have no intention of letting matter triumph over mind, and the body triumph over the spirit, in their case.

This being the point of view of the Suffragettes, the most modern of all modern women, it will be seen that out of the present impasse in sex matters, there is only one way – chastity for men, guaranteed and confirmed by the greater independence which the Vote will give to women.

Appendix: the truth about the Piccadilly Flat

In the Piccadilly Flat Case, with its foul revelations and its still fouler concealments, is summed up the whole case against Votes for Women.

The Anti-Suffragist theory of life and of the position of women leads straight to the hideous state of affairs of which the Flat Case is an illustration.

The Anti-Suffragist believes that women are of value only because of their sex functions, which functions he also believes are to be used at the orders and in the service of men. To state the same thing in other words, the Anti-Suffragist man regards women as a subject sex created entirely for sex uses. Incidentally he expects woman to act as unpaid domestic servant; or, if he is rich, to promote his individual interests in society or politics; and he is not unwilling that she shall work in his factory at a starvation wage, unless he can find machinery to do the same work more cheaply.

As he does not hesitate to tell her, the Anti-Suffragist is of opinion that apart from her sex activity the world would get on quite well without her. He does not realise that the same thing might at least as truly be said of men by women.

We repeat that the Anti-Suffragists see in woman, sex and nothing more. Women they hold to be solely and simply females – a sub-human species useful in so far as female, but not otherwise. These females they divide into two classes. Those belonging to the first class are expected to give birth to legitimate children. They are not recognised by the law as 'persons,' and they are not recognised as legal parents of their own children. They are called 'wives.' The second class inhabit Piccadilly Flats and other similar resorts. They are called 'prostitutes.' They are used for the physical satisfaction of men. In a short time they become diseased and ugly and unfit for use, and that is the end of them! Their ranks are constantly recruited as a result of the starvation wages paid for honest work, and by means of fraudulent advertisements, bogus marriages, kidnapping, and other tricks.

In addition to the wives who are neither persons nor parents, and in addition to the prostitutes, there are other women who are described by the Anti-Suffragists as 'superfluous women.' Wives are needed, think the Anti-Suffragists, because some men, at any rate, may decide to have a home and family. Prostitutes are needed because of that exaggerated development of the sex instinct which is supposed to be natural where men are concerned. For the rest of womenkind the Anti-Suffragist sees no use at all. In fact, he has a peculiar fear and horror of them.

The demand for Votes for Women means a revolt against wrongs of many kinds – against social injustice and political mismanagement as they affect both men and women. But more than all it is a revolt against the evil system under which women are regarded as sub-human and as the sex-slaves of men. In short, as we have already stated, the demand for Votes for Women is an attack upon everything that is represented by the Piccadilly Flat Case.

The facts in that case are not rare and exceptional. There are many such flats. There are many such women as those who were its inmates. There are thousands upon thousands of men such as those who frequented it. Numbers of these men are respectable husbands and fathers. They pretend that after visiting such places they are morally and physically fit to return to their homes and to associate with their cleanminded and clean-living wife and daughters.

Let us take the facts as disclosed in the well-nigh secret proceedings at the Clerkenwell Sessions. The girls who were found in the flat were little more than children. If the age of consent were 21 – as it ought to be, seeing that a girl's property is protected till she is 21 – if it were even 18, the very fact of having immoral intercourse with them would have made the men visiting the flat liable to imprisonment. One of the girls is now only 17 years of age, and it is several months since her connection with the flat first began. Another is not much more than 18. Their 'extreme obvious youth,' as it was described in court, was, however, a positive advantage from the point of view of the 'gentlemen' ('gentlemen' was the term employed throughout the case) who were customers at the flat. These British husbands and fathers had, some of them, asked in writing that their victims should be innocent young girls!

All evidence as to how and when these unhappy children were ruined in the first instance was withheld from the court. But the inference is that a male frequenter of the flat was responsible, at any rate in one case.

The newspaper accounts of the matter, scanty as these were, are enough to show that this flat was a veritable den of iniquity, and one of the lawyers admitted as much when he said 'that all sorts of practices were carried on there, and indeed the girls say that they were resorted to, and the instruments that were found were in fact used there.'

The men patrons of the Piccadilly Flat, after their share in degrading young girls, after wading through physical and moral filth, went home, and doubtless forbade any 'meddling with the Suffrage question.' This prohibition, we may be sure, was supplemented by an attack upon the methods of the Suffragettes, and a statement concerning the means that ought to be adopted to suppress these militant women. Heaven help and pity the wife of such a man! She is put in danger of acquiring loathsome disease, and the marriage into which she entered in love and trust is desecrated.

The majority of women do not want the vote, people say. If that be true it is because so many women do not even yet know the facts about their own position. But day by day they are learning the truth, and the number of Suffragists is growing in consequence. The Anti-Suffragist forces have done their best to keep the truth hidden, but now they are, in spite of themselves, helping to make it known. The Piccadilly Flat Case is an instance of this. The conniving of men with men to keep the facts of this case concealed from them – that has been to women a great revelation. Here, they plainly see, is a matter which concerns a great many men, and concerns also some who hold very high positions. Only men of great influence and power would have been successful in getting the assent of the authorities to hush up this case. And even then, unless it had been a whole system, and not an isolated and exceptional matter that was involved, this hushing up could not have been achieved. Everybody knows that important men were supporting the Piccadilly flat. A great many people know *who these men are*.

These are the questions which women are asking: Why were women kept out of the police court when this case was being more fully investigated than it was in the final, hushed-up trial? Why were no men punished, although evidence against them was in the hands of the police? Was this because there is truth in the rumour that a man very prominent in political and social life is implicated? Why was the defendant in this case put in the second division, while Miss Annie Kenney and her fellow-conspirators were put in the third division? Why was she given a sentence of only three months' imprisonment, while Mrs Pankhurst was sent to three years' imprisonment?

The leniency shown to this woman, who has not merely destroyed property, but has trafficked in flesh and blood, is very remarkable when contrasted with the severity shown to Suffragettes. It is easy to see how Queenie Gerald and all others engaged in the same dreadful trade will interpret this leniency. They will believe that men wish them to read into it the following message:

'We must for the sake of appearances send you to prison occasionally. But you shall not stay there very long, and you shall not be too uncomfortable while you are there. This little interlude in the pursuit of your lucrative occupation will not, we hope, deter you, or discourage you and your fellow-traders from carrying on the business in future. We regard you and your trade as necessary institutions, and as a source of great gratification to us.'

The Piccadilly Flat Case shows the enemies of Women's Emancipation hiding, like the ostrich, with their heads in the sand. If this case had been fairly and squarely fought out before the public, women's suspicions would have been less aroused. As it is, they have been put thoroughly on the alert. They are wanting to know how many more of these plague-spots London contains – for plague-spots they are, spiritually and physically.

In these places men's ideas about women become tainted, and there arise diseases which are handed on to healthy and unsuspecting wives and innocent children.

Why should this be, and what is the justification of it? As we have said, women's suspicions are aroused. The venom and obstinacy with which their demand for the vote is being resisted is to them a warning that there is more in this question than even they themselves suspected at the beginning. All over the world it is vice that finds its interest in the subjection of women, and this is so in our own country no less than in every other.

Let all women who want to see humanity no longer degraded by impure thought and physical disease come into the ranks of the Women's Social and Political Union, and help to win the Vote!

The Government and White Slavery

No wonder the Government resist the enfranchisement of women! The reason of their Anti-Suffrage policy is plain. We should as soon expect the White Slave traders to welcome Votes for Women, as we should expect the Government to welcome that reform.

The fact is that the Government are themselves White Slave-mongers and upholders of vice. That is why they dare not meet the judgment of women voters.

That the Government are bad employers and are thus responsible for driving women into slavery, is a notorious fact. Working women have no power to elect Members of Parliament, and so cannot get the protection of an adequate fair wage clause such as working men, through their votes, can obtain. Sweating is, therefore, rampant in connection with the employment of women on Government contracts. But that is not all, and that is not the worst.

The Government are directly responsible for a large measure of White Slavery. They are, in effect, *procurers of women* for the vicious pleasures of men in the Army and Navy.

The state of affairs in India is thus described by the Friends' Association for Abolishing State Regulation of Vice:

'The following system is now in existence practically throughout the Indian cantonments – the permanent military stations:

'1.Certain houses, set aside for immoral purposes, are definitely permitted by the local authorities of the Government of India in the cantonments, with the understanding that the keepers of these houses will abide by the regulations of the Cantonment Code.

'2. When a British soldier is found by the medical officer of the regiment to be suffering from disease caused by vice, he is questioned as to the supposed origin of that disease, and if the woman accused lives in one of these houses she is forthwith surgically examined by the medical officer, and, if found diseased, is turned out of the house, with the choice of either leaving the cantonments or of proceeding to the "voluntary" hospital belonging to the Government. She is not allowed to return to her original residence until discharged from the hospital in a supposedly "fit" state to resume her former occupation.

'Under such regulations the British Government does that which no Government ought to do, gives a vested interest in houses of this kind. The occupation of a keeper of a house of ill-fame, under such circumstances, is absolutely legalised. This tends greatly to the slavery of the women occupying such houses.

'From a purely medical point of view, under such a system, the Government affords a false security, and holds out a wrecker's light to men frequenting such houses. The impossibility of the avoidance of the malady, except by avoidance of its cause, is becoming more and more recognised by experts.'

Many of the White Slaves of these brothels, sanctioned and supervised by the Government, are, it is said, mere children. How are they obtained, and what happens to them when they become hopelessly diseased and thus 'unfit for use' by the officers and soldiers?

The British Committee of the International Federation for the Abolition of the State Regulation of Vice have lately had a correspondence with the India Office, in which they have urged in vain that the present infamous system shall be ended.

The Government's abominable conduct where the womanhood of India is concerned has only to be known to make British women more determined than ever to win the vote. Under the rule of men, Indian women have been and are being enslaved, degraded, destroyed.

These awful wrongs are being visited upon innocent women and children in the mother country. Many soldiers return from India diseased, and they infect their unhappy wife and offspring.

The evil is stated by the Friends' Society for Abolishing State Regulation of Vice in the following terms:

'There are now 70,000 young Englishmen, soldiers, stationed in these cantonments. They are sent out from this country at the rate of 13,000 every year, and after five years of education in the principles of State-sanctioned vice, they are sent back to this country at the same rate, less the number of deaths, and, their time being expired, are scattered all over the towns and villages of the land, there to spread the leaven of this teaching. Further than that, Indian officers who have served on these Cantonment Committees, when they come back to England, in large numbers of cases become members of various public bodies, up to Parliament itself, and so form a leaven in the ruling circles of Society, similar to that set at work by their subordinates amongst the mass of the population.'

If all women realised these facts more plainly there would be no Anti-Suffragists left. We doubt whether there would be left even Anti-Militants!

Let women consider the words of an ex-official who for many years had charge of the Government chaklas or brothels. Said he to Dr Louisa Martindale, author of *Under the Surface:*

'I cannot speak too strongly against them. Many a young boy or man comes out to India pure and good. It is the presence of the Government chaklas that first puts it into his head to lead a vicious life. Many resist for a time, but when they see their friends and their superior officers making use of these, and when they are given to understand that the medical inspection makes it safe for them to go, sooner or later they give way and follow the example of the rest. But to start with – they don't want it.'

Miss Elizabeth Robins in her book, *Where Are you Going to?* makes a charge against the naval authorities to which no answer has been forthcoming. It will be remembered that the sister of little Bettina, who is swept innocent and unsuspecting into the whirlpool of vice, is herself saved by a man who tells her of the real nature of the house into which she and Bettina have been entrapped. In order to enlighten her, he tells her of how the very Government of the country fosters and encourages vice. Into the mouth of this man Miss Robins puts her charge against the naval authorities. First she refers to the case of India. She makes the man say:

'Take India – I've been there. I know an official who had charge of the chaklas. You don't know what chaklas are? Your father knew. If you'd gone riding round the cantonments you'd have seen. Little groups of tents. A hospital not far off. Women in the tents. Out there it's no secret. They're called "Government women." The women are needed by the Army. So there you are.'

Then the indictment runs on:

'Even Governments (he said) had to recognise human nature and shape their policies accordingly. I was too young to remember all that talk in the Press some years ago about the mysterious movements of British battleships in the Mediterranean. Instead of hanging about Malta the ships had gone cruising round the Irish coast. Why? The officials said, "For good and sufficient reasons." The chorus of criticism died down. The "reasons" were known to those who had to know. Not enough women at Malta. The British fleet spent some time about the Irish coasts. "Human nature!" '

So a Government who have nothing but insult, treachery, and torture for women are ready to minister to the vices of men.

The soldiers and sailors may ask for healthier quarters or higher pay, and these things may be denied to them because they cost money; but their vices the Government are quite willing to encourage because they cost nothing more than the slavery, disease, and death of *women*.

For such a condition of affairs the only cure is Votes for Women. When women have political power, equal with that of men, they will not tolerate the exploitation of their sisters in India and elsewhere. Nor will they themselves submit to exploitation. They will secure such economic independence and prosperity as shall save them from the danger of being driven to live by the sale of their sex.

As the natural custodians of the interests of the race, and as the natural lawgivers on matters of morality, they will insist that by men, as well as by women, sex power be regarded as a trust, and be only rightly and reverently used.

Sylvia Pankhurst

The Woman's Dreadnought

Published by the East London Federation of the Suffragettes
(8 March 1914)

Our Paper

The name of our paper, *The Woman's Dreadnought*, is symbolic of
the fact that the women who are fighting for freedom must fear
nothing. It suggests also the policy of social care and reconstruc-
tion, which is the policy of awakening womanhood throughout the
world, as opposed to the cruel, disorganized struggle for existence
amongst individuals and nations from which Humanity has
suffered in the past.

This first advance number of our paper is to be sold at a penny,
but when *The Woman's Dreadnought* begins to be published as a
regular weekly newspaper, on Saturday, April 4th 20,000 copies
will be issued freely each week in East London and as far as
possible, the publishing expenses will be covered by the prices
charged for the advertisements displayed in our columns. It is by
the advertisements that every newspaper is made to pay its way.

The Woman's Dreadnought is published by the East London Federation of the Suffragettes, an organization mainly composed of
working women, and the chief duty of *The Dreadnought* will be to
deal with the franchise question from the working woman's point
of view, and to report the activities of the votes for women movement in East London. Nevertheless, the paper will not fail to
review the whole field of the women's emancipation movement.

The East London Federation of the Suffragettes

Some of our readers may ask, What is the East London Federation
of the Suffragettes? And when and why was it formed?

These are the facts.

In October 1912, Mrs Drummond and I agreed that the work of arousing the working women of East London to fight for their own enfranchisement must be seriously and systematically attacked. Mrs Drummond was not able to give much time to the enterprise, but I went down to the East End daily, and between us we induced some of the West London Local Unions, who have money and leisured members, to help in breaking up the ground. Hence the Kensington W.S.P.U. opened a centre of work in Bethnal Green, the Chelsea W.S.P.U. worked in Stepney and Limehouse: the Paddington W.S.P.U. in Poplar, Lincoln's Inn House paid the rent of a shop in Bow Road, and I collected a body of workers for that district. A big procession and demonstration in Victoria Park was held on November 10th 1912.

Immediately after the demonstration came the Bow and Bromley by-election, caused by the resignation of Mr George Lansbury, the Labour Member of Parliament for the constituency. As all the world knows, Mr Lansbury resigned his seat in order that he might be free to put up an uncompromising fight against the Government on the question of Votes for Women. He felt that as a Member of the Parliamentary Labour Party he was not free to make that fight, and he therefore wished to represent the constituency as an Independent Member or not at all.

The Election Campaign, into which the W.S.P.U. threw itself vigorously, and in which every other Suffrage Society joined, made Bow and Bromley people think a good deal about Votes for Women, but Mr Lansbury was not returned.

Soon after the by-election and originally at my suggestion, preparations began to be made for the Working Women's Deputation to Mr Lloyd George. Though volunteers for the Deputation were invited from all over the country, by far the largest number came from East London, and the various East London districts were the most systematically worked.

Of the thousands who had volunteered for the Deputation, only twelve were finally chosen to go to Downing Street. These included a Poplar laundress, a home-worker who made pinafores at sweated rates in Bow, a waste rubber worker from Poplar, and the wife of a labourer earning 22s. a week, who had eight children and lived in a wretched two roomed tenement in Bethnal Green, for which she paid 5s. a week in rent.

On the eve of the discussion of the Suffrage Amendments, the Deputation of Working Women waited on Mr Lloyd George and Sir Edward Grey. Mr Lloyd George assured the women that the prospect of the Votes for Women admendments being carried was so good as almost to amount to a certainty. Sir Edward Grey spoke to the same effect: but that very night, whilst the women were assembled in various public halls, and fifty of them by special permission, were gathered together in the Grand Committee Room of the House of Commons, the Speaker let fall his bombshell. He announced that if any of the Women's amendments were carried, the whole Reform Bill would be out of order.

The House adjourned and Mr Asquith took time to consider the situation. On the following Monday he announced that the Reform Bill would be withdrawn, and that though the Liberal Government still intended to introduce Manhood Suffrage later on, women must rely on the efforts of Private Members to secure their Enfranchisement. Mr Asquith also withdrew his oft-repeated promise that the Government would make itself responsible for any Private Member's Bill to give Votes to Women after it had passed its second reading unaided.

When the Working Women's Deputation was over, most of the West London workers left the East End, and all financial aid from the W.S.P.U. headquarters was finally withdrawn.

I was determined that the East End work must go on. Lady Sybil Smith and I had collected some money for big popular open-air meetings during the summer and autumn, and as that money was not all spent, we had used it to further the East End campaign. A few pounds still remained and with them as a nucleus I decided to take the risk of opening a permanent East End headquarters in Bow.

Miss Emerson and I went down there together one frosty Friday morning in February to hunt for an office. The sun was like a red ball in the misty, whitey-grey sky. Market stalls, covered with cheerful pink and yellow rhubarb, cabbages, oranges and all sorts of other interesting things, lined both sides of the narrow Roman Road. The Roman, as they call it, was crowded with busy, kindly people. I had always liked Bow. That morning my heart warmed to it for ever. We decided to take a shop and house at 321, Roman Road, at a weekly rental of 14s. 6d. a week. It was the only shop to let in the road. The shop window was broken right across, and was only held together by putty. The landlord would not put in new glass, nor would he repair the many holes in the shop and passage flooring because he thought we should only stay a short time. But all such things have since been done.

Plenty of friends at once rallied round us. Women who had joined the Union in the last few weeks came in and scrubbed the floors and cleaned the windows. Mrs Wise, who kept the sweet shop next door, lent us a trestle table for a counter and helped us to put up purple, white and green flags. Her little boy took down the shutters for us every morning, and put them up each night, and her little girls often came in to sweep. A week after the shop was opened Miss Emerson and I were arrested. We went to prison on Friday night, February 14th, and our fines were paid on Saturday at noon. We had been hunger-striking, and as soon as we had broken our fast we went back to Bow. We found Mrs Lake scrubbing the table, and as many other members as the shop would hold talking about us, and wondering how we were getting on.

On the following Monday, February 17th we held a Meeting at the Obelink, and after it was over Mrs Watkins, Mrs Moor, Miss Annie Lansbury, and I broke an undertaker's window. Mr Will Lansbury broke a window in the Bromley Public Hall, and Miss Emerson broke a Liberal Club window. We were all six arrested, and sent to prison without the option of a fine.

That was the beginning of Militancy in East London. Miss Emerson, Mrs Watkins and I decided to do the hunger-strike, and hoped that we should soon be out to work again. But though Mrs Watkins was released after ten days, Miss Emerson and I were forcibly fed, and she was kept in for seven weeks, although she had developed appendicitis, and I for five. When we were once free we found that we were too ill to do anything at all for some weeks.

But we need not have feared that the work would slacken without us. A tremendous flame of enthusiasm had burst forth in the East End. Great meetings were held, and during our imprisonment long processions marched eight times the six miles to cheer us in Holloway, and several times also to Brixton gaol, where Mr Will Lansbury was imprisoned. The people of East London, with Miss Dalglish to help them, certainly kept the purple, white and green flag flying.

Early in April the anti-Suffragist Government entered on a strenuous campaign of Suffragette persecution. Mrs Pankhurst was sentenced to three years' penal servitude on April 2nd. Miss Annie Kenney was summoned under a musty old Statute of Edward III, which was directed by that monarch and his Parliament against 'pillers and robbers form beyond the sea,' and was now raked up by the Liberal Government to prevent her speaking at the Albert Hall Meeting on April 10th. Mrs Drummond and Mr George Lansbury, who spoke at that Meeting, were summoned because of their speeches under the same old Act. Miss Kenney and Mrs Drummond were afterwards charged with conspiracy, but Mr Lansbury was ordered to either bind himself over in heavy sums of money to make no more such speeches, or to go to prison for three months. He appealed against the magistrates' decision. Meanwhile the Government had not only tried to prohibit the printing of *The Suffragette* newspaper, but had prohibited the W.S.P.U. meetings in Hyde Park. The police kept the Suffragette platforms out of the Park, but they could not prevent the women speaking. Nevertheless, anti-Suffragist hooligans and police together might have given the speakers a bad time but for the help of the East London dockers, who fought to protect the women. Sunday after Sunday.

On Sunday, May 25th, 1913 was held 'Women's May Day' in East London. The Members in Bow, Bromley, Poplar, and neighbouring districts had prepared for it for many weeks past and had made hundreds of almond branches, which were carried in a great procession with purple, white and green flags, and caps of Liberty flaunting above them from the East India Dock gates by winding ways, to Victoria Park. A vast crowd of people – the biggest ever seen in East London – assembled in the Hyde Park of East London to hear the speakers from twenty platforms.

A few days later the East London Federation of the Suffragettes, or East London Federation of the W.S.P.U. as it was then called was formerly set up to unite for greater strength the local Unions that had been formed in Bow, Bromley, Poplar, Stepney and Hackney, Canning Town has since been added to the number. The Federation Council consists of the Hon. Secretary, the Hon. Treasurer, the Hon. Financial and Hon. Meetings Secretaries, the Hon. Advertisement Manager, the District Secretaries and Organisers, and two elected representatives of the Members in each district.

On Sunday, June 29th 1913 the East London Federation organised a big procession to Trafalgar Square, in which Suffrage Societies and Trades' Unions and Labour organisations joined. There was an immense crowd in the Square. But of what use was one more big Meeting where so many had been held? The 'Cat-and-Mouse' Act had just been passed and under it Mrs Pankhurst and a number of other hunger-strikers were being ruthlessly dragged back and back to prison. Their lives were at stake. Emily Wilding Davison, feeling their peril, had given her own life to make the nation think. On June 4th she had flung herself into the midst of the Derby racehorses and had been killed. In face of such happenings what was the use of talking? The need was for an emphatic public protest. I asked the people to go and hoot the Cabinet Ministers and if they were able to do more than hoot – to imprison the Cabinet Ministers in their official residences as they had imprisoned more than 2,000 women Suffragists until the Ministers would agree to give Women the Vote.

I had hardly finished speaking when the people were streaming off down Whitehall and soon they were hooting and shouting 'Votes for Women' outside Mr Asquith's house. Police reinforcements were immediately hurried across from Scotland Yard to force the people away and a sharp struggle took place in which five men were arrested.

The following Thursday, July 3rd I too was summoned under the antique Statue of Edward III to appear at Bow Street on July 5th. I did not consider it my duty to obey, and instead I went away for the weekend and then made my way to the Bromley Public Hall in Bow Road, where I had promised to speak. After the Meeting the people rallied unanimously, and fought to protect me from the detectives, who had come with a warrant for my arrest. Eventually I was taken prisoner with five others. One of these was Miss Mary Richardson who on July 4th had been struck with the flat of his sword by one of the King's equerries when she was trying to present a Petition to the King.

After remaining the night at Bow Street. I was sentenced next morning to three months imprisonment, because I would not promise not to make militant speeches. On reaching prison I started the hunger-and-thirst strike.

On being released the following Sunday I was received as a guest by Mr and Mrs Payne at 28, Ford Road, Bow. Letters of sympathy, flowers and presents of all kinds were showered on me by kindly neighbours. One woman wrote to say that she did not see why I should ever go back to prison when every woman could buy a rolling-pin for a penny.

I had tremendous welcomes, both in Bow and Poplar, when I spoke during my week's licence. On the Monday after the licence expired I got to the Bromley Public Hall Meeting in disguise, and so splendidly did the good people fight with me to forward Votes for Women, and smash the 'Cat-and-Mouse' Act that detectives and policemen were held at bay and I was rushed away into safety by the crowd.

On Sunday, July 27th the East London Federation organised another great March to Trafalgar Square. The Square was densely packed with people. It was said that no meeting so large had been held there since the eighties.

In spite of a veritable host of policemen and detectives, I was able to get there in disguise and just at the moment when the principal superintendent of police was asking if I had arrived and his lieutenants were replying in the negative I was taking my seat on the back of one of Landseer's lions. When I came undisguised from a sheltering group of friends, the people greeted me with cheers and eagerly agreed to go to Downing Street to carry our Women's Declaration of Independence to the Prime Minister's official residence.

I sprang from the plinth. Friends down below caught me and closed around me, forcing the police away All the vast gathering swarmed behind.

At the top of Whitehall policemen on horseback met us. We rushed between them and pressed on.

A taxi-cab was standing in the middle of the road. The people opened the door and asked me to ride away thinking that thus I might elude the police. I said 'No. I am going with you to Downing Street.' The cab door was shut. We pressed on nearly to Downing Street but reinforcements from Scotland Yard – a great company – came upon us. I was dragged away by detectives, dragged off to Holloway. The crowd was beaten back and twenty-seven people were arrested.

Next day Mr Lansbury's appeal against the sentence imposed upon him under the Act of Edward III was decided against him and he was ordered to surrender to his bail on Wednesday, July 30th, two days later. He went up from Bow to Bow Street with a host of friends and was carried off to gaol but on adopting the hunger strike he was released on a 'Cat-and-Mouse' licence the next Saturday and has not yet been taken back. Feeling was running very high at the time in East London and vast meetings and processions were organized in Mr Lansbury's honour as well as to forward Votes for Women and break down the 'Cat-and-Mouse' Act.

On August 10th the Free Speech Defence Committee, a composite body on which sit many Radical and Labour Members of Parliament and Labour leaders, announced a demonstration in Trafalgar Square to protest against the Government's many attempts to suppress the rights of free speech and public meeting and especially against the prosecution of speakers under the Act of Edward III. I was asked to speak with Mr Lansbury and Mr Scurr and Mrs Cohen (who had also been summoned under the Act, though never sent to prison) on condition that I would pledge myself not to go to Downing Street. I replied that I could not agree to this condition and issued a leaflet 'To Lovers of Freedom' saying that after the Free Speech people had done their talking. I should be present in the Square to go with those who cared to come to Downing Street. This I did, and the vast majority of those present went with me as far as we could go. When we were beaten back by the mounted police, eighteen people besides myself were arrested and the windows of a motor bus were broken.

These demonstrations of Militant popular support were a fine answer to those who were saying that public opinion was against the women in their fight for liberty.

On August 15th Parliament was prorogued and there came a season of quiet propaganda work and holidays, but at the end of October we learnt with horror that Mary Richardson and Rachel Peace were being forcibly fed in prison.

On October 13th the East London Federation held a packed Meeting in Bow Baths. I got there in disguise. The people held the front door against the police and detectives, but I had not been speaking ten minutes when policemen sprang on to the platform from behind the curtains with truncheons drawn. The people shouted 'Jump, Sylvia, jump!' I jumped as they told me, from the platform into the audience and turned for a moment half dazed with the shock to see policemen with truncheons and those we believe were detectives with loaded sticks, striking the people who were crowded on to the platform and smashing the chairs. Mrs Mary Leigh was knocked insensible, Mrs Ives was held up by the collar and struck with a truncheon so that her arm was broken. Miss Forbes Robertson, sister of the great actor, also had her arm broken and many unknown men and women were seriously hurt. The people in the gallery retaliated by throwing chairs down on to the police. People in the audience then stole up behind me, put somebody's hat and coat on me and led me out that I might speak in Poplar Town Hall next night.

As Miss Emerson was leaving the hall a man we believe was a detective who was annoyed because the people called 'Puss! Puss!' to him, struck her on the side of the head with a lead-weighted instrument. Mr Mansell-Moulhn the noted surgeon stated on examining her that Miss Emerson's skull was fractured and that if the blow had been struck an eighth of an inch further back she would certainly have been killed.

Next night I was recognised by the detectives who crowded the steps of the Poplar Town Hall and a couple of hundred policemen had closed round me before the people could get to me. A man and his wife who rushed towards me were arrested.

I was released after nine days. Though obliged to be carried to speak at Bow Baths and Poplar Town Hall on a stretcher during my week's licence. I was able to be up and doing at the end of the week. A few days after the expiration of my licence I spoke at the Royal Albert Hall and the Hackney Baths and was so well protected by the people that I was able to get away in safety.

On November 5th 1913 a Meeting was held to inaugurate the People's Army which is an organisation that men and women may join to fight for freedom and in order that they may learn to cope with the repressive methods of the Government servants.

On my way to this Meeting I happened to call at Mr Lansbury's house in St Stephen's Road. The house was immediately surrounded by detectives and policemen and there seemed no possibility of escape. But the people of 'Bow' on hearing of the trouble, came flocking out of the Baths where they had assembled. In the confusion that ensued the detectives dragged Miss Daisy Lansbury off in a taxi, and I went free.

When the police authorities realised their mistake, and learnt that I was actually speaking in the Baths, they sent hundreds of men to take me, but though they met the people in the Roman Road as they came from the Meeting I escaped. Miss Emerson was again struck on the head, this time by a uniformed constable, and fell to the ground unconscious. Many other people were badly hurt. The people replied with spirit. Two mounted policemen were unhorsed and many others were disabled.

Twice shortly afterwards I spoke in Canning Town Public Hall and each time went free, the police, though present in large numbers to take me, preferring not to attack. One Sunday afternoon I spoke in Bow Palace and marched openly with the people to Ford Road. When I spoke from the window afterwards a veritable forest of sticks was waved by the crowd. The police had evidently guessed that we were armed, and so treated us with respect.

At last the police won the day. It was at my eighth Meeting, which was held at Shoreditch Town Hall, a district in which the East London Federation had never held a meeting and in which even for this Meeting but little advertising had been done. We had grown over-confident.

As a result of the police raid on Bow Baths on October 13th and the police treatment of the people on Nov. 5th the Poplar Borough Council unjustly refused to let for Suffragette meetings Bow Baths; the Bromley Public Hall and the Poplar Town Hall – the only large public halls in the Poplar Borough.

Whilst I was in prison after my arrest at Shoreditch, a Meeting of Protest against the refusal of the public halls to the Suffragettes was held in Bow Palace on Sunday afternoon, December 14th. After the Meeting it was arranged to go in procession around the district and to hoot outside the houses of hostile Borough Councillors. When the processionists turned out of Bow Rd. into Tomlin's Grove they found that the street lamps were not lighted and that a strong force of police were waiting in the dark before the house of Councillor Le Manquais. Just as the people at the head of the procession reached the house, the policemen closed around them and arrested Miss Emerson, Miss Godfrey and seven men, two of whom were not in the procession, but were going home to tea in the opposite direction. At the same moment twenty mounted police came riding down upon the people from the far end of Tomlin's Grove, and twenty more from the Bow Road. The people were all unarmed. They had no 'mouse' to save, and had expected no trouble. There were cries and shrieks and people rushed panic-stricken into the little front gardens of the houses in the Grove. But wherever the people stopped the police hunted them away. I was told that an old woman who saw the police beating the people in her garden was so much upset that she fell down in a fit and died without regaining consciousness. A boy of 18 was so brutally kicked and trampled on that he had to be carried to the infirmary for treatment. A publican who was passing was knocked down and kicked and one of his ribs was broken. Even the bandsmen were not spared. The police threw their instruments over the garden walls. The big drummer was knocked down and so badly used that he is still on the list for sick insurance benefit. Mr Atkinson, a labourer, was severely handled and was then arrested. In the charge room Inspector Potter was said to have blacked his eye. Mr Atkinson afterwards brought an action for assault against the inspector but though Potter was committed for trial he was not convicted.

Such happenings show the need that the People's Army should be efficiently drilled and trained. Above all they prove that a voice in controlling the Government should be open to every man and woman and vigilantly used by every one.

Since the New Year opened the people of Canning Town have again made it possible for me both to speak and to come safely away from their Town Hall although wanted by the police.

I have also been able to take part in the Poplar by-election. I lived for the time at our Committee rooms, where we held two Women's Meetings every afternoon, having to turn the audience out at half-time to make room for more people. We also spoke to enthusiastic gatherings from the window every night.

On the eve of the poll we organised a great Votes for Women Procession in which the other Suffrage Societies took part down the dingy East India Dock Road. I marched in the Procession and spoke afterwards to a vast Open Air Meeting at the Dock gates. It was evident that most of the people there were prepared to act the part of bodyguard if necessary. There were many detectives watching by the road, but no more than half a dozen constables were to be seen. It had been widely advertised that I was to be there.

Why was no attempt made to arrest me? Why did not the detectives and policemen come cutting their way through the people with loaded sticks and truncheons. Why? Perhaps because this was the eve of the poll in Poplar, and it is better not to break the electors' heads the night before they vote.

The detectives were heard to say: 'We did not get her this time. There were too many people. There has been too much fighting in the East End.'

What clearer proof of the unpopularity of the 'Cat-and-Mouse' Act can be needed than the fact that the Government fears to enforce it in sight of electors on the eve of polling day?

Early in 1914 the east London Federation of the W.S.P.U. changed its name and became the East London Federation of the Suffragettes. We made this change at the request of others. Our policy remains what it has always been. We are still a Militant non-party organisation of working-women.

Some people tell us that it is neither specially important that working-women should agitate for the Vote, nor specially important that they should have it. They forget that comparatively the leisured comfortably situated women are but a little group, and the working-women a multitude.

Some people say that the lives of working-women are too hard and their education too small for them to become a powerful force in winning the Vote, many though they are. Such people have forgotten their history. What sort of women were those women who marched to Versailles?

Those Suffragists who say that it is the duty of the richer and more fortunate women to win the Vote, and that their poorer sisters need not feel themselves called upon to aid in the struggle, appear in using such arguments to forget that it is *the Vote* for which we are fighting. The essential principle of the vote is that each one of us shall have a share of power to help himself or herself and us all. It is in direct opposition to the idea that some few, who are more favoured, shall help and teach and patronise the others. It is surely because we Suffragists believe in the principle that every individual and every class of individuals has a right to a share both in ruling and in serving and because we have learnt by long and bitter experience that every form of government but self-government is tyranny – however kindly its intention – that we are fighting for the Vote and not for the remedying of some of the many particular grievances from which women suffer.

It is necessary for women to fight for the Vote because by means of the Vote, if we combine in sufficient numbers to use it for definite ends, we can win reforms for ourselves by making it plain to Governments that they must either give us the things we want or make way for those that will. Working-women – sweated women, wage slaves, overworked mothers toiling in little homes – these of all created beings, stand in the greatest need of this, the power to help themselves.

One of the principal reasons why it is essential that working-women should rise up in a body and work strenuously for the vote is that when the Franchise Question at last comes up for actual settlement the anti-Suffragists in Parliament will struggle to reduce the number of women voters as far as possible. Any restrictions that they may seek to impose are practically certain to operate most hardly against the poorest women, and the only thing that can safeguard their position is a big and active working-women's Franchise Agitation.

The Reformers of old *worked* to extend the boundaries of human freedom, because they believed the principle to be right, but they *fought and suffered and strove with desperate courage*, because they were spurred on by the knowledge that they or their fellows were suffering and in need. So is it to-day with those who want the Vote.

We have a tremendous task before us. We are only fighting with the courage with which men fight the Government, and men in the mass will only see the suffering and the fighting of the men. Only when we bear infinitely more than men and struggle infinitely harder, will men care enough or understand enough to help women to be politically free. So we must go on striving and try always to see the greatness of our aim.

How Shall We Get the Vote?

(*WD*, 21 March 1914)

Votes ought to have been granted to women at least a generation ago. The reform is long overdue. In 1870, Jacob Bright's Women's Enfranchment Bill passed its Second Reading by a majority of thirty-three votes but the then Liberal Government sent an urgent whip to their followers to defeat the Bill in the Committee stage.

Ever since then Votes for Women have been held back, by a handful of men at the head of either the Liberal or Conservative Party – whichever happened to be in power at the time. Why have the party leaders blocked the way to Votes for Women? Partly because every British Government has hitherto made it a rule to *talk* as much as possible and to *do* as little as it can, but chiefly because the leaders of each Party have always feared that the woman's vote might not be beneficial to their own Party game. The Liberals have said: 'The women will vote Tory'. But if the Conservatives had thought that they would certainly have made voters of the women long ago.

But whatever they may say in excuse the deep root reason why the politicians have stubbornly set themselves against women's suffrage is that they know that the coming women voters will insist upon wide spread social reform.

The Party politicians are afraid of women.

As a matter of fact in those states and countries where women vote, they have been less influenced than men on the lines of the bad old Party system, and have concentrated their attention very largely on securing improved social conditions and better laws for women and children and especially for widows and orphans, who stand in greatest need of adequate protection by the State.

But how are we to get votes for women? We have waited fifty years, we will not wait a hundred. How are we to force that stubborn handful of men in the Cabinet to give way? One of the things most necessary to success in this as in every other cause, is a big determined popular movement. It is not merely a movement capable of holding big meetings that is wanted. Big meetings have been held for years without moving the Government by a hair's breadth. A movement is needed with a spirit of enterprise and fight.

It must be a movement of large masses of the common people wherein each one will do what she or he can to protest against the present exclusion of women from any part or lot in the Government of the country and the making of the conditions under which they live.

In protesting against the outlawry of women all must do as much as their own conscience tell them that they can do.

To hoot a Cabinet Minister and smash up his meeting for him even if one cannot find it in one's heart or courage to stone him; to fight to shield a prisoner under the cruel Cat and Mouse Act, even if at last she should be taken; to join a raid on Downing Street though the attempt should fail; all these things in their own way will help the cause because they show popular discontent.

In these things the people of East London have led the way and pointed it out to people of other parts. We must do more of these things, for Cabinet Ministers hate them and who can say when the last straw will come and they give in.

The Trafalgar Square Protest on March 8th was a good beginning for the season. We must keep it up. We must show that time cannot wear away our zeal and our determination and we must become stronger and more determined until we are able to make the Government afraid. We must each one of us strive and strive and do our individual part to make our movement grow.

Here in East London each one of us must grow more and more impatient. Indeed there is most grievous need for change. Nowhere else are women so horribly sweated as amongst us and the underpayment of women's labour lowers the status of all.

To Quicken the Pace

What can we do to quicken the pace? We can make ourselves more formidable. What do the workers do when they want their wages raised? Do they merely talk amongst themselves or hold meetings? Do they merely send petitions to their employers? No. They go on strike. We can do that too. And we can strike against whatever thing we please. We might decide to strike against paying our taxes but here in London where we are mostly poor, but few of us pay direct taxes, and so for us that kind of strike will not do. We might as women decide to strike against doing our daily work in the home – how often that has been suggested – but that would injure the children and that too will not do. Moreover the Government would not care for that kind of strike in the East End, for it would only make poor homes more uncomfortable and every Government that ever has been in this country hitherto has been most bent on safeguarding not the homes of the poor but the interests of the rich.

Therefore, our strike for the vote must be directed against something which will embarrass the rich of whom the Governments in both Houses and of both Parties are so largely compounded and from whom they draw their immense Party funds.

The only thing against which the mass of women can strike effectively is the payment of their rent. The 'No Vote, no Rent' strike is the working woman's most powerful weapon. In using this weapon she needs, if she is married, her husband's co-operation. This co-operation should surely be given gladly for the mass of women, whether wage earners themselves or not, are always ready to back up the strike of men. The women in the jam, biscuit tin and other East London factories came out in a body to help the transport workers when they were on strike a while ago. The Dublin women came out from Jacob's factory to help the Irish transport workers and in every strike that ever was the mothers who usually stop at home have been ready to go out charing or washing or to take in homework to make ends meet.

Surely every right thinking man wants his wife, his mother and his sisters to have a vote and will be willing to back them up when the women go on strike.

When Will 'No Vote, No Rent' Begin?

What will be the best time to begin the 'No Vote, No Rent', strike? If as it is rumoured there is to be a general election in May or June it will be best to start as soon as the election is over in order that the new Government that will be formed may at once be faced with the 'No Vote, No Rent' deadlock and will realize that the wisest course is to put votes for women in the King's Speech right away. It is quite certain that with a strong 'No Vote, No Rent' strike in progress no anti-suffrage Prime Minister will be allowed to take office. Mr Asquith will either have to get converted or be thrown overboard and the Government will speedily seek to quell the trouble by introducing a Votes for Women Bill.

If the Government intends to hang on until 1915, however, we must strive to wrench Votes for Women from them this very year. In that case the strike ought to begin as soon as we are ready. In any case we must be prepared for the right moment when it comes. We do not mean to begin to strike until we have a nucleus of several thousand people pledged to join us. A thousand families in Leeds have struck because their rents were raised. No one has yet been evicted and the strike has continued since January. When the 'No Vote, No Rent' strike begins we must have not one thousand persons in scattered districts as they are in Leeds, but several thousands living not far apart. Then we shall be very safe against eviction. At the same time we shall collect a good bank balance in case of any instances of individual victimisation just as, since last autumn, we have taken the precaution of establishing a prisoners' families and fund for the dependents of those who may be arrested in fighting for the cause.

We pledge ourselves that we will not start the strike until a large number of strikers are ready. It is time that we began to take the names of those who will join the 'No Vote, No Rent' strike. On the day that it is announced those who will join should fill in this form and bring or send it to the Central Office of the East London Federation of the Suffragettes, at 321 Roman Road, Bow. The names and addresses will be kept absolutely secret.

It is when the spirit of affectionate comradeship and sympathetic tolerance dies out of any organisation that it becomes arid and stereotyped and that its usefulness ceases to extend. But those of us who can learn the lesson will find that in practising it for our cause, we have also made better and happier human beings of ourselves.

On Wednesday night, March 11th I was in my cell weary and despondent wondering, wondering, wondering what we should do next to get the vote. Wondering and wondering how to increase the power and numbers of our own Federation of the Suffragettes and the general popular movement for the vote amongst both men and women in East London. Wondering, hoping and perhaps a little doubting and fearing too. Suddenly, I heard a band playing and knew that friends from East London were close by. I heard your voices and knew that your message was 'no surrender, pull together, we shall win'.

And the moral is that we must never cease to work and strive together, and that we must believe, believe with every fibre of our being, that victory is near. So we shall win!

To the Abbey

This Sunday, March 22nd we intend to march together to the Evening Service at Westminster Abbey to pray for Votes for Women and the Saving of the Hunger Strikers. I have written to the Dean of Westminster to tell him that we are coming, and to ask him to adapt the service to the occasion.

The Procession will form up at 18 Ford Road, Bow at 3.45p.m. and start at 4.15. I shall be with you in the Procession though I cannot possibly be strong enough to walk by then. This day is especially appropriate for our purpose as it is 'Mothering Sunday'. The old custom of visiting one's mother and making her a present on this Sunday is now being revived by people of all sorts and conditions. It is therefore well that we should choose this day for offering up our prayers, that the mothers of the nation should have an equal share with the fathers in the dignity and responsibility of Law making and of caring for the nation's children.

Let us assemble in large numbers to pray to God for our great Cause, and to show the religious people of power and influence in Westminster how earnest is our desire and determination to win Votes for Women this year.

The Hunger and Thirst Strike and its Effects

(*WD*, 11 April 1914)

Increasingly wearing and painful grows the Hunger and Thirst Strike with every 'Cat and Mouse' repetition.

One is generally more or less bruised and knocked about in being re-arrested, and the strong force of the police having compelled one back to prison, one finds oneself in the cell again, feeling weak and cold and sick the first night.

One may do what one can to protest; one may refuse to lie on the bed and determine to walk up and down all the night; but faintness overpowers one, and every now and then one falls or stumbles involuntarily to one's knees with blackness and pain and rushing noises. Stealthy drowsiness creeps over one as the first acuteness of the faint passes, and one dozes a few moments, to wake cramped and stiff, and drag oneself to one's feet.

But if, finding protest useless, one lies down on the bed, one cannot sleep; it is so cold. If one takes the hot water bottle that the wardress probably offers, it seems only to burn, not warm, one place and leaves that place cold as before when it is moved. There are pains in the back and limbs, and the head aches.

At half past five in the morning, when the wardress opens the cell door to see that all is well before she goes off duty, one is still awake, but after that one falls into a hazy half sleeping, half waking state which lasts, perhaps, for an hour or two, perhaps for the greater part of the day, in spite of the passing in and out of wardresses and cleaners, and the visits of the doctor, governor and matron.

If one remains quiescent, the time passes mostly between this dull drowsiness of the day, which is dispelled by periodical attacks of acuter pain and the restless wakefulness and more frequent pain of the night. Perhaps one seems a little better the second day and night, but gradually the feeling of weakness and illness grows. One's mouth and throat are terribly parched. One's tongue is dry, hot and rough, and thickly coated. The saliva becomes more and more thick and yellow and a bitter tasting phlegm keeps coming up into one's mouth. It is so nasty that it makes one retch violently, as though one were going to be sick, but sick one cannot be.

The urine is each day more scanty. It is thick and dark, and passed with difficulty. The bowels do not move during the whole time one is in prison.

There is great pain in the small of the back, pain in the chest, and a sharp stinging liver pain in the right breast. Griping pains come suddenly in the stomach and abdomen.

One sees each day that one has grown thinner, that the bones are showing out more and more clearly, and that the eyes are grown more hollow.

The circulatory system is out of order. The skin looks goose-fleshy and shrivelled. The hands and feet are dull purple with bright red splashes.

If one leaves one's bed one grows faint and giddy, and as the days pass there comes at last a constant singing in the ears when one is lying flat, which changes if one stands up, to a deafening roaring noise and pressure in the head and in the ears as one breathes. As one holds one's breath one seems to hear the pulses in the head throb with the beating of the heart.

The pulse becomes quick and irregular. One has palpitations and pain in the region of the heart. If one refuses to lie and take things quietly, all these symptoms are aggravated and the imprisonment becomes a nightmare like torture of pain and misery, the actual danger to life being greatly increased.

Some hunger and thirst strikers develop nervous diseases, such as Chorea or St Vitus' Dance. The nervous system of all must necessarily undergo a severe strain.

When one is told that the order for release on a week's licence has come, one is asked to take some nourishment before leaving the prison. The officials frequently offer all sorts of things to eat, but, if one is wise, one drinks first some hot water and afterwards a small quantity of hot water and milk in equal proportions.

As soon as one has begun to drink the hot water, one's face and hands and arms become hot and fiery red. One forgets one's weakness in the excitement of being free to leave the barred window and the iron door and those four small walls of whitened brick, to go home to friends and work again.

That first night out of prison, sleeping draughts prove useless. All the pulses throb, one is hot or cold. Eager thoughts, plans for work, hopes, fears and worries crowd into one's brain. Pains now with everything at hand to ease them, seem more acute than when one was in gaol.

Next day one feels as though one had been under a steam roller. Too weak to sit up without someone to help one, and wanting to lie all the time quite flat. It will probably be a week before one can stand without feeling faint.

It is long before the digestive functions are again in working order. For at least a week, frequently for much longer, it is impossible to obtain a natural motion of the bowels. Acute flatulence persists indefinitely and headaches come almost daily for some. Pimples on the face and body are frequent, and small pimples frequently cover the scalp. Dry eczema-like patches often appear on the skin. For many days after release one's hands and wrists are often swollen and burning like a chilblain, except when they are cold. For a few days the extremities remain very red, then grow to look bloodless and waxlike. Heart and nervous symptoms frequently persist for some considerable time. Even after apparent recovery a number of illnesses may develop months after her Thirst and Hunger Strike. Miss Gladys Evans who had been imprisoned in Mountjoy Prison in Ireland, was found to be suffering from a serious Kidney trouble, which her medical adviser stated to be the result of the Thirst Strike. Appendicitis is constantly looked for by the hunger strikers' doctors.

All this because the Government does not wish to give women the vote!

What Happened on May 24th

(WD 6 June 1914

After the detectives had thrown me violently on to the floor of the cab, they were at first very angry. One of them twisted my arms and bent back my wrists to hurt me, but when I called out to tell the people that they were hurting me they stopped. Four of the big men crowded into the cab and sat on the seats with me all twisted up on the floor amongst their feet. They held me down for a while and then said I could sit on the seat. All the way to Holloway they clutched my wrists tight and pressed their knees against mine to stop me moving an inch.

At first they used very ugly language both towards me personally and towards you. They sneered at you and said you were all afraid of them. I said that they had had to come dressed as costers in order to get into the crowd unnoticed. They said they would not come in decent clothes to such a verminous place as Bow – they used very, very objectionable words. They said that you were roughs and anarchists, and that I was an anarchist and ought to have known better than have come down to the East End to play on your 'evil passions'. I said that you would all of you be ashamed to do their horrible work and I told them I knew that they had been to all the houses in Ford Road trying to get someone to take them in to lodge there, so that they could watch me and that at every house they had been refused, although they had offered a 'small-fortune' and many of the people were poor enough to need money very badly.

One of the detectives seemed ashamed at their attempts at bribery and said: 'It's all in the game'. Another sneered and said that he wouldn't stay in the dirty houses in Ford Road.

I said that in that case it was a shame that you, the people, should have to live there, and that it was all the more reason women should get the vote soon to help to make things better. 'You'll never get the vote' they jeered, but one of them whom I had heard say something nice about our East London women before said: 'Oh yes, they'll get it'. When we got to Holloway and two of the others got out of the cab, the same man said: 'The best part about it all is that the people down there think so much of you and are prepared to fight for you and to make sacrifices for you.'

I said: 'They do it for the cause, but perhaps now you understand them, you will try to treat them better all round.' He answered: 'Oh, I never had anything against them.' Then he said: 'I am trying to get a vote myself and I am sure I shall think more about it because of all this, than I should have done.'

I asked: 'Why haven't you had a vote before,' he said: 'Because my parents were poor and when I first came to London I was living in a section house.' I supposed that a 'section house' is a sort of barracks where the police live, but I did not ask.

Presently one of the other detectives, who was standing waiting by the cab, offered me a copy of the *Suffragette*. He said: 'You see we read it.'

Before that they had asked me about the WOMAN'S DREADNOUGHT and how I found time for it.

One thing that the detectives said was important. They admitted that at the Poplar Election and on some other occasions they had come up to take me, but had not done so because there were too many friends prepared to fight around me.

On Sunday, May 24th I and I think most of us thought, though why I cannot explain to myself, that the detectives were not coming and that I was not wanted any more. So our fighters were walking each with their own sections, or were attending to the cart of little children, the may poles the banners, the papers, or some other thing. We were none of us on the alert for an attack and the detectives were clever enough to know it. They were clever too in keeping away out of sight and allowing only a few uniformed police to be in evidence until the moment when we reached the Park gates, which were suddenly shut in our faces and the mounted police turned upon us.

Next time we must put some friends who understand horses in the front row.

In Prison

When I got to my cell I felt bruised and worn out, as one usually does.

Next morning I heard some of the new wardresses being drilled under my window. There is a great contrast between those who have just come and those who are fully trained and I think the regular drilling must very largely account for the change. They become so much more upright and firm looking and their shape and carriage improve tremendously.

Their drill is not like that of soldiers, for they have exercises to develop every part of the body. The same is true of the police.

Only one of the exercises that I saw the wardresses do suggested fighting, and when they were doing this I heard their instructor say: 'Do it as though you were hitting someone's face', she added as she counted up to eight, 'the person's supposed to be dead by that time.'

How terrifying it must be for poor cowed women spending their first days in prison to hear such a joke!

Of course the days dragged very wearily as they always do, but on Tuesday night I heard the drum and fife band and knew that friends from East London had come to say 'no surrender'. I remembered that they had walked six long miles to get there after a hard working day.

A Minimum Wage
for Women

(*WD*, 12 September 1914)

Many people are saying that on the other side of this war we shall come into a new regenerate world; an international commonwealth of happiness and well-being in which the squalor and misery of to-day will be unknown.

How precious and long desired is that vision, how white are its dear feet upon the mountains of imagination! With fancy's flowers we embroider its glades, and its skies fill with sun and song. Its children are lovelier than the blossoms and more joyous than the birds. Our hearts yearn for such a peace from this world of dreary actuality.

Life does not change like a dream vision, its battlements are *hard and cruel facts*. Yet do not shake your head over the 'new world' vision and turn away from it saying it cannot be. It is too beautiful, too sorely needed to be cast aside, either for lack of care or lack of hope. Neither sit dreaming and fancying that all the forces of evolution make for good.

We are the evolutionary forces, we with our small wills together striving. We, banding together, can hasten our country's upward growing and joining our hands across the seas to countless others, we each of us playing some small upward part, can hasten the great growth international.

Away on the field of war and the scenes of murder, where kindly fathers kill poor mothers' dear young sons in spite of the awful negation of humanity and civilisation in which they are joining, men learn, forced by the hand of stern necessity to play a hero's part. On the field of war, we are told all men of a side are as brothers, sharing alike in sleep and rations: each helping each, and privates and officers alike ready to go to an almost certainty of death, to carry a wounded comrade out of the range of fire.

Stern virtues such as these we who are left at home must practise, if we would make that 'new world' possible after the war. We cannot wait until the war is over, we must begin toiling and building now. We must apply ourselves to the difficult task of rooting up long standing abuses and cope as well with the new emergencies and troubles that arise.

In the first place let us try always to realise that every human being has a right, not merely to a bare existence, the mere food to keep life coursing within the body, but to comfort and joy and the means for upward development.

If, as it may be, even barest necessities grow scarce amongst us during the war, then we must not allow some to go half-starved whilst others live in plenty, but must share here at home as we are told they do away there on the field of war.

In the meantime, while as yet famine does not stare us in the face and may not, let us strive to enforce generally a decent standard of payment for work and for relief.

In Australia where women have the vote a widowed mother is entitled to 5s. a week for each child, it costs more than that to maintain it in the Workhouse, that she may keep it with a decent standard of simple comfort, beside her in the home.

Most pitiful is the plight of many British soldier's and sailor's families. One fragile woman from Ranwell Street, Bow, came to us to-day. She has three little children aged four and a half, three years, one year and nine months and is expecting another soon. Her husband is a Reservist and was called up when war began. She had 20s. from him and 22s from the Soldier's and Sailor's Families Association. The War Office have sent her £1 19s. 6d., i.e. 9s. 1d. a week for the month of September. 'They said it wasn't as much as I ought to have,' she said, 'but they were getting short of money'. The Soldier's and Sailor's Association had told her to wait until they should come to visit her and she did not know whether she will get any more from them. She was terribly worried, '9s. won't keep us,' but she made excuses for the War Office, they were 'busy' she thought. And then she cried, she had heard that 'a lot of Mr Regiment have fallen down.'

The husband of a woman living in Ford Road had the order from his firm 'enlist or go'. He joined the Territorials and went into training at the barracks in Tredegar Road. The firm *promised* him 5s. a week whilst he was at the war, but in the meantime he had nothing. There are six little ones whose ages vary from 10 years to 8 months, the baby is wasting, another child has abscesses in her head. The rent is 7s. No money has come from the War Office. The Soldier's and Sailor's Association told the woman to wait until a visitor called upon her.

'When she came to us on Monday there was no food in the house.'

On Wednesday she came again. Still there was no money from the War Office. The visitor from the Soldier's and Sailor's Association had been, but had left without giving her anything, merely saying that she *might* get some money on Saturday.

Surely the British Nation is able, surely it should be willing to grant a fixed payment of £1 a week to soldiers' and sailors' wives who have no more than two children and where there are more than two children to 10s. a week for the mother and 5s. a week for each child: £1 a week for a mother whose son, who has been her support has gone to the war, 5s. a week for the brothers and sisters who have been supported by soldier and sailor brothers.

The men who are out fighting at the bidding of their country's Government are entitled to the knowledge that their families are removed from want. The women whose husbands and sons will probably never return to them, are entitled to this small return for all the anxiety and grief that they must suffer.

One of the most glaring and far reaching evils menacing society has for long been the under-payment of our women. For many years after this war the proportion of women wage-earners is bound to be increased because so many, many men who took their part in the world's work and were the bread winners of families will have lost their lives. If the present gross under-payment of women's labour is allowed to continue the 'new world' after the war will be worse, an infinitely worse one than the world that we know to-day. Let us demand that the standard of women's wages be raised immediately. Let us band ourselves together to insist on a minimum wage for women of 5d. an hour, or £1 for a full week's work. It is little enough especially in these days of high prices!

We women can all do our part in getting this minimum enforced. Numbers of us are members of Boards of Guardians Town Councils, Local Representative Committees for distress and so on and there is hardly a woman's society that is not organising on its own account some kind of employment scheme to cope with the present distress. Through all these avenues we can press for this women's minimum wage of 5d. an hour or £1 a week.

Do not be led away by those who tell you that if you pay a fair wage you will be obliged to employ a smaller number and that a larger number will be forced to starve. Those for whom no work can be found the State must be forced to care for, and by paying a miserable pittance to a large number you will be helping to keep down the standard for the Nation. Also you will not be helping as you might to prevent unemployment, for every woman who is paid a decent wage is able to buy clothes and other manufactures and in this way to provide employment for other people.

In all that we do to relieve distress at this juncture, hard though the effort is, as case after case of misery comes upon us we must remember always the 'new world' that we must build and strive to secure that the integrity of our Nation for which men fight, shall be an integrity worthy of preservation for all time.

The Sweating Scandal

(W.D. 24 October 1914)

Girl as bookkeeper required by West-end stores, excellent opening for beginner; good writer and typist essential; salary to start 4/-, Apply, HERBERT & Co. 102 Great Portland Street, near Oxford Circus, W.

The above advertisement was brought to me by a little group of girls at our Hackney meeting! 'What are we to do,' they said, 'when such wages are offered to us? It costs a girl perhaps £15 to get her training and then she is asked to work for 4s. a week.'

One of them told me that she was out of employment, but that she would be ashamed to accept such a wage for skilled work. 'But what are we to do? they said with heart searching pathos, 'people think we can live on almost nothing, what are we to do?'

Then they said that some Hackney ladies had started a little sewing guild to keep some of them going. 'We don't know what we'll be paid. Perhaps they can't pay us very much. Perhaps we're slow as it's not our regular trade. But the ladies do patronize us so.' 'They oughtn't to patronize us so, ought they, when we're working for our money?' one of them said and looked up at me with her pretty wistful face.

'What are we to do?' they said again. I could only answer: 'My dears *something* must be done.'

Lying on the table when I came on to the platform was a woman's letter:

'Being in need, not having had a substantial meal since August 23rd, I asked for temporary aid. On October 6th, a woman called and after asking me fifteen questions and noting the replies on a form and getting eight of my testimonials reaching back over 24 years, and getting good personal character for me from my late employers, she offered me employment as a charwoman.

'I went to her house and was instantly set to work turning out bedrooms, etc.

'Beginning on Monday, I worked all through the week from 9 till 3, and on Friday till 6 having one light meal, dinner only given to me. On Saturday I came away still without payment and leaving the house spotlessly clean. I have been in good service. On Monday I was paid 4s. 6d. for the seven days work. The woman who used to do the work that I did was paid 2s. a day, and she had a husband in regular employment. I am a widow.

'When I complained she said we "ought to be glad to take anything." Of course being sent from the committee she made her own case good with them, and had me under her thumb to do exactly as she liked with.'

And this is charity!

At G. B. Kent and Sons, Brush Factory in Victoria Park Rd., women and girls are employed just now on a War Office order of brushes for our soldiers.

I have seen the brushes that they are making, oval shaped brushes with brownish black bristles. The bristles are supplied to the workers all roughly tumbled together, lying this way and that, and the women have to pick out from the mass a certain quantity of them, pat and push this into a neat little bundle, twist wire round the bundle, push it into a hole in the wooden brush back and fasten off with wire behind: 163 little bundles must they make and wire and fix into 163 holes for one penny.

Working very quickly they can make two brushes in an hour and the brushes are paid for at the rate of 1s. 2d. a dozen, which works out at a little over 2¼d. an hour.

The women and girls work in the factory from 8 a.m. to 6 p.m. and take more brushes home with them to do at night because they cannot live on what they can earn after being in the factory ten hours each day.

One, who had worked five years at the trade and was considered extraordinarily quick, earned 11s. 1d. one week. Three shillings worth of this was done after she left the factory. She stayed up working each night till ten o'clock. She had earned more than any of the others. Another had earned 7s. 5d., 1s. 3d. of it at home, another 6s. 9d., 1s. of it at home.

Their fingers, especially the last ones, were sore and disfigured with the wire, some of them grown all swollen and stiff so that they will never be able to straighten them out any more. Some of them had sore eyes, a common thing they said, from working so many hours, especially with dark coloured bristles. Two of the girls, who had worked four-and-a-half years at the trade had specially bad eyes.

They told me that these same soldiers' brushes when given out by Kent and Sons to women to make in their own homes, are paid for at the rate of 1s. ½d. a dozen instead of 1s. 2d.

When the bristles are put in by machinery, these same brushes are paid for at 9d. a dozen. The women who do it earn a little more than the others, but the machines are very hard to work. There is a treadle to press with the foot and a heavy weight to lift, not many women can be got to do it.

The women employed at japanning the brushes in the same factory earn but 6s. or 7s. a week; as girls they begin at 4s.

Here is sweating indeed, and sweating seems almost universal amongst women employed in War Office contracts.

The Army contractors are making huge sums of money out of the War. When will the Government see to it that this exploitation of the women who are piling up the profits of these contractors is made to cease? When will the people of the country unite to insist that this shall be? Women, even without the vote that we need so much, we can unite in leading this demand!

The newspapers have chronicled in much detail, the visits of Queen Mary to the workrooms established in connection with the fund called by her name, and these same chronicles have told the world of the work that is being done. The excuse most frequently given for the underpayment of women in the Queen's Workrooms, *for every one admits that a maximum wage of 6d. is underpayment* is that the employment is only intended to be temporary and the women are being trained.

But what is being done to secure that the employment shall be only temporarily needed, what other work is being provided for the women? Alas, the Nation is providing none. The War, Lord Kitchener tells us, is likely to be a long one. The Central Unemployed Body for London tells us that the tale of workless women in London is being augmented by 4,000 every week. What prospect is there of any but relief work being found for those thousands? Alas, at present none.

As for the training, the chronicles of the Queen's progress have revealed to all what it consists of, chiefly the making of well to do people's old clothes into garments for the poor. The triumph of one workroom was the manufacture of a pair of little boy's trousers out of a woman's blouse. 'Some must waste and others must work,' is the motto of such efforts.

But the main point is that a woman cannot learn to earn a living from such teaching. For factory work the main essential is speed, not cogitation as to how to turn one garment into another, but how to fashion many and many gross of garments from many and many bales of stuff.

Another excuse made by those who defend the sweated rates paid to women in Queen Mary's workrooms is that half a loaf is better than no bread. But why should no bread or half the bread that is necessary, be the choice of the daughters of the richest country in the world?

Men and women who use this pitiful half loaf argument, or who hear it without a protest, are you content that masses of women and children should be having far less than enough to eat, whilst as yet there is plenty of food in the country for us all? Even if a scarcity should come upon us, would you not rather we should share alike?

Women, those of you who are organising workrooms, do not shelter yourselves behind the sweating practised by other people. Do not bolster up the sweating scandal – pluck out the beam from thine own eye!

How to Meet Industrial Conscription

(WD, 20 March 1915)

To the women whom they have refused to grant the rights of enfranchised citizens, the Government, through the President of the Board of Trade, has issued an appeal to enlist for War service.

The Women's Societies which the Government has so often flouted are urged to lend their aid in marshalling the volunteers.

Registers of women who are prepared to undertake any kind of paid work, industrial, agricultural, clerical, etc., are to be kept at the Labour Exchanges, and registration forms are being sent out to the women's organisations. Those who register must state their ages and whether they are married, widowed, or unmarried; if they have ever done any paid work, and if so, what and when, and in whose employ: if they are free to work whole or part time, or to leave their homes; whether there is any kind of work that they are willing or able to do, and whether they are willing to train for work which they have not previously done.

In view of this appeal, which is being made to women by the Government – appeals by Government usually tend to become irresistible demands – it is surely time that all the women's organisations, trade union, political, educational and social, should come together to discuss this important matter and formulate their demands to safeguard the position of women of all ranks in the labour army.

The men who signed the Army forms that were sent round to the householders, found themselves called up for service, sometimes much to their surprise. The women who sign their names on the War Service Register will probably find themselves called up too, whether they wish or not. Shall we allow them to go without fair conditions first being assured?

The Government, through Mr Lloyd George and Lord Kitchener, has announced that it is about to take extensive control of industry.

The Government makes it plain that it is determined that the provisions of munitions of war both for Great Britain and the Allies, shall absorb all our entire national energies, so that all our people may become part of a great war machine engaged either in fighting, supplying the wherewithal to fight, or in providing necessaries of food, clothing, housing and transport for the soldiers or armament makers.

In order to conciliate the British workmen (who, by their votes, have been made the ultimate arbiters of the nation's destiny, though they scarcely realize their power), Mr Lloyd George has held conference with the Great Trade Unions which, as yet, are almost entirely controlled by men. The Government has promised that limits shall be set to the profits of employers, and that good wages and fair conditions of labour shall be ensured.

Various increases in wages have been made, and negotiations are taking place in regard to demands for much larger increases. The Trade Union leaders and Labour Members of Parliament occupy a position of grave and anxious responsibility at this time, for on their handling of the situation the position of millions of workers largely depends.

Perhaps an even vaster responsibility rests on the shoulders of women who are leaders of women at this time. As yet, the working woman, the sweated drudges of the world, are but poorly organised, and all the women's suffrage and other political and local organisations must lend their aid at this crisis in securing the best possible terms for the masses of women workers on whom the future of our race so largely depends.

It is more urgently imperative than ever that every woman who works for her living should join a Trade Union, in order that she may have a strong organisation to protect her interests, and that she may help to protect the interests of other women.

A national conference of women should be called immediately to formulate demands for the regulation of the industrial enlistment of women. Here are some of the demands which would, undoubtedly, be adopted by such a conference.

(1) As the Government is already by far and away the largest employer of labour in the country, and may soon be almost the sole employer, it is absolutely imperative that *women who are to be enlisted as recruits in the National War Service shall have the Vote at once.*

(2) That fair wages shall be assured to women. *That where a woman is employed on work hitherto done by men she shall receive the wage hitherto paid to men, in addition to any war bonus or increase in wages which might have been paid for the work now in the case of men*

employees. That in no case shall an unskilled woman be employed at a lower wage than the current rate to men unskilled labourers.

(3) The Government has announced its determination to put an end to industrial disputes and proposes that, where the parties concerned fail to come to an agreement:

> 'The matter shall be referred to an impartial tribunal, nominated by His Majesty's Government, for immediate investigation and report to the Government with a view to a settlement.'

The Women's Conference would undoubtedly demand that women should have strong representation on this tribunal, and that in all disputes in regard to women's employment, a woman of standing and experience (the nation has many such to draw upon) should be the chairman of the tribunal, or in case of the appointment of a sole arbiter, a woman should be the arbiter of the dispute.

(4) That proper safeguards in regard to hours, wages, and conditions be arranged in connection with representatives of the women concerned, and that no woman shall be compelled to work under conditions which the representative of the organisation to which she belongs, reports to be unsatisfactory.

This is a moment of very vital importance to women, calling for all our energy and resource, all our earnestness, all our solidarity.

Let us band ourselves together sinking our differences – to build up a position of dignity and security for our sisters, in order that as free citizens they may give their services to the nation willingly and with enthusiasm.

Stand by the
Woman Worker

(*WD*, 27 March 1915)

In the Conference at the Treasury between Mr Lloyd George and the Trade Union representatives, the question of women's labour was not clearly faced. The agreement arrived at in regard to unskilled men, who may replace the skilled workers who have gone to the War, is quite plain and explicit. Unskilled men are to be paid precisely as their skilled predecessors were. But the words of the agreement in regard to women's labour are vague and ambiguous. They imply that men's wages shall not suffer because women are employed, but they do not give any assurance that women, like unskilled men, are to receive the same rates hither to paid to the men whom they replace.

We have written to the Prime Minister, Mr Lloyd George, and the President of the Board of Trade, Mr Runciman, to ask what the words in regard to women's labour mean, and whether there is to be equal pay for equal work. We are told that our letter is being considered. We, therefore, conclude that the Government has not yet made up its mind.

It cannot be stated too emphatically that pledges to dispense with women who have been employed at a lower rate, in order to take on men at a higher wage after the War is over, are absolutely worthless. After the War is over, employers who find that women are working satisfactorily, or even partially so, at half the wage of men, will say that they cannot afford to replace the women by men at a higher wage. Contract prices, price lists, and the organisation of buying and selling will by that time have been re-adjusted in accordance with the prevailing cost of labour, and employers will protest that they are unable to raise wages, especially if, as is probable, a period of trade depression ensues, and in view of the enormous War taxes which will have to be paid.

The only possible way to safeguard the interests of the men wage earners themselves and to prevent women from being cruelly and unjustly sweated and exploited, is to insist that there shall be equal pay for equal work without distinction of sex. A pledge to this affect must be obtained from the Government and the fulfilment of the pledge must be secured by constant and determined vigilance.

It is also imperative that representatives of women's labour shall be placed on the tribunals which the Government is setting up for dealing with trades disputes and that where a sole arbiter is appointed, and the dispute is concerning women's labour, the sole arbiter shall be a woman.

The importance of these points is very clearly shown by the fact that the Treasury conference left the vital question of women's labour in its present vague and undigested form.

To secure that women workers receive fair treatment, it is even more essential than ever before that they should be strongly organised into Trade Unions. to all women, whatever may be their conditions, these things are of importance. In the past the woman worker has been the sweated drudge of the labour market. Frequently she is put to dull mechanical work, which gives her no opportunity for self-development and the exercise of initiative. But even when her work is skilled she is almost invariably paid much less than if she had happened to be a man. Her competition is hated and feared by the workmen and by their wives, because entrance into any form of work lowers the wages and so brings down the subsistence level for the family.

Because of the prevailing custom of underpaying women, widows with dependent children, and families supported by wage-earning daughters, are plunged into poverty and the entire status of womanhood is debased.

The miserable plight of women wage earners has spurred on both Suffragettes and Suffragists in their efforts to obtain the Vote. But here again, the masses of women submerged in a sea of hopeless poverty, the masses of others just able to keep above the privation line by working too hard and too long for a bare subsistence, and this bad old system of discounting, as of minor importance, all that women do, have enormously added to the difficulty of securing enfranchisement.

Suffragists know that the possession of citizen rights is essential to full social development, but economic and political enfranchisement go hand in hand, and well organised bodies of either men or women, are best able and fitted to win them both.

A letter, purporting to be written by a woman, has appeared in the Press urging that because women are unsuited for the firing line, they are less valuable to the community than men, and therefore must not demand equal pay for equal work when employed in civilian occupations. Is it more value to the body politic then to kill, than to bring new life into the world?

Women who write in this strain are essentially of the blackleg type. They are dangerous to themselves, to other women and to the community.

The present is a great opportunity for placing women's labour upon a sounder basis. Women should band themselves together to seize it. If they fail to do so, the position of the woman wage earner and the effect of her position upon our whole social life will become worse instead of better.

We Must Persevere

(WD, 24 July 1915)

What made the Suffragette movement? For what cause did we defy conventions and go to prison?

It was because we were sick at heart for the miseries of the people; because we wished to free our sisters and brothers from the slavery of want; because we believed the votelessness of women to be a drag on the wheels of progress, contributing towards their social and industrial bondage, and proving a source of weakness to all the vast masses of people, who, struggling for existence in the labour market and because of their comparative lack of political knowledge and organisation, cheated in the political field, yet by their toil build up and sustain the fabric of our State.

We wanted women to stand the comrades and equals of men, both legally and industrially, in order that side by side with men, they might not carry on the world in its accustomed way, but build it up into something new and infinitely better than its present self.

It was for a world where human beings should count more than commerce, a world without poverty and exploitation, and the needless deaths of little children that we were longing. When we went to prison we found there our sisters stunted and spoilt by the harsh and unequal organisation of our social life.

We were consumed with yearning to help our sisters, to call on each one of them to come and join our ranks. To those who were happy and unfortunate we said: 'Come out from your homes, for you are needed': to those who were heavy with the burden of life we said: 'Pool your experience with ours and let us hope for a better future dawn in your factory and slum.'

It was for this that we toiled for the Suffragette movement: and the old struggle is before us still. Now, with the War at its height, the poorest are being exploited to pile up extra War profits, the women are being sweated and used as the instruments to blackleg men and undermine the general standard of wages.

The Government and the great Party press lent their aid in the getting up of a demonstration for War Service for Women, and Government Registers compiled for national purposes, were placed at the disposal of the organisers of a political group for this purpose.

Long columns in the newspapers were used to advertise it and Mr Lloyd George spoke to the processionists from the platform specially erected on Government premises. But, even so, the Procession was not so large as many held by women fighting against heavy odds.

And now that the pageantry is over, and the bands have ceased to play, what do Mr Lloyd George's words to those Saturday processionists amount to?

He said that the offer made by the deputation that women should replace men in industry during the War would be accepted gradually and in time. This probably means that the women will be taken on, as at present, when, and as, the manufacturers find it profitable to engage them, without any forcing by the Government.

In regard to the vital point as to the wages at which women are to be brought in to replace men, Mr Lloyd George's reply was altogether unsatisfactory. It means that unless we can produce a change of heart in the Government the employment of women in munition factories at wages of from 8s. to 14s. or 15s. a week is to continue, and that the trades that were good trades, as trades go, for men, are to be turned into sweated industries for women.

Men, women and children by the million will suffer for the Government's betrayal of the woman worker, unless we can fight the equal pay battle through to victory.

The difficulties of the struggle are very great. Thousands of women are unemployed, the National Register forms will be brought round to them, as to others. These forms ask for volunteers to do Government work. The women hear that War Service is needed and *they* are needing bread. Naturally they will reply that they are willing to give War Service. But, once they have done so, their liberty of action will have disappeared, and they will be obliged to work when and where they are told, however low the wage.

Therefore, we must urge all women, if they fill up the forms at all, to state most clearly that they will not undertake any kind of work, except under clearly defined safeguards.

But, it must be remembered that, should the National Register be but the prelude to compulsory industrial service, as seems probable, the demand for safeguards would be in vain, for all whom the authorities might choose to select for service would then be taken to work by force, whether they would or no, and in spite of any conditions that they might have laid down.

There are many people who intend to refuse to submit to compulsory industrial service, should it come, because they hold the present conditions of labour to be grossly unjust, and hope that by their abstention they will be able to induce the Government to insist on fairer terms. There are others who would refuse to submit to compulsion for conscientious reasons. Many of both these classes are willing to fill up the National Register forms, giving the particulars asked for, and stating that they decline to do Government work, except under certain conditions.

But those who intend to fill up the forms must remember that, if compulsion comes, and the National Register forms have been filled up without protest, the hardships of compulsion will inevitably fall on the shoulders of those least able to protect themselves. The struggle against compulsion, if any struggle is made, will fall to the people who are without influence and unknown, for the Government will not seek to forcibly introduce into factories at sweated wages, either men or women, who have means and influence, or who are known as politicians and agitators.

This is a point that needs most thorough consideration and deep and earnest thought.

I believe in collectivism, in the collective action of a free people agreeing on equal terms to subordinate the separate individual wishes for the benefit of the whole.

But in the present arrangements of the Government, under which already the poorest and most helpless workers are being more firmly bound by a system of infamous sweating, I see not the collective action of free people for the common welfare, but the enslavement of the many for the profit of the few.

We must gird ourselves anew for the struggle. We have the old fight still to make.

Death-Rate of Mothers

(WD, 6 November 1915)

The Maternity and Infant Clinic should be of vital importance to the nation, because of the opportunity and encouragement it should give to the doctoring and nursing profession of studying the scientific problems of pregnancy and child-bearing, and the nurture of infant life, from the point of view of securing health and the most perfect development, rather than of curing illness.

The science of curing illness is as yet in a very early stage; the science of preventing illness is only just beginning to be thought a science at all.

The busy general-practitioner has not time to specialise in the complex problems of maternity and infancy; the special hospitals for women and children only deal with those who are already ill; but the Maternity and Infant Clinics should gradually provide the world with new stores of valuable information. It is not only the poor woman who has need of the Maternity and Infant Clinic, though let us always remember that, as the poor woman is in the vast majority, the race must stand or fall by her. Even in well-to-do homes, the feeding, clothing, and general treatment of the baby is often not wisely planned. Even the well-to-do expectant mother often ignorantly disregards the laws of health, and fails to realise the need of expert advice on innumerable matters, not merely at the time of the confinement, but also during pregnancy and whilst she is nursing the child.

Science Held Back by Poverty

The scientific work that the Mother and Infant Clinics should be doing is heavily handicapped by the sordid poverty in which the mothers and children live. It is a mockery to speak of the higher forms of child nurture, when one finds that a husband and wife, a four months' old baby, and seven other children have to be maintained on a wage of 23s. a week; or when a penniless widow with a prematurely born child a few days' old, and several other little children applies for aid!

We of the E.L.F.S. find in our four East London Clinics that the work that we are obliged to do is largely that of providing milk and food for those who are hungry, and clothes for those who have scarcely the wherewithal to cover themselves.

It is disheartening to talk to an expectant mother of careful feeding when she is scarcely able to get enough food of any kind to keep herself and family alive. It is useless to talk to her of modern hygienic clothing when she scarcely ever buys a new garment for herself, but has to get what she can second-hand at very rare intervals indeed. It is difficult to talk to her of fresh air and sanitation, when the entire household is packed away into from one, two, three, or four tiny rooms; when the water supply is defective, and the house badly built and in disrepair; and when she cannot afford either fuel enough to keep the rooms warm by day, or warm and light bedcovering by night.

It is absurd to weigh the undernourished infant, or to give medical advice to a starving woman, unless one can provide what the mother and baby need. Mothers and babies in the 20th century ought not to have to go for charity to the Clinic because the family income is not large enough to supply the elementary needs of life!

But it is useless to give a bottle of medicine where a meal is needed, and clinics that prescribe the amount of milk that is to be given to the baby, without having the power to provide the milk, where necessary, will find their efforts absolutely thrown away in a large proportion of cases.

Appalling Mortality of Mothers

The report of Dr Newsholme on maternal mortality in connection with child-bearing, just published by the Local Government Board, points out that 'each death before the age of 60, or even 70, represents waste of national wealth in the form of life.' It is an appalling thing that one mother should die, both in the counties and the county boroughs of England and Wales, for every 250 live children born, and that of those babies, for whose sake there is such a heavy mortality amongst mothers, over 90,000 should die before they are a year old.

Mortality from all causes, apart from that of child-birth, is undoubtedly highest amongst the working class, and the rate of mortality rises as the share of food and comfort and the quantity of cubic air-space available for each individual diminishes; but the statistics on mortality from child-bearing in Dr Newsholme's report do not clearly bear out this principle, which applies, without fail, to death from every other cause.

It must be remembered that statistical comparison between district and district tends to be misleading, because side by side with the dwellings of the rich, we often find the poorest slums. Nevertheless, the following table which I have compiled from statistics given by Dr Newsholme, and which give both the rate of child-bearing mortality, and of infant mortality, which may fitly be called the poverty barometer, is very striking:

	1913	
	Child-bearing mortality per 1000 Births	Infant Mortality per 1000 Births
Hampstead	4'47	73
Stoke Newington	3'03	81
Lewisham	3'01	76
Shoreditch	2'62	155
Bermondsey	2'06	133

This table shows that whilst Hampstead has the lowest rate of infant mortality in the Metropolitan boroughs, it has also the highest rate of child-bearing mortality.

It would seem that the old wives' tale about the women who work hard having an easier time in childbirth is borne out by these figures, as far as they go. But remember that the old wives' tale also says that the woman who works too hard before her child is born, may not have much trouble at the actual birth, but suffers later on. Moreover, everyone who knows anything of their lives is aware that the majority of working women suffer chronically from want of rest and care during childbirth, and this has been proved by the National Insurance Act.

Mr Newsholme states that syphilis is responsible for a large percentage of child-bearing mortality, and this may partially account for the mortality being higher in some of the West London boroughs than in the working-class communities of the East End.

Death from Overwork

But whilst Hampstead with its 4'47 deaths of mothers per 1,000 births has the highest child-bearing mortality rate of the London boroughs, many districts have a still higher rate, and nine towns have a child-bearing mortality rate of more than six per thousand births.

These towns in which the child-bearing mortality rate is highest are:

	1913	
	Child-bearing Mortality per 1000 Births	Infant Mortality per 1000 Births
Dewsbury	8'54	131
Rochdale	7'21	106
Burnley	6'57	174
Blackburn	6'55	148
Bury	6'49	141
Halifax	6'23	83
Merthyr Tydfil	6'11	126
Huddersfield	6'07	104
Oldham	6'06	141

It will be noticed that, with the exception of Merthyr Tydfil, where housing conditions are exceedingly bad, all these towns are centres of the textile industry, in which a large proportion of the married women go out to work in the spinning and weaving factories.

We need not wonder at this. Any one who considers the matter must expect it. Factory life, as it is today, it both arduous and monotonous. It makes a larger drain than is consistent with physical and mental well-being upon the physique, both of men and women. The hours are too long, and, especially in the textile factories, the atmosphere is overheated, and the noise of machinery is deafeningly loud. There is a perpetual pressure of monotonous work that must be done at too high a rate of speed.

The care of the working-class home to-day is also an arduous business. The house is usually badly built, small and overcrowded. The cooking, washing and house-cleaning, scrubbing floors and so on, together with caring for the children, have all to be done in too small a space, and with insufficient utensils and materials.

It really is not possible for one woman with a large family to perform unaided all these various domestic duties in an efficient way, and we know that the factory work alone is also more fatiguing than it should be for a worker who has nothing else but factory work to do. Surely there can be no doubt then, that a woman must suffer who has to perform both these too great tasks, and, in addition has laid upon her the strain of child-bearing.

We need not be surprised that, as Dr Newsholme complains, some of the women who have the double load to carry should feel themselves driven to the practice, which is so disastrous both to mother and child, of taking drugs to prevent another increase in the family. It is tragic that women should even wish to do this, but under present conditions we need not wonder that they do.

The Danger of Underpaying Women

That a woman who has learnt a trade should continue to ply that trade after marriage, earning a good wage, and out of it paying someone else to do the domestic work of her home, is one thing; that a woman should be responsible for caring for her home and should, at the same time, go out into the labour market, to work for half the wage that would have to be paid to her if she were a man, is another.

The employment of women to do men's work at a lower wage is a terribly serious matter. Unless checked it will lower the existing wage standards for men until it becomes impossible for homes to be maintained except where both husband and wife are earning and the wife is also saving expense by working in the home. This system of double work for the wife means death to both mothers and children.

Where the maternity mortality rate is high, the rate of still births is naturally also high.

It is natural that a high birth-rate should tend to produce a high mortality amongst both mothers and children, for the mother who has many children born in quick succession has to face a tremendous drain upon her vitality. If she is overworked and underfed she will be the less able to meet the calls upon her and to give force to the new life.

Statistics will not carry us very far until the occupation of the parents, the weekly income of the family and the cost of living in the district are co-ordinated with the mortality rates and the ages of the mother and her children.

A study of the child-bearing mortality statistics lead us, as we should expect, to the conclusion that in the main the rate is highest, firstly, where the birth-rate is very high, where there is poverty and overcrowding, and where the married women are obliged, through economic need, to work for money, either outside or within their homes, as well as attending to domestic cares.

Secondly, the rate is high in country districts whre skilled aid in the hour of danger is not easily obtained.

Backward Local Authorities

The backward state of the Public Health departments of many districts may be gathered from the statistics given by Dr Newsholme in regard to puerperal fever. This disease became notifiable in 1899 and statistics from each sanitary area in regard to it have been published in the annual reports of the L.G.B. since 1911. So lax has been the administration that in 26 counties and county boroughs the number of cases notified has been actually fewer than the number of deaths from the disease. In eleven districts the deaths and notifications were equal, and in only 23 counties and county boroughs were twice as many cases of puerperal fever notified as there were deaths from the disease. Yet in Manchester, where the midwives are under municipal supervision, the deaths from puerperal fever were only 19 per cent. of the cases notified.

To-day the majority of children are still helped into the world by midwives, not by doctors, and in many districts the vast majority of the midwives are still untrained handy women. For the whole of England and Wales the number of trained and untrained midwives is estimated by the Central Midwives' Board to be equal.

The Sweated Midwife

The life of a midwife is a very arduous one, and quite naturally, as working married women have so little money, the pay is wretchedly low.

Before the National Insurance Act, the average pay for care of mother and child during the entire confinement varied from 5s. to 7s. 6d. It has now been raised from 10s. to 15d., or occasionally to 20s. Women in East London tell us that fees have gone up since the War, midwives are evidently suffering from the higher cost of living like their clients.

Dr Janet Lane Claypon, one of the Local Government Board

Maternity and Infant Welfare Inspectors, estimates that no midwife earns more than £90 a year, and that the majority make much less.

The Maternity Inspector for Hertfordshire, reports that in that county the average earnings of the midwives in 1907 were 4s. 4½d. per week each and in 1913, 5s. 0½d.

We need not wonder that in some districts there is a serious shortage of midwives, and that their numbers are diminishing.

A midwife's training costs about £30, and out of her small earnings, she must buy drugs and apparatus, and must keep herself supplied with clean cotton uniforms. Her work is very hard, and makes large demands upon her for tact, adaptability and patient kindness.

It is exceedingly harmful, both in its effect on the midwife and on the babies whom she attends, that she should live in the sordid poverty to which, unless she has private means, the midwife is obviously condemned.

The Medical Officer of Health for Radnorshire, reports that 12 or nearly half, the midwives practising in the county were over 60 years of age, and that two were old age pensioners.

Municipal Midwives and Maternity Hospitals

Whilst the condition of the working classes remains as it is, the only way of improving the position of the midwife, is to attach her to some institution, which will make itself responsible for paying her an adequate salary.

The fact that child-bearing mortality is comparatively low in the London boroughs, is undoubtedly due, in a large measure, to the free provision of midwives by various institutions.

Municipalities, everywhere, should have their staffs of midwives, to send out free in every case, and there should be a free municipal maternity hospital in every district.

There ought to be no red tape or inquisitional rules, no stigma of charity, connected with these necessary institutions. Some private societies refuse to extend their help to mothers who are not married, and to those, whom they, in the light of their necessarily imperfect knowledge, consider careless.

Such distinctions ought not to be made. The fact that a woman has practically no legal claim upon her child's father, makes it the more necessary that she and her child should be able to secure help from the community. If a mother should be temperamentally careless, it is the more important that she should come into contact with those whose scientific training has made them realise the importance of taking infinite pains.

Wanted – Free Public Nurseries

Just as each district has its free schools to accommodate all the children of the neighbourhood so, eventually, every district must have its free nursery to accommodate all the children whose mothers are obliged to leave them there, either regularly, because the mothers are wage-earners, or occasionally, because the mother is ill, or for some other cause.

Some people will fear that if free nurseries were provided, and every mother might leave her child there whenever she pleased, large numbers of mothers would habitually cease to care for their children; but in practice fears of this kind always prove groundless. The vast majority of mothers are very much more solicitous for their children's welfare than anyone else ever is, and the average mother takes a genuine pleasure in her babies. To think otherwise is to under-estimate human nature in an unwarrantable way.

Wanted – The Mothers' Vote!

Mr Walter Long speaking at the Guildhall recently, said that his mission was to ask the women of England to help in saving infant life. The women of England, handicapped by their votelessness, have been striving for many years to build up maternity and infant welfare centres, and to interest successive Governments in the work. They have succeeded in inducing the Local Government Board to move only a little way, and to provide only an infinitesimal part of the cost.

If the women of the country had the power of the Parliamentary Vote, and if women were elected in larger numbers to the various local bodies, they could speed up the machinery of maternity and infant welfare work in a way that would surprise Mr Long!

Much greater than the good that infant welfare centres can do, or hope to do, with all their efforts, is the harm that is being done by the rising prices of coal and food, and even rent, facts that are causing misery to far more mothers and children than any charity can reach.

Expert instruction to poor mothers on natal and anti-natal problems is useful in its way. But more urgently needed is instruction by those same poor mothers, to legislators and administrators, on the practical War-time problems of rearing babies in the slums!

That most needed of all instruction will never be given effectively until the mothers of slum babies become a coherent political force, armed with the Vote.

One Woman, One Vote

(WD, 27 November 1915)

The newspapers have been busy with forecasts of the Parliament and Registration Bill.

The *Manchester Guardian* first suggested that it might embody the principle of 'one man, one vote.'

The *Daily Telegraph* said:

1. It will prolong the existence of the present Parliament until a reasonable period after the War.
2. It will preserve the position held by the Plural Voting Bill before the breaking out of hostilities.
3. It will ensure that the next General Election shall take place on a new register, compiled to meet the altered conditions of the country.

The *Telegraph* further stated that a compromise had been arrived at between the Liberals and Tories in the Cabinet, as a result of which the Bill would include *not only one man, one vote; but also one vote, one value.*

The *Telegraph* explained that 'under a Coalition Government, such a settlement is of course not impossible'. Since then, there has been a hitch, and the Bill has been postponed.

We agree that under a Coalition Government most things are possible, unless people outside care enough to raise a great protest.

In this case, there are people outside who are caring very much indeed.

The people outside are voteless women, who have been clamouring for enfranchisement, in increasing numbers and with growing impatience since 1865.

Women are not concerned to oppose 'one man, one vote,' or 'one vote, one value.' Indeed, every suffragist who has a logical brain, must realise that these are but parts of the same democratic demand for equal representation, which we ourselves are making;

but, certainly, we are determined that when the next alteration of the franchise comes, the women's claim to vote must be met.

Every Suffrage Society has approached the Government either publicly or privately, on this matter. Each one has said that the Woman's Suffrage movement will spring into action, vigorous and formidable, to do battle for the Vote, if and when the franchise issue shall be raised.

So far, well. But it is our business to see that those declarations can be made good.

Words that cannot be followed up by deeds are things that we must beware of. We must educate, agitate, organise, until the forces of the public opinion we have created become overwhelming otherwise time and the politicians will steal a march on us, and we shall see the franchise door open and shut, and the women still left out in the cold.

American women have probably thought, in the past, that the work that they are obliged to accomplish before they can win the franchise is infinitely greater than ours. In State after State they must first convert the members of two legislative chambers and in many cases must secure the passage of the measure by a two-thirds' majority twice in succession. Then they must convert the majority of an immense electorate, living scattered over tremendous territories. This entails expensive journeys under difficulties of great heat, or intense cold, blizzards and deep snows or floods, which cause trains to be hours, even days, behind the scheduled time. The electorate which has to be reached is constantly being added to, and a large proportion of the immigrant electors cannot speak either English, French, or German, and come from lands where neither men nor women have the Vote.

But American women have this advantage: they know that the task before them is nothing less than the conversion of the majority of the men of the United States.

In this country Suffragists too often are led into the pit-fall of imagining that wire-pulling and keeping in touch with plausible politicians will win the Vote for them, without the necessity of ranging up on the side of the woman's movement the vast majority of the men and women.

Sooner or later we Suffragists must recognise that we cannot win without the pressure of the people, the politicians will only help us when they must.

We must get out amongst the people, and make them realise that women need votes, and that men, and the nation, need the equal comradeship of men and women.

We must prepare the ground for a great campaign for a vote for every woman and for every man.

E. Sylvia Pankhurst

Our Letter to Asquith

Dear Sir,

It is widely rumoured in both the Liberal and Conservative press, that the Government's proposed Bill to amend the Parliament Act, will not merely be a measure to delay the next General Election, but also a Franchise and Registration Bill, which will establish the principle of one man one vote and one vote one value.

The East London Federation of the Suffragettes, on whose behalf I write, waited upon you on Saturday, June 20th, 1914, at a time when women believed that the day of their enfranchisement could not much longer be delayed.

You replied to that deputation in most sympathetic terms, promising to give the case presented to you 'very careful and mature consideration.' You stated that you understood the case of the working women who waited upon you to be 'that the economic conditions under which women labour in a community like, for instance, the East End of London, are such that, either in the way of legislation, or perhaps in the way of administration, we cannot get substantial and intelligent reform, unless women themselves have a voice in choosing representatives for Parliament.' You admitted that the case has been illustrated by evidence to show 'that it is not a mere rhetorical statement, but does correspond to the actual facts of East End life.'

You stated that when the franchise was given to women it must be by means of a democratic measure and that, 'if the change has to come, we must face it boldly and make it thorough going and democratic in its basis.'

In these words you entirely summed up our own case.

We agree with you that every man should be enfranchised; we ask that every woman should be enfranchised too.

The case of Votes for Women has grown more urgent since the war. Women are deeply concerned in the war question because their husbands, sons and brothers are fighting at the front. Very many thousands of women are concerned in the matter of war pensions and allowances, and in the formation of the committees which will have so much power over the control of the lives of soldiers' and sailors' dependants, the majority of whom are women and children.

Women suffered more greatly than men from unemployment at the outbreak of the war; they were vitally affected by the efforts of the Government to deal with unemployment.

Above all, women are daily coming more and more into the industrial world because of the war, and the industries of the country cannot be maintained without them, and, as you have pointed out, they play an indispensable part in the production of munitions. If industrial troubles come after the war, the women will still more urgently need the protection of political power.

It is the women who are suffering most greatly from the high cost of living, and as they form a growing majority of the home population, the injustice of excluding them from enfranchisement becomes more serious every day.

These matters are felt most urgently by the women on whose behalf I write. We therefore ask you to receive a deputation of our members on an early date in order that we may lay our case before you, as we did in June 1914.

As we believe that other women's organisations may also approach you we should be willing to agree to a joint deputation, if this would meet your wishes, and make it easier for you to accede to our request.

Faithfully yours,

Why Wait?

(WD, 22 January 1916)

That serpent of the Garden of Eden was surely a manifestation of the spirit that to-day animates the politician. Surely his object was to destroy our Mother Eve's frank, confident simplicity and directness, by filling her mind with suspicious fears, and through them, persuading her to adopt his own guileful strategy and compromise. Certainly fear and suspicion are the predisposing causes of most of the evil that is done in the world to-day.

The people of Germany fear Russia, the people of England and France fear Germany, and so the populace have allowed themselves to be plunged into war, which brings upon them the very outrage that they have dreaded.

'Suppose the invaders were to come; suppose the War were brought to our own homesteads,' wail the elders, and possessed by this fear, they send out to die the youths with their lives before them, who are infinitely more precious to the State than the old, whose day is drawing to an end.

Fear often leads people to do evil that their hearts shrink from. Freedom was never won by fear, but fear is a frequent cause of tyranny and the tame acceptance of oppression.

Courage is needed to fight for liberty, we are all agreed as to that, but we often fail to realise that frankness and courage carry us further than sublety.

The pioneers, who have stood out fearlessly for each measure of freedom, are often forgotten when the honours of victory come to be conferred, the laurels falling to the politicians who hung back till the battle had been won. The reformers have gone forging on ahead to some new struggle. Perhaps already they are covered with new obloquy, but it was their unflinching courage, not the strategy of the timid, that won the old reform. It is such courage that will win the new, and the greatest and most essential part of

294

the needed courage is that of being prepared to assent to the liberty of others, as well as demanding it for ourselves.

The agitation that preceded the first Reform Act of 1832 was undoubtedly greater and more widespread than any later franchise agitation, and, obviously, only a very tremendous movement could have stormed the then almost impregnable fortress of privilege, on which no democratic leverage, such as is at present possible, could be brought to bear.

What tactics did those old franchise reformers use in arousing the great agitation that they needed? Was their demand for something very safe and small, that would be most acceptable to the most timid and moderate sections of those who desired a change and perhaps would placate even some of those who were lined up with the forces of reaction?

No, the old reformers suggested no compromise, they demanded 'universal suffrage,' and, by that claim for absolute justice, they aroused a volume of enthusiastic popular support, which would not have been forthcoming for any narrower issue. That fact may well be considered now, for the fight for the first Reform Bill began at the close of the Napoleonic wars, and though the Reform Bill was not what the reformers asked for, it was a tremendous achievement for the time and marked a new era in British history.

The women's suffrage movement, even at its inception, probably lost much popular support, because it asked merely that women should be admitted to the existing restricted franchise, instead of demanding votes for all women. Certainly the restricted demand damps popular ardour now, for politicians of all parties have come to admit that the existing franchise for men is illogical and out-of-date; and everyone knows that it would exclude an enormously greater number of women than of men, if it were extended to both on technically equal terms.

It has been left very largely to the anti-suffragists to point out that to divide a million and a quarter votes amongst 13 million women would leave the vast majority of women still disfranchised, and would leave women still in a position of great electoral inferiority as compared with men. The anti-suffragists have naturally made great capital out of this fact, indeed their only effective card has been to characterise the women's suffrage movement as undemocratic, because of its advocacy of a restricted measure.

But the leaders of the suffrage societies have refused to adopt a wider demand, on the ground that if women were to ask for the vote on more advantageous terms than those on which men actually have it, women would get nothing. Meanwhile the old demand has brought us nothing!

It has been said that we women have no business to suggest alterations in the men's franchise, until we have secured admission to it, and that to ask for a better franchise than the men have got, would be to demand a 'fancy franchise.'

But the sanctity that is supposed to attach to the claim for the vote 'as it is or may be granted to men' has been more than once disregarded by suffrage leaders. In 1890-1, the National Union of Women Suffrage Societies supported Mr Woodall's Bill, which definitely stated that married women should be allowed to vote, although the women's suffrage movement was violently divided on the question. In 1910-12, all the then existing suffrage societies combined in support of the Conciliation Bill, which offered considerably less than even technical equality to women.

Why, then, should we tenaceously cling to the phrase 'as it is or may be granted to men,' when a wider franchise is proposed? How can those suffragists who accepted the Conciliation Bill refuse to adopt the demand for womanhood suffrage, on the ground that it would establish a new franchise qualification?

An old fable used to be current about the working men who were in the habit of asking at public meetings: 'Will my wife get a vote under your Bill?' and when told 'No!' would answer: 'Then I'm with you!'

We have always doubted this story, because the men who have asked *us* that question have always expressed disappointment on learning that the Bill would not enfranchise their wives. But if men still exist who are specially anxious that their own wives should not vote, there can surely be no woman so foolish as to fancy that those men are possessed of really genuine enthusiasm for the spinster's vote!

We were always wearied by the argument that a woman should have a vote *because* she paid rates and taxes, and we protest that in the Women's Suffrage Movement much precious energy has been dissipated, in narrowing down our demands to meet the views of half-hearted persons, who cannot bring themselves to agree that every one of us should have a vote. We believe that no mistake can be greater than that of holding back the enthusiastic vanguard to keep pace with the rear.

It is said that if we ask for the vote for every woman we shall be obliged to ask for it for every man, and certainly the Womanhood Suffrage demand must imply complete Adult Human Suffrage, whether it be expressed or no. Here an objection is raised. It is declared that we must not allow ourselves to be '*used*' to get more votes for men, who are in a stronger position than we are to secure what they need for themselves.

But indeed, dear women, is it sensible or right to say this when we are asking men to help actively in getting votes for us? So long as *they* say that they are not going to trouble themselves to get votes for women, where are we? They are in possession of the franchise, and it is only through them that we can gain admission to it.

Of course, we all agree that we women would help men to get the franchise if the positions were reversed, but, as it is, Suffragists urge that men ought to be content to wait for a further extension of the franchise until *some* women have been admitted to it, after which we might together join hands in demanding a wider franchise for us all.

But why should we wait? Why have two, or more, lengthy struggles to secure two or more Acts of Parliament, when one justly framed measure would settle the franchise question once for all?

Do Suffragists love so much this weary hammering at the shut franchise door, accompanied by perpetual whining about our outcast place amongst the idiots and the criminals, that they should wish to lengthen it? Are they content to put off the time when we can begin to *do* things with out vote a single hour longer than they need? Does any Suffragist consider that if one woman in thirteen had a vote, we should be justified in abandoning the franchise struggle? Does any Suffragist imagine that with one vote in thirteen, we should be able to work the changes that we might, if a vote were extended to every woman in the land?

And again, what would become of our claim to technical equality to the vote 'as it is now, or may in the future be granted to men,' if a franchise Act should be passed to give votes to soldiers and sailors as has already been done in Australia?

But, and this is the greater of their objections, Suffragists fear that the men who to-day are voters will conspire to cheat the women, to use the great franchise movement that the women will rouse up, to get votes for men alone, and to leave the unfortunate women out in the cold.

It is the old Serpent at his work again, tempting our Mother Eve to refrain from the great demand for Human Suffrage, which alone could enfranchise the vast majority of women, because of the possible wrong that someone else might do.

It is said that in various Continental countries this is exactly what has happened, the women have agreed to ask for Adult Suffrage for both men and women, but men alone have won the vote. We might ask ourselves in which of those Continental countries has there ever been a votes for women movement, comparable in its wide spread organisation to that of the men's franchise movements in those countries, or to the women's movement here. As a matter of hard fact, however, the International Woman's Suffrage Alliance and its affiliated Societies have always stood, hitherto, for the enfranchisement of the women of each country on the terms open to the men. It is a fact that in no country have women secured admission to the franchise on *any* terms until the property qualifications for men had been swept away. Those who imagine that the granting of Adult Suffrage would make it harder for women to gain the vote should consider this.

But we wish that we might hear no more of these stories of selling the Women's Suffrage Movement. No movement can be sold if its members will stand true, though any movement may fail, as ours has done again and again in the past, for lack of strength.

If we cannot get behind it a popular demand strong enough to force the Government to concede it, no form of demand can safeguard us from getting left out in the cold!

The experience of the last thirty years might well teach us that what we have to dread, more than the prospect of a Reform Bill going through without us, is the apathy and inaction, which has made it possible for successive Governments to refuse to deal with the franchise in any way.

We have got to fight that apathy, rouse the nation to enthusiasm, make every woman feel that this is her fight and the fight of all humanity!

We must make every woman thrill with the idea that the battle for Human Struggle is part of the great struggle for upward human evolution, in the course of which dominance and compulsion, exploitation and poverty, will be abolished, and the false ideals that divide into warring sections the people and the peoples, shall be cast aside.

Not carping suspicion, not cold, hair-splitting politician's logic, can carry us on to victory in this fight, but the broad refusal to compromise or bargain, and the call to every human being to join in winning equality for us all.

We must fight for the franchise, not to keep this harsh old world as it is, but as a tool which shall help us to make it new.

Let us step out from the ruts that the politicians have made for us, and strive to see life with new eyes.

A Question of Tactics

(WD, 29 January 1916)

The reason for narrowing down the women's suffrage claim to the demand for votes on the terms on which they are at present extended to men, was the hope of pushing through, as a Private Member's measure, a little Bill of one clause, which merely provides that, for all purposes connected with voting at Parliamentary elections, 'words importing the masculine gender shall include women.'

In devising the Bill it was recognised that a Private Member's Bill must be as short as possible, and, if possible, should confine itself to one issue, because, even in 1870, when the Bill was first introduced by Jacob Bright, the time allowed for Private Members' business was very limited, and their power to prevent this being wasted by obstuctionists was very small.

The power and prestige of the Private Member has waned since 1870, and everyone is now agreed that no Private Member's Bill can become law, unless the Government of the day is actively interested in it. Moreover the refusal of the Speaker to give the Closure in order that a vote might be taken on the Conciliation Bill, except on condition that the measure went no further than a Second Reading and his declaration that the women's suffrage amendments to the Reform Bill were out of order, show us that votes for women cannot be secured by a Private Member's Bill or amendment.

All the Suffrage Societies are now agreed in demanding a Government measure. Therefore, the reason for a one-clause Bill has disappeared, as the Government has all the time of Parliament at its disposal. It is the duty of Suffragists to prepare the way for a Government measure, to work and struggle to hasten its coming, and to see that it is the biggest and broadest measure possible when it comes.

In the dim past, which dates from the birth of the Women's

Suffrage Societies in 1865-6, Suffragists adopted a non-party attitude. They strove to conciliate the Conservatives and Liberals, and
also the Irish, endeavouring to win supporters from every side, in
the hope that votes for women might go through as a non-party
measure, championed by a Private Member.

The ideal of the Suffragists in those days was that the opposing
parties should mean nothing to them. I remember hearing Mrs
Fawcett say, in 1904, that the Government and Opposition were
to Suffragists merely 'the Ins and the Outs.'

In 1905-6 came a change – the W.S.P.U. arose with an anti-
Government policy (afterwards adopted by numbers of other new
societies) which was avowedly designed to make votes for women
a Party question, in order that it might be taken up and passed
through by a Party Government as one of its own measures.

A Conservative Government was going out, a Liberal Government was coming in. For those who had determined to make
Votes for Women a party measure, the question to be decided was
whether they should aim at hitching their cause to the Conservative
or the Liberal and progressive forces.

If the former course were chosen, it would mean that the women
must wait for enfranchisement until the incoming Liberal Government should be overthrown and the Conservatives should come
in; whereas there was possibility of achieving success during the
reign of the new Government, if Votes for Women could be made
a Liberal measure. Undoubtedly Votes for Women, like every
other extension of the franchise, naturally belongs to the
progressive programme whether the existing temporary exponents
of the progressive parties may be willing to place it there or no.
It is true that Conservative Governments have from time to time
introduced progressive measures, for instance the Reform Act of
1870 and the Factory Acts. Moreover the Liberal Party is riddled
with hypocrisy and many of the grossest of the re-actionaries
abound in its ranks.

But the choice was not actually between the ephemeral leaders
of the Liberal and Conservative Parliamentary Parties. It was as to
whether Votes for Women was to be put forward as something
that would aid in keeping things as they are, and in bolstering up
property and privilege; or whether Votes for Women was to come
as an extension and reinforcement of the power of democracy and
the development of the equal right of every human being to mould
the conditions of our collective life.

To succeed in making Votes for Women a Party question it was
necessary to make precisely that choice, if the necessary leverage
were to be obtained.

The choice was never definitely made, and the object of securing that Votes for Women should be a Party measure was not achieved.

At first, and later, from time to time, it seemed that the militant suffragists had chosen to ally themselves unofficially with the progressive forces, but gradually there came a decided bias towards reaction. The Non-Militant National Union of Suffrage Societies showed a more constant though, also, more cautious tendency towards progressivism. On the whole the suffrage societies have continued to justify their oft-repeated assertion that they are non-Party, in the broad sense of being neither progressive nor reactionary, although Votes for Women is in itself progressive.

This non-Party attitude is, in our opinion, a negation of the demand for a Party measure. In making this assertion we do not wish to imply that to secure a Party measure it is necessary for suffragists to be subservient to, or even definitely allied to any political organisation. But we contend that if suffragists are to succeed in securing the adoption of Votes for Women as a progressive measure, they must be still more progressive than the progressives: if they desire to make it a reactionary measure, they must be still more reactionary than the reactionaries.

Suffragists who wish to remain impartial, sitting on the fence between the great issues of popular liberty, as against autocratic compulsion, should refrain from calling for a Party measure and from attacking the Government, if they would be logical and achieve results. They should return to the old practice of being all things to all men. Their duty undoubtedly is to press for Votes for Women, now, during the War, to be carried as an agreed non-Party measure. Alas the chance of success appears to be small and yet this is the best chance the non-Party solution is ever likely to get.

Those who wish to have Votes for Women brought in as a bulwark of reaction and privilege, and who either have the capacity of thinking clearly enough to devise a logical policy, or whose innate tendencies lead them that way, are now to be found crying out for both industrial and military compulsion, and the suppression of national and international co-operative tendencies and popular liberties. They may be applauded for what is called their partriotic fervour; but, though everything is possible of course, it is unlikely that the Party of reaction will confidently espouse Votes for Women as a reactionary measure!

We, who believe that Votes for Women must come with the onward march of democracy, and that it can only come as a part of the democratic demand, must not fear to show that we are on the side of democracy on every predominant issue. Moreover we must modernise and democratise our demand.

Some suffragists put forward a host of such sayings as that 'this is a conservative country,' and that British Governments always 'take two bites at a cherry,' to induce us to adhere to the old demand for:–THE VOTE ON THE SAME TERMS AS IT IS, OR MAY BE, GRANTED TO MEN.

We point out that votes on those terms would enfranchise less than two million women, and urge that we want the married woman to have a vote, but they tell us to be practical, and insist that 'you cannot remove the sex bar and the property bar at the same time.'

We say that *they* are refusing to be practical, and to bring their ideas up to date. They refuse to recognise the significance of the fact that the 'Reform Act' introduced by the Liberal Government in 1913, would have established what was almost manhood suffrage for men, *and would have been passed into law, but for the situation created by the Votes for Women question.*

Manhood suffrage having come so near to enactment as that, it would be folly to imagine that it will be long postponed. Therefore unless we are to surrender the demand for Votes for Women on the same terms as it is *or may be* granted to men, we must prepare the ground for womanhood suffrage.

When the 1913 Reform Bill was before Parliament, it was seen that the country, nay, even large sections of the Suffrage Movement, were unprepared to demand equality under it, which would have amounted to little less than Womanhood Suffrage.

Large sections of the Suffrage Movement actually advocated taking less than equality, and admitted that they would be satisfied with any measure of enfranchisement, however small. They failed to realise that the measure of justice which reformers can wring from Governments is in direct proportion to the breadth and strength of the reformers' demand.

Experience of suffragist policy when faced with the Reform Bill, and the opinions now expressed by prominent suffragists, point irresistibly to the conclusion that, to meet the next franchise Bill, working women must organise without delay to support their own claim.

Most of the existing suffrage societies are mainly middle-class; they fail to realise the importance of securing that all women shall be enfranchised, and lack the strength and enthusiasm to fight for this broad claim.

Working women are those who suffer most by any property barriers to the franchise. They alone can be depended on, in the mass, to insist that such barriers shall be broken down. It is essential that working women should organise for womanhood suffrage. They should either form suffrage groups or committees in their existing working-class organisations or start special working women's suffrage societies and federations all over the country.

The East London Federation of the Suffragettes, which as our readers know, is a working woman's organisation, the object of which is to obtain the vote for every woman over 21, will gladly give what assistance it can in the matter to the working women of other districts.

Write to us if we can help!

The Opportunity

(WD, 3 June 1916)

Women who want the vote must now put forth all their energies to toil for it. We shall never win the franchise without great effort, and at some periods all out striving seems powerless to advance our cause, though we persevere in case we should lose ground. But now an opportunity to win the franchise is developing, and if we are not alert and strong of purpose it will slip from our grasp.

From the opening of hostilities until recently it seemed as though the question of the franchise could not be brought into the legislative arena until the close of the War. But now it appears that the powerful machinery of the two great capitalist political Parties has been set in motion to introduce a franchise measure.

Why this is being done we do not know; we do not know whether it is but the outward showing of some political bargain that is being made, whether the politicians are determined to have a general election during the war, or whether they believe that the war is ending and are preparing for an election as soon as peace is declared. But whatever may be the reason, the franchise measure is now announced to appear after Whitsuntide, and *The Times* threatens to cause trouble to the Government should it delay.

Though the forthcoming Bill is spoken of in the Press as a Registration Bill, its object is supposed to be to sweep away existing franchise anomalies and extend the vote to additional numbers of men. The Liberal papers say that the Bill will 'establish manhood suffrage'; the Tory papers say it will 'give votes to our soldiers and sailors.' If it does either the one thing or the other it will be in reality a franchise Bill, whatever it may be called. *The Times* says that two Bills may be required.

If the proposed measure, or measures, alter the basis of the men's franchise, and women are not able to secure the vote whilst the change is being made, we shall find it exceedingly difficult to secure the reopening of the franchise question in Parliament for a long time to come. Moreover, the next election, whether it happens to take place during or after the War, will be of most critical importance and we must leave no stone unturned to ensure that women shall take part in it.

Many people still find it difficult to believe that the franchise will be touched during the war. They say that the possibility of a General Election is too remote to be taken seriously, that, there-fore, the Parliamentary register is not likely to be altered for the present, and that, in short, they are content to 'wait and see' what will happen before they begin to act. But there is one fact that it is absolutely necessary to remember, if we mean to win when the time comes: it is that once the Government has committed itself to an open pronouncement of its intentions in regard to the fran-chise, only a truly overwhelming pressure will suffice to induce Cabinet Ministers to take back the scheme that they have put forward and to substitute another. If we can bring the pressure at our disposal to bear on the Government *before* its members have declared themselves, our victory will be the more easily attained.

We use the word victory, for it must be victory and not failure. In the difficult times before us our need for the franchise will be greater even than it has been in the past. We must not delay an unnecessary hour in preparing for the crisis that is surely approaching, for whether the trial of strength may arrive a few weeks or a few months hence, it will certainly come before we have done all that it would be well to do in order to insure success.

In the American States, where every man has the right to cast a vote in deciding whether women shall be admitted to the fran-chise or not, the Suffragists know that they have before them the task of converting a majority of the entire male population. It is with the spirit displayed by those women who have accomplished this task in State after State that we must work now. We must shrink from no drudgery that will secure that an individual or an audience has been converted, a paper sold, or a resolution passed.

The women who earn their living in the factories, the men who work beside them and who inevitably are affected by their conditions, the soldiers' wives, the mothers of the young conscripts, all these must be aroused to the crisis that is before us. Demonstrations and conferences must be held, petitions organised from every district; the demand must be sent to Parliament that there shall be no Registration Bill, no half-measures, but a Fran-chise Bill to give a vote to every woman and man over 21. The next few weeks are of vital importance; we must use them in working for Human Suffrage with all the energy that we possess.

Appendix:

Outstanding Events in the Suffragette Campaign 1903–14

(From Antonia Raeburn, *the Militant Suffragettes*, Michael Joseph, 1973)

1903
October 10 Inaugural meeting of the Women's Social and Political Union.

1904
May 12 Mrs Pankhurst holds a protest meeting outside the Houses of Parliament following the talking out of a Women's Suffrage Bill.

1905
October 13 Christabel Pankhurst and Annie Kenney are thrown out of the Manchester Free Trade Hall and subsequently imprisoned.

1906
January General election and return to power of a Liberal Government. Suffragettes campaign against Churchill as Liberal candidate for N.W. Manchester.
February 19 First London meeting of the Suffragettes at the Caxton Hall. A deputation of women arrives at the House of Commons to find the doors of the Strangers' Entrance closed to them.
February Mrs Pethick Lawrence joins the movement.
April 25 Keir Hardie introduces a women's suffrage resolution in Parliament. Suffragettes in the Ladies' Gallery protest as Members ridicule the measure.
May 19 First great women's suffrage demonstration. The Prime Minister, Sir Henry Campbell Bannerman, receives a deputation

of three hundred and speaks of opposition to women's suffrage within the Cabinet.

June 21 Annie Kenney and two working women are sentenced to six weeks' imprisonment for attempting to call on Asquith after his refusal to receive a deputation.

August At Cockermouth, Christabel establishes the W.S.P.U. by-election policy.

September The W.S.P.U. open official headquarters at Clement's Inn.

October 23 Opening of Parliament. Rebuffed members of a women's suffrage deputation protest in the Lobby of the House of Commons. The arrested include Mrs Pethick Lawrence and Mrs Cobden Sanderson. All are sentenced as common criminals. Several are shortly released from prison having broken down, and under public pressure the Home Secretary transfers the others from the second to the first division, thereby recognising them as political prisoners.

1907

February 13 First Women's Parliament at the Caxton Hall. A Suffragette deputation to the House of Commons persists against a force of mounted police to try to reach the House. The confrontation results in over fifty arrests.

March 8 W. H. Dickinson's Women's Suffrage Bill is rejected.

September Mrs Despard, Teresa Billington Greig and Edith How Martyn break away from the W.S.P.U. to form the Women's Freedom League.

October The Pethick Lawrences bring out the first number of *Votes for Women*.

1908

January 17 While Suffragettes chained to railings cause a diversion, Mrs Drummond attempts to get into a Cabinet Council meeting at 10 Downing Street. The authorities in sentencing the women to imprisonment revert to placing them in the second division.

February 11, 12, 13 Three-day session of a Women's Parliament. Suffragettes try to reach the House by a Trojan Horse method. The first arrest of Mrs Pankhurst (February 13).

February 28 A Women's Suffrage Bill put forward by Mr York Stanger is carried by a majority of one hundred and seventy-nine votes.

June 21 Great Hyde Park meeting. Purple, white and green become the Suffragette colours.

June 30 The public is asked to support a Suffragette deputation to

Parliament. Huge crowds watch Suffragettes being turned away from the House. Two women break windows of 10 Downing Street in protest.

October 11 In Trafalgar Square the public are invited to help the Suffragettes to 'rush the House of Commons'.

October 13 Mrs Pankhurst, Christabel and Mrs Drummond are arrested and eventually imprisoned with some thirty other Suffragettes who had tried to 'rush the House'.

October 28 Two Women's Freedom League members chain themselves to the grille of the Ladies' Gallery in the House of Commons. Officials, unable to detach the women, have to wrench the pieces of grille out of the surrounding stonework. The House is temporarily closed to strangers.

October Start of an organised campaign of heckling cabinet ministers.

December 22 Triumphal procession round the West End to celebrate the release of the leaders.

1909

February 18, 24 Deputations to Parliament from the Women's Freedom League and the W.S.P.U. Mrs Despard, Mrs Pethick Lawrence and Lady Constance Lytton are among the arrested. Their preferential prison treatment causes public comment.

March 19 Second reading of Geoffrey Howard's Electoral Reform Bill proposing votes for women. Despite the vote in favour, Asquith states that such a Bill would only be acceptable as a Government measure.

March 22 Lancashire Suffragettes lead an unsuccessful deputation to the House.

May 13/26 The Women's Exhibition at the Prince's Skating Rink in Knightsbridge.

June 29 The 'Bill of Rights' deputation. Mrs Pankhurst and eight well-known women attempt to take a petition to Parliament, claiming that: 'It is the right of the subject to petition the King.' The deputation is rejected and a highly organised manoeuvre follows. Windows of Government offices are broken and one hundred and eight arrests are made. In the police court the women claim that their action is justified by the Bill of Rights. While all but the stone throwers are remanded, the case is referred to the High Court. The test case of Mrs Pankhurst and the Hon. Mrs Haverfield is heard in December. They are found guilty and fined and the cases of the other ninety-two women are dismissed.

July 5 Marion Wallace Dunlop, in prison for stamping a passage from the Bill of Rights in St Stephen's Hall, begins a hunger strike in protest against second-division treatment.

July 13/14 Stone throwers in Holloway mutiny and adopt the hunger strike. The majority are released within a week.

August 13 M.P.s and the Home Secretary visit Holloway accompanied by one of the hunger strikers. Prison conditions about which the Suffragettes complained are soon afterwards improved.

August/September Cabinet ministers, waylaid and pestered by Suffragettes, are closely guarded in public, and Suffragettes are banned from Liberal meetings.

September 17 Barricades are erected in Birmingham in anticipation of Suffragette disturbances during Asquith's visit. In defiance the Suffragettes shower down stones from the roof of the hall where the Prime Minister is to speak.

September 24 The start of forcible feeding in Birmingham causes a public outcry. Within a few days H. N. Brailsford and H. W. Nevinson resign their positions on the *Daily News* in protest.

October 9 Militant demonstration on the occasion of Lloyd George's visit to Newcastle. Among the twelve women imprisoned, Lady Constance Lytton and Jane Brailsford receive preferential treatment.

1910
January General election. A Liberal Government is returned with a reduced majority.

January 14 Lady Constance Lytton, disguised as Jane Warton, leads a protest demonstration in Liverpool and is imprisoned and forcibly fed without a thorough medical test. She is released, seriously strained, on January 23 when her identity is discovered.

February 14 The Suffragettes declare a truce in view of the proposed Conciliation Bill drawn up by Lord Lytton and H. N. Brailsford.

March 15 Churchill rules that political prisoner treatment shall be given to all offenders whose crimes do not involve moral turpitude.

June 14 The Conciliation Bill is introduced in Parliament by D. J. Shackleton.

June 18 Ten thousand Suffragettes march in a two-mile-long procession from the Embankment to the Albert Hall. The public is sympathetic.

June 21 Asquith receives deputations from constitutional suffragists and from anti-suffragists.

July 11/12 A debate on the Conciliation Bill results in a majority of one hundred and thirty-nine votes in favour of the proposals. No time is allowed for a further reading during the session.

November Differences between the Lords and the Commons necessitate the dissolving of Parliament.

November 18 Black Friday. Suffragettes try to gain assurance from the Prime Minister of a future for the Conciliation Bill. He refuses to meet their deputations, and in subsequent attempts to reach the House of Commons the Suffragettes meet with violence and brutality from police and plain-clothes men. Several women are seriously injured and two later die as an immediate result of their treatment. Altogether one hundred and nineteen arrests are made, but charges against the offenders are withdrawn next day at the direct instruction of Churchill.

1911

Coronation Year. The Suffragettes resume their truce.

January 21 Dr Ethel Smyth gives the first performance of her newly composed 'March of the Women' and presents the piece to Mrs Pankhurst.

April 2 Suffragettes boycott the national census. All-night activities are organised by groups who are absent from home at the time of enumeration.

May 5 The Conciliation Bill is again debated and the vote shows a majority of members in favour.

June 17 All suffrage societies unite in a procession of forty thousand supporters from every class and profession. The demonstration includes historical and empire pageants. There is general anticipation of victory.

November 7 By announcing a Manhood Suffrage Bill, Asquith 'torpedoes' the conciliation proposals.

November 17 Asquith receives a deputation of Suffragettes and suffragists after announcing that women would only be included in an amended Manhood Suffrage Bill. He refuses to make any concessions.

November 21 Mrs Pethick Lawrence attempts to lead a deputation to the House of Commons from the Caxton Hall but all ways are blocked by police. An organised stone-throwing raid on the windows of shops and Government offices follows involving two hundred and twenty-three arrests.

1912

March 1 Mass window smashing in the West End. After persistent warnings which gain no response from the Government, the Suffragettes announce that they intend to use the 'argument of the stone', and give notice of a demonstration on March 4. Unannounced, a manoeuvre led by Mrs Pankhurst is carried out on March 1. Mrs Pankhurst is arrested.

March 4 A further outbreak of window smashing takes place.

March 5 Police raid the W.S.P.U. headquarters at Clement's Inn. The Pethick Lawrences are arrested, Christabel escapes to France and Annie Kenney secretly becomes the chief organiser in London.

May 15/22 Mrs Pankhurst and the Pethick Lawrences are tried at the Old Bailey and sentenced to nine months' imprisonment.

June 19 A Suffragette hunger strike begins in Holloway as a protest against the preferential treatment of the leaders.

June 22 Large numbers of Suffragettes in Holloway are fed by force. Mrs Pankhurst defiantly prevents the authorities from feeding her, while other Suffragettes barricade their cells and Emily Wilding Davison throws herself over the prison staircase.

June 24 Mrs Pankhurst and Mrs Pethick Lawrence are released.

June 27 Pethick Lawrence is released from Brixton.

June 18 A hatchet is thrown into Asquith's carriage on the occasion of his official visit to Dublin. Suffragettes attempt to fire the Theatre Royal where Asquith is speaking. For their part in the protest Mary Leigh and Gladys Evans are sentenced on August 7 to five years' penal servitude. Both women hunger strike and are released within nine weeks.

July 19 Helen Craggs is arrested for attempted arson.

August 21 Pethick Lawrence has been made responsible for damages involved in the Suffragette window-smashing outbreaks. Bailiffs enter the Mascot, the Pethick Lawrences' country home.

September 12 Christabel's whereabouts become public.

October 17 At an Albert Hall meeting Mrs Pankhurst outlines a new militant policy and W.S.P.U. members hear of the split between the Pankhursts and Pethick Lawrences.

October 18 The first number of *The Suffragette* appears.

November 9 Letter-box damage begins.

November 11 George Lansbury resigns from Parliament on the women's suffrage issue. After a strongly supported election campaign he loses the seat on November 26.

November/December Widespread letter-box attacks.

1913

January 23 A deputation of working women led by Mrs Drummond put their case before Lloyd George and Sir Edward Grey and demand proof of the ministers' professed support for women's suffrage. In the House of Commons the Speaker rules against a woman's suffrage amendment to the proposed Electoral Reform Bill.

January 28 Militant demonstration by the working women's deputation.

January/February Golf greens are ruined and telegraph wires are cut.

February At a series of Suffragette meetings Mrs Pankhurst openly encourages a policy of stronger militancy.

February 12 The burning of the Regent's Park refreshment kiosk is the first incident in a continuous programme of Suffragette damage to empty buildings.

February 19 Lloyd George's newly built house at Walton Heath is damaged by a bomb and Mrs Pankhurst is arrested on February 24 in connection with the outrage. She accepts full responsibility.

March 18 After a public outcry against the latest forcible feeding of Suffragettes, a majority of Members are against the practice and many think that the women should be left to die. On this point McKenna firmly disagrees, foreseeing mass Suffragette martyrdom.

March 25 The Prisoners' Temporary Discharge Act (the Cat and Mouse Act) is introduced to prevent Suffragette hunger strikers from securing unconditional release.

April 3 Mrs Pankhurst is sentenced at the Old Bailey to three years' penal servitude.

A record of a typical week of attacks on property which follow Mrs Pankhurst's imprisonment. ★

April 3 Four houses are fired at Hampstead Garden Suburb. Three women damage the glass of thirteen pictures in the Manchester Art Gallery. An empty railway carriage is wrecked by a bomb explosion at Stockport.

April 4 A mansion near Chorley Wood is completely destroyed by fire. A bomb explodes at Oxted station.

April 5 The burning of Ayr racecourse stand causes an estimated three thousand pounds' damage. An attempt to destroy Kelso racecourse grandstand is discovered.

April 6 A house at Potters Bar is fired. A mansion is destroyed at Norwich.

April 7 An attempt to fire stands on Cardiff racecourse is discovered. Fire breaks out in another house in Hampstead Garden Suburb. In the ruins of Dudley Castle the Suffragettes charge one of the ancient cannons and cause a shattering explosion.

April 8 'Release Mrs Pankhurst', cut in the turf at Duthie Park, Aberdeen. The word 'release' is twelve feet high.

April 9 A haystack worth a hundred pounds is destroyed near Nottingham.

April 9 Annie Kenney is arrested. Grace Roe secretly takes her place.
April 12 Mrs Pankhurst is released under the Cat and Mouse Act.

A record of Mrs Pankhurst's imprisonment under the Cat and Mouse Act.

1913	April 3	Imprisonment.
	April 12	Release.
	May 26	Rearrest at Woking.
	May 30	Release.
	June 14	Rearrest before Emily Wilding Davison's funeral.
	June 16	Release.
	June 21	Rearrest at the London Pavilion.
	June 24	Release.
	December 4	Rearrest at Exeter.
	December 7	Release.
	December 13	Rearrest on Dover Express.
	December 17	Release.
1914	March 9	Rearrest at Glasgow.
	March 14	Release.
	May 21	Rearrest outside Buckingham Palace.

May 26	Release.
July 8	Rearrest at Lincoln's Inn House.
July 11	Release.
July 16	Rearrest at 2 Campden Hill Place while setting out on a stretcher to attend a W.S.P.U. meeting.

1913

April 15 The Home Office prohibits Suffragette open-air meetings. Suffragettes defy the order and police make little attempt to enforce the rule.

April 16 Mrs Drummond and Lansbury are arrested for disturbing the peace.

April 30 The W.S.P.U. Headquarters are raided, heads of department are arrested and police confiscate copy for the forthcoming *Suffragette*. Grace Roe eludes the police and organises the printing of an edition of *The Suffragette* which appears on sale next morning. Grace Roe, disguised and in hiding, continues to operate as Mrs Pankhurst's chief organiser in London.

May/June Continual demonstrations are held in defence of free speech and the freedom of the Press.

June 4 Derby Day. Emily Wilding Davison stops the King's horse and is seriously injured. She dies on June 8.

June 14 Emily Wilding Davison's funeral.

June 9/17 Annie Kenney and the arrested Lincoln's Inn staff are tried for conspiracy and sentenced to long terms of imprisonment. They are sent to distant and separate gaols but shortly return to London on release after hunger striking.

July/August Mrs Pankhurst and Annie Kenney defy the Cat and Mouse Act and between periods of imprisonment they escape from closely guarded recuperating quarters and address W.S.P.U. meetings at the London Pavilion. During the July meetings either one or the other is rearrested.

July 10 The Piccadilly Flat case. The lenient sentencing of a procuress under the new White Slave Traffic Act causes the W.S.P.U. to investigate undisclosed facts in the case and to embark on an anti-prostitution campaign.

July/August Many sections of the public protest against the Cat and Mouse Act.

August 3 Protest chanting begins in churches. Suffragettes interrupt the Litany at St Paul's with prayers for Mrs Pankhurst.

August Mrs Pankhurst, Sylvia Pankhurst and Annie Kenney go abroad.

September 13 During a performance of *Androcles and the Lion* the Suffragettes make analogies between their position and that of the Christian martyrs. Interruptions are later made at other plays.

October 11 Mrs Pankhurst leaves France for her third visit to the United States. She is held up as an undesirable at Ellis Island on October 20; she is admitted to the country by order of the President.

October/November Annie Kenney and Sylvia Pankhurst return to England. They appear in public between imprisonments and accompanied respectively by the Bodyguard and the People's Army, they defy arrest. Finally, weakened by prison experiences, they each speak at meetings from a stretcher.

December 4 Mrs Pankhurst returns from America and is arrested at sea.

December 5 The clergy protest against renewed forcible feeding.

1914

January 26 After serious reports about the condition of Suffragettes in Holloway, Mrs Dacre Fox organises deputations to bishops asking them to take action.

January 28 The Bishop of London investigates conditions in Holloway and interviews Suffragette prisoners. He finds nothing to justify reports of ill treatment.

February Further deputations to bishops are organised.

February 7 Christabel announces that Sylvia's East End Federation, which has worked persistently in conjunction with the Labour Party, is no longer connected with the W.S.P.U.

February 10, 21 With the help of the Bodyguard Mrs Pankhurst escapes from guarded houses having first publicly announced from a balcony her intention of doing so.

February 20 A statement in *The Suffragette* alleges that tests on released prisoners show evidence of bromide drugging.

March 10 Mary Richardson slashes the Rokeby Venus in protest against the brutal rearrest of Mrs Pankhurst at Glasgow on the previous day. Public galleries are temporarily closed.

May 21 A mass Suffragette deputation goes to Buckingham Palace. After a fierce confrontation with the police, an organised window-smashing campaign takes place. Police discover a Suffragette arsenal at a Maida Vale flat.

May 23 Police raid Lincoln's Inn House and Grace Roe is arrested. Olive Bartels, disguised as a widow, takes her place, running the organisation from a series of changing bases.

June 11 At a debate in the House McKenna refers to militancy as 'a phenomenon absolutely without precedent in our history'.

June 16 At a meeting at the Holland Park Skating Rink, fifteen thousand pounds is raised. Annie Kenney is smuggled into the hall, and after speaking she leaves in disguise undetected.

June 20 Asquith receives a deputation from the East End Federation.

August 10 Six days after world war is declared all Suffragette prisoners are unconditionally released. Mrs Pankhurst suspends militancy and calls on her followers to help defend the country.

Index

Index

Manhood Suffrage, 243; *see also*
suffrage (male)
Manhood Suffrage Bill, 135, 310
Mansell-Moulhn, 248
March of the Women, The, 8
marriage, 25, 72, 157, 180, 210–13
married women's vote, 167, 171,
174, 176, 302
Marshall, Francis Hugh Adam,
199, 212–15
Martindale, Louisa, 239
Martin, Selina, 120–1
Martyn, Edith How, 307
martyrdom, 16, 312
Massy, Colonel Percy H. H., 108
Maternity and Infant Clinic, 281
May, Mrs, 108
Melville, Dr C. H., 203
methods of suffragettes: argument,
160–1; arson, 4, 311, 312–13;
'boisterous', 30; bombs, 312;
bye-elections, 43–4, 307;
Cabinet Ministers' meetings,
45–7, 143–4, 146, 246, 254, 308,
309; chains, 308; conferences,
305; demonstrations, 9, 59, 81,
142, 155, 305, 306; deputations
to Commons, 47–8, 51–2, 306,
307–8; letter-box attacks, 311;
meetings, 10, 19, 21, 24, 25, 29,
31, 51, 58, 107, 145, 147, 245;
militant, 13, 42, 117, 123, 128–9,
141–3; persuasion, 160–1;
petitions, 21, 31, 133–4, 144–5,
305; processions, 250, 257;
protests at meetings, 45–7;
rushing the Commons, 60–1;
strikes, 254–5; truces, 309, 310;
window-smashing, 4, 147,
183–4, 185, 244; *see also* hunger
strikes
Middleton, 15
midwives, 286–7
militancy, 128–9, 153–62, 185,
315, *see also* methods of
suffragettes
Mitchell, David, 12
Mitchell, Hannah, 16

Moor, Annie, 108
Moor, Mrs, 244
Morley of Blackburn, 1st
Viscount, 70
Morrow, Dr A. Prince, 202–3,
210–13, 216, 223
mortality rates, 283, 285, 287
Mother and Infant Clinics, 281
motherhood, 2, 6, 157, 221–4, 229,
281–9
Mott, Valentine, 214
Murphy, Agnes, 111
Murray, James, 110–11
Muskett, Mr, 79

National Insurance Act, 286
Nationalist Party, 30
National Register, 279–80
Navy, 237–40
Neisser, Albert Ludwig
Siegmund, 216
Nevinson, Henry Wood, 6, 108,
309
Newsholme, Dr, 282–3, 285, 286
newspapers, 47, 290, 304, 309, *see
also* press boycott
New Zealand, 20, 30
Noeggerath, 202, 212, 218–19
Non-Militant National Union of
Suffrage Societies, 301
Norris, Jill, 12
Norway, 20
nurseries, 288

O'Connor, Fergus, 177
Outragettes, 185–6

pacifism, 2
Paget, Sir James, 207
Pankhurst, Christabel: bye-
election policy, 307; cross-
examinations, 81–5, 86, 88–9;
Dangerfield's account, 4; escape
to France, 311; examination of
witnesses, 110–13; expels East
London Federation, 315;
Gladstone examination, 101–7;
Great Scourge, 13–15, 187–240;

321